The Oxford
Of English Verse
1250–1900

Chosen & Edited by
Arthur Quiller-Couch

1921

Copyright © 2013 Read Books Ltd.
This book is copyright and may not be
reproduced or copied in any way without
the express permission of the publisher in writing

British Library Cataloguing-in-Publication Data
A catalogue record for this book is available from the
British Library

Arthur Quiller-Couch

Sir Arthur Thomas Quiller-Couch was born on 21st November 1863, in Bodmin, Cornwall, England. He was educated at Newton Abbot Preparatory College, and subsequently at Clifton College, Bristol. Quiller-Couch undertook his university education at Trinity College, Oxford, and on completing his degree in 1886 became a lecturer (in classics) at the college.

Quiller-Couch only remained at Oxford for a short time however and soon moved to London in order to gain valuable journalistic experience. Despite this short tenure, he still managed to publish a well received book, *Dead Man's Rock* (1887); a romance in the vein of Robert Louis Stevenson's *Treasure Island*. Quiller-Couch published most of his books under the pen name of 'Q', and his first publication was followed up with *Troy Town* (1888), a comic novel set in a fictionalised version of Fowey (Cornwall). From his Oxford days Quiller-Couch was known as a writer of excellent verse. With the exception of the parodies entitled *Green Bays* (1893), his poetical work is contained in *Poems and Ballads* (1896). In 1895 he published an **anthology** of sixteenth and seventeenth English lyricists, *The Golden Pomp*, followed in 1900 by the *Oxford Book of English Verse, 1250–1900*.

During his 'journalistic phase' in London, he contributed to the *Speaker,* before again moving – this time to Cornwall, in 1891. Quiller-Couch settled in Fowey, Cornwall and became an active political member of the Liberal Party. As a result of this work he was knighted in 1910, and in 1928 was made a Bard of Gorseth Kernow, taking the Bardic name of *Marghak Cough* ('Red Knight'). He was also appointed Commodore of the Royal Fowey Yacht Club in 1911.

It was in 1910 that Quiller-Couch published one of his best known works though; *The Sleeping Beauty and other Fairy Tales from the Old French*. As a result of scholarship and research such as this, he was appointed to the King Edward VII Professorship of English Literature at the **University of Cambridge** in 1912, and retained it for the rest of his life. Simultaneously he was elected to a Fellowship of Jesus College, Cambridge. His inaugural lectures as the professor of English literature were turned into the book *On the Art of Writing* (1916), and it was largely due to Quiller-Couch's tireless enthusiasm and diplomacy that the Cambridge English faculty grew into the success it is today.

Quiller-Couch was also a noted literary critic, publishing editions of some of Shakespeare's plays (in the *New Shakespeare*, published by **Cambridge University Press**) and several critical works, including *Studies in Literature* (1918) and *On the Art of Reading* (1920). He edited a successor to his verse anthology: *The Oxford Book of English Prose*, which was published in 1923. He left his **autobiography**, *Memories and Opinions*, unfinished; it was nevertheless published in 1945.

Arthur Quiller-Couch died in a road accident on 12th May 1911, at the age of eighty, after being hit by a jeep near his home in Cornwall. He is buried in Fowey's parish church of St. Fimbarrus.

TO

THE PRESIDENT

FELLOWS AND SCHOLARS

OF

TRINITY COLLEGE OXFORD

A HOUSE OF LEARNING

ANCIENT LIBERAL HUMANE

AND MY MOST KINDLY NURSE

PREFACE

FOR this Anthology I have tried to range over the whole field of English Verse from the beginning, or from the Thirteenth Century to this closing year of the Nineteenth, and to choose the best. Nor have I sought in these Islands only, but wheresoever the Muse has followed the tongue which among living tongues she most delights to honour. To bring home and render so great a spoil compendiously has been my capital difficulty. It is for the reader to judge if I have so managed it as to serve those who already love poetry and to implant that love in some young minds not yet initiated.

My scheme is simple. I have arranged the poets as nearly as possible in order of birth, with such groupings of anonymous pieces as seemed convenient. For convenience, too, as well as to avoid a dispute-royal, I have gathered the most of the Ballads into the middle of the Seventeenth Century; where they fill a languid interval between two winds of inspiration—the Italian dying down with Milton and the French following at the heels of the restored Royalists. For convenience, again, I have set myself certain rules of spelling. In the very earliest poems inflection and spelling are structural, and to modernize is to destroy. But

PREFACE

as old inflections fade into modern the old spelling becomes less and less vital, and has been brought (not, I hope, too abruptly) into line with that sanctioned by use and familiar. To do this seemed wiser than to discourage many readers for the sake of diverting others by a scent of antiquity which—to be essential—should breathe of something rarer than an odd arrangement of type. But there are scholars whom I cannot expect to agree with me; and to conciliate them I have excepted Spenser and Milton from the rule.

Glosses of archaic and otherwise difficult words are given at the foot of the page: but the text has not been disfigured with reference-marks. And rather than make the book unwieldy I have eschewed notes—reluctantly when some obscure passage or allusion seemed to ask for a timely word; with more equanimity when the temptation was to criticize or 'appreciate.' For the function of the anthologist includes criticizing in silence.

Care has been taken with the texts. But I have sometimes thought it consistent with the aim of the book to prefer the more beautiful to the better attested reading. I have often excised weak or superfluous stanzas when sure that excision would improve; and have not hesitated to extract a few stanzas from a long poem when persuaded that they could stand alone as a lyric. The apology for such experiments can only lie in their success: but the risk is one which, in my judgement, the anthologist ought to take. A few small corrections have been made, but only when they were quite obvious.

PREFACE

The numbers chosen are either lyrical or epigrammatic. Indeed I am mistaken if a single epigram included fails to preserve at least some faint thrill of the emotion through which it had to pass before the Muse's lips let it fall, with however exquisite deliberation. But the lyrical spirit is volatile and notoriously hard to bind with definitions; and seems to grow wilder with the years. With the anthologist—as with the fisherman who knows the fish at the end of his sea-line—the gift, if he have it, comes by sense, improved by practice. The definition, if he be clever enough to frame one, comes by after-thought. I don't know that it helps, and am sure that it may easily mislead.

Having set my heart on choosing the best, I resolved not to be dissuaded by common objections against anthologies—that they repeat one another until the proverb δὶς ἢ τρὶς τὰ καλά loses all application—or perturbed if my judgement should often agree with that of good critics. The best is the best, though a hundred judges have declared it so; nor had it been any feat to search out and insert the second-rate merely because it happened to be recondite. To be sure, a man must come to such a task as mine haunted by his youth and the favourites he loved in days when he had much enthusiasm but little reading.

> A deeper import
> Lurks in the legend told my infant years
> Than lies upon that truth we live to learn.

Few of my contemporaries can erase—or would wish to erase—the dye their minds took from the late Mr. Palgrave's

PREFACE

Golden Treasury: and he who has returned to it again and again with an affection born of companionship on many journeys must remember not only what the *Golden Treasury* includes, but the moment when this or that poem appealed to him, and even how it lies on the page. To Mr. Bullen's *Lyrics from the Elizabethan Song Books* and his other treasuries I own a more advised debt. Nor am I free of obligation to anthologies even more recent—to Archbishop Trench's *Household Book of Poetry*, Mr. Locker-Lampson's *Lyra Elegantiarum*, Mr. Miles' *Poets and Poetry of the Century*, Mr. Beeching's *Paradise of English Poetry*, Mr. Henley's *English Lyrics*, Mrs. Sharp's *Lyra Celtica*, Mr. Yeats' *Book of Irish Verse*, and Mr. Churton Collins' *Treasury of Minor British Poetry*: though my rule has been to consult these after making my own choice. Yet I can claim that the help derived from them—though gratefully owned—bears but a trifling proportion to the labour, special and desultory, which has gone to the making of my book.

For the anthologist's is not quite the *dilettante* business for which it is too often and ignorantly derided. I say this, and immediately repent; since my wish is that the reader should in his own pleasure quite forget the editor's labour, which too has been pleasant: that, standing aside, I may believe this book has made the Muses' access easier when, in the right hour, they come to him to uplift or to console—

ἄκλητος μὲν ἔγωγε μένοιμί κεν· ἐς δὲ καλεύντων
θαρσήσας Μοίσαισι σὺν ἀμετέραισιν ἱκοίμαν.

PREFACE

My thanks are here tendered to those who have helped me with permission to include recent poems: to Mr. A. C. Benson, Mr. Laurence Binyon, Mr. Wilfrid Blunt, Mr. Robert Bridges, Mr. John Davidson, Mr. Austin Dobson, Mr. Aubrey de Vere, Mr. Edmund Gosse, Mr. Bret Harte, Mr. W. E. Henley, Mrs. Katharine Tynan Hinkson, Mr. W. D. Howells, Dr. Douglas Hyde, Mr. Rudyard Kipling, Mr. Andrew Lang, Mr. Richard Le Gallienne, Mr. George Meredith, Mrs. Meynell, Mr. T. Sturge Moore, Mr. Henry Newbolt, Mr. Gilbert Parker, Mr. T. W. Rolleston, Mr. George Russell ('A. E.'), Mrs. Clement Shorter (Dora Sigerson), Mr. Swinburne, Mr. Francis Thompson, Dr. Todhunter, Mr. William Watson, Mr. Watts-Dunton, Mrs. Woods, and Mr. W. B. Yeats; to the Earl of Crewe for a poem by the late Lord Houghton; to Lady Ferguson, Mrs. Allingham, Mrs. A. H. Clough, Mrs. Locker-Lampson, Mrs. Coventry Patmore; to the Lady Betty Balfour and the Lady Victoria Buxton for poems by the late Earl of Lytton and the Hon. Roden Noel; to the executors of Messrs. Frederic Tennyson (Captain Tennyson and Mr. W. C. A. Ker), Charles Tennyson Turner (Sir Franklin Lushington), Edward Fitz-Gerald (Mr. Aldis Wright), William Bell Scott (Mrs. Sydney Morse and Miss Boyd of Penkill Castle, who has added to her kindness by allowing me to include an unpublished 'Sonet' by her sixteenth-century ancestor, Mark Alexander Boyd), William Philpot (Mr. Hamlet S. Philpot), William Morris (Mr. S. C. Cockerell), William Barnes, and R. L. Stevenson; to the Rev. H. C. Beeching for two poems

PREFACE

from his own works, and leave to use his redaction of *Quia Amore Langueo*; to Messrs. Macmillan for confirming permission for the extracts from FitzGerald, Christina Rossetti, and T. E. Brown, and particularly for allowing me to insert the latest emendations in Lord Tennyson's non-copyright poems; to the proprietors of Mr. and Mrs. Browning's copyrights and to Messrs. Smith, Elder & Co. for a similar favour, also for a copyright poem by Mrs. Browning; to Mr. George Allen for extracts from Ruskin and the author of *Ionica*; to Messrs. G. Bell & Sons for poems by Thomas Ashe; to Messrs. Chatto & Windus for poems by Arthur O'Shaughnessy and Dr. George MacDonald, and for confirming Mr. Bret Harte's permission; to Mr. Elkin Mathews for a poem by Mr. Bliss Carman; to Mr. John Lane for two poems by William Brighty Rands; to the Society for Promoting Christian Knowledge for two extracts from Christina Rossetti's *Verses*; and to Mr. Bertram Dobell, who allows me not only to select from James Thomson but to use a poem of Traherne's, a seventeenth-century singer rediscovered by him. To mention all who in other ways have furthered me is not possible in this short Preface; which, however, must not conclude without a word of special thanks to Dr. W. Robertson Nicoll for many suggestions and some pains kindly bestowed, and to Professor F. York Powell, whose help and wise counsel have been as generously given as they were eagerly sought, adding me to the number of those many who have found his learning to be his friends' good fortune.

October 1900   A.T.Q.C.

CONTENTS

NUMBER		PAGE
1–7.	Anonymous. XIII–XIV Century	1–10
8.	Robert Mannyng of Brunne. b. 1260, d. 1340.	10
9.	John Barbour. d. 1395	10–11
10–12.	Geoffrey Chaucer. b. ? 1340, d. 1400	11–14
13.	Thomas Hoccleve. b. 1368–9, d. ? 1450.	14–15
14.	John Lydgate. b. ? 1370, d. ? 1450.	15
15.	King James I of Scotland. b. 1394, d. 1437	15
16–17.	Robert Henryson. b. 1425, d. 1500	16–25
18–21.	William Dunbar. b. 1465, d. ? 1520	25–33
22–29.	Anonymous. XV–XVI Century	33–57
30–31.	John Skelton. b. ? 1460, d. 1529	57–59
32–33.	Stephen Hawes. d. 1523	59–60
34–38.	Sir Thomas Wyatt. b. 1503, d. 1542	60–65
39–41.	Henry Howard, Earl of Surrey. b. 1516, d. 1547	65–68
42.	Nicholas Grimald. b. 1519, d. 1562	68–69
43–44.	Alexander Scott. b. ? 1520, d. 158–.	69–71
45.	Robert Wever. c. 1550	72
46.	Richard Edwardes. b. 1523, d. 1566	72–73
47.	George Gascoigne. b. ? 1525, d. 1577	74–75
48.	Alexander Montgomerie. b. ? 1540, d. ? 1610.	75–77
49.	William Stevenson. b. 1530, d. 1575	77–78
50–72.	Anonymous. XVI–XVII Century	79–99
73–74.	Nicholas Breton. b. 1542, d. 1626.	100–102
75–78.	Sir Walter Raleigh. b. 1552, d. 1618	102–104
79–84.	Edmund Spenser. b. 1552, d. 1599	104–129
85–86.	John Lyly. b. 1553, d. 1606.	129–130
87.	Anthony Munday. b. 1553, d. 1633	130
88–95.	Sir Philip Sidney. b. 1554, d. 1586	131–136
96.	Fulke Greville, Lord Brooke. b. 1554, d. 1628	136–137
97–100.	Thomas Lodge. b. ? 1556, d. 1625.	137–141
101–102.	George Peele. b. ? 1558, d. 1597	141–143
103–105.	Robert Greene. b. 1560, d. 1592	143–145
106.	Alexander Hume. b. 1560, d. 1609	146–150
107.	George Chapman. b. 1560, d. 1634	150
108–109.	Robert Southwell. b. 1561, d. 1595	151–153
110.	Henry Constable. b. ? 1562, d. ? 1613	153

CONTENTS

NUMBER		PAGE
111-113.	Samuel Daniel. b. 1562, d. 1619	153-159
114.	Mark Alexander Boyd. b. 1563, d. 1601	160
115.	Joshua Sylvester. b. 1563, d. 1618.	160-161
116-120.	Michael Drayton. b. 1563, d. 1631	161-173
121.	Christopher Marlowe. b. 1564, d. 1593	173-174
122.	Sir Walter Raleigh. b. 1552, d. 1618	174-175
123-164.	William Shakespeare. b. 1564, d. 1616	175-200
165.	Richard Rowlands. b. 1565, d. ? 1630	200-201
166-167.	Thomas Nashe. b. 1567, d. 1601	201-203
168-176.	Thomas Campion. b. ? 1567, d. 1619	203-209
177.	John Reynolds. XVI Century	209-210
178-180.	Sir Henry Wotton. b. 1568, d. 1639	210-212
181.	Sir John Davies. b. 1569, d. 1626	212-213
182-183.	Sir Robert Ayton. b. 1570, d. 1638	213-215
184-194.	Ben Jonson. b. 1573, d. 1637.	215-225
195-202.	John Donne. b. 1573, d. 1631	225-231
203.	Richard Barnefield. b. 1574, d. 1627	232
204.	Thomas Dekker. b. 1575, d. 1641.	233
205-206.	Thomas Heywood. b. ? 157-, d. 1650	233-235
207-217.	John Fletcher. b. 1579, d. 1625	235-241
218-220.	John Webster. d. ? 1630	242-243
221.	William Alexander, Earl of Stirling. b. ? 1580, d. 1640	243-244
222.	Phineas Fletcher. b. 1580, d. 1650.	244
223.	Sir John Beaumont. b. 1583, d. 1627	245
224-232.	William Drummond, of Hawthornden. b. 1585, d. 1649	245-250
233.	Giles Fletcher. b. 158-, d. 1623	250-252
234.	Francis Beaumont. b. 1586, d. 1616	252
235.	John Ford. b. 1586, d. 1639.	253
236-239.	George Wither. b. 1588, d. 1667	253-260
240-246.	William Browne, of Tavistock. b. 1588, d. 1643	260-264
247-275.	Robert Herrick. b. 1591, d. 1674	264-284
276-277.	Francis Quarles. b. 1592, d. 1644.	285
278-280.	Henry King, Bishop of Chichester. b. 1592, d. 1669	286-290
281-286.	George Herbert. b. 1593, d. 1632.	290-295
287-288.	James Shirley. b. 1596, d. 1666	295-296
289-295.	Thomas Carew. b ? 1595, d. ? 1639	297-301
296.	Jasper Mayne. b. 1604, d. 1672	301-302
297-298.	William Habington. b. 1605, d. 1654	302-304
299-300.	Thomas Randolph. b. 1605, d. 1635	305-308
301-303.	Sir William Davenant. b. 1606, d. 1668.	308-309
304-306.	Edmund Waller. b. 1606, d. 1687.	310-311

CONTENTS

NUMBER		PAGE
307-324.	John Milton. b. 1608, d. 1674	311-347
325-328.	Sir John Suckling. b. 1609, d. 1642	347-350
329.	Sir Richard Fanshawe. b. 1608, d. 1666.	350
330-333.	William Cartwright. b. 1611, d. 1643	351-353
334.	James Graham, Marquis of Montrose. b. 1612, d. 1650	353-354
335.	Thomas Jordan. b. ? 1612, d. 1685.	354-355
336-342.	Richard Crashaw. b. ? 1613, d. 1649	355-370
343-348.	Richard Lovelace. b. 1618, d. 1658	370-374
349-353.	Abraham Cowley. b. 1618, d. 1667	374-380
354.	Alexander Brome. b. 1620, d. 1666	381
355-361.	Andrew Marvell. b. 1621, d. 1678.	382-394
362-365.	Henry Vaughan. b. 1621, d. 1695.	395-399
366.	John Bunyan. b. 1628, d. 1688	399
367-392.	Anonymous : Ballads	400-459
393.	William Strode. b. 1602, d. 1645.	459
394.	Thomas Stanley. b. 1625, d. 1678.	460
395.	Thomas D'Urfey. b. 1653, d. 1723	460-461
396.	Charles Cotton. b. 1630, d. 1687	461
397.	Katherine Philips ('Orinda'). b. 1631, d. 1664	462
398-402.	John Dryden. b. 1631, d. 1700	462-471
403.	Charles Webbe. c. 1678	472
404-405.	Sir George Etherege. b. 1635, d. 1691	472-473
406.	Thomas Traherne. b. ? 1637, d. 1674	473-475
407.	Thomas Flatman. b. 1637, d. 1688	475-476
408.	Charles Sackville, Earl of Dorset. b. 1638, d. 1706	476-478
409-410.	Sir Charles Sedley. b. 1639, d. 1701	479-480
411-412.	Aphra Behn. b. 1640, d. 1689	480-481
413-416.	John Wilmot, Earl of Rochester. b. 1647, d. 1680	481-484
417-418.	John Sheffield, Duke of Buckinghamshire. b. 1649, d. 1720	485-486
419.	Thomas Otway. b. 1652, d. 1685.	486
420.	John Oldham. b. 1653, d. 1683	487
421.	John Cutts, Lord Cutts. b. 1661, d. 1707	487
422-428.	Matthew Prior. b. 1664, d. 1721	488-493
429.	William Walsh. b. 1663, d. 1708.	493
430.	Lady Grisel Baillie. b. 1665, d. 1746	494-495
431-432.	William Congreve. b. 1670, d. 1729	495-496
433.	Joseph Addison. b. 1672, d. 1719.	496-497
434-435.	Isaac Watts. b. 1674, d. 1748	497-500
436.	Thomas Parnell. b. 1679, d. 1718.	501
437.	Allan Ramsay. b. 1686, d. 1758.	501-502

CONTENTS

NUMBER		PAGE
438.	William Oldys. b. 1687, d. 1761	503
439.	John Gay. b. 1688, d. 1732	503
440-442.	Alexander Pope. b. 1688, d. 1744	504-507
443.	George Bubb Dodington, Lord Melcombe. b. 1691, d. 1762	508
444-445.	Henry Carey. b. ? 1693, d. 1743	509-511
446-447.	William Broome. d. 1745	511-512
448.	James Thomson. b. 1700, d. 1748	512
449.	George Lyttelton, Lord Lyttelton. b. 1709, d. 1773	512-513
450-451.	Samuel Johnson. b. 1709, d. 1784	513-516
452.	Richard Jago. b. 1715, d. 1781	516
453-456.	Thomas Gray. b. 1716, d. 1771	516-528
457-460.	William Collins. b. 1721, d. 1759	528-533
461-463.	Mark Akenside. b. 1721, d. 1770	534-537
464.	Tobias George Smollett. b. 1721, d. 1771	538
465.	Christopher Smart. b. 1722, d. 1770	538-542
466.	Jane Elliot. b. 1727, d. 1805	542-543
467-468.	Oliver Goldsmith. b. 1728, d. 1774	543-544
469.	Robert Cunninghame-Graham of Gartmore. b. 1735, d. 1797	544-545
470-471.	William Cowper. b. 1731, d. 1800	545-547
472.	James Beattie. b. 1735, d. 1803	548
473.	Isobel Pagan. b. 1740, d. 1821	548-54
474.	Anna Lætitia Barbauld. b. 1743, d. 1825	549-550
475.	Fanny Greville. XVIII Century	550-551
476.	John Logan. b. 1748, d. 1788	551-552
477.	Lady Anne Lindsay. b. 1750, d. 1825	552-553
478.	Sir William Jones. b. 1746, d. 1794	554
479.	Thomas Chatterton. b. 1752, d. 1770	554-550
480-482.	George Crabbe b. 1754, d. 1832	556-557
483-492.	William Blake. b. 1757, d. 1827	558-566
493-506.	Robert Burns. b. 1759, d. 1796	566-577
507-508.	Henry Rowe. b. 1750, d. 1819	578-579
509.	William Lisle Bowles. b. 1762, d. 1850	579
510.	Joanna Baillie. b. 1762, d. 1851	580
511.	Mary Lamb. b. 1765, d. 1847	581
512.	Carolina, Lady Nairne. b. 1766, d. 1845	581-582
513-514.	James Hogg. b. 1770, d. 1835	582-594
515-541.	William Wordsworth. b. 1770, d. 1850	594-618
542-548.	Sir Walter Scott. b. 1771, d. 1832	619-628
549-555.	Samuel Taylor Coleridge. b. 1772, d. 1834	628-658
556.	Robert Southey. b. 1774, d. 1843	658-659
557-576.	Walter Savage Landor. b. 1775, d. 1864	659-667

CONTENTS

NUMBER		PAGE
577-579.	Charles Lamb. b. 1775. d. 1834	668-672
580-581.	Thomas Campbell. b. 1777, d. 1844	672-675
582-585.	Thomas Moore. b. 1779, d. 1852	675-678
586.	Edward Thurlow, Lord Thurlow. b. 1781, d. 1829	678-679
587-588.	Ebenezer Elliott. b. 1781, d. 1849	679-681
589-591.	Allan Cunningham. b. 1784, d. 1842	681-683
592.	Leigh Hunt. b. 1784, d. 1859	683
593-595.	Thomas Love Peacock. b. 1785, d. 1866	684-687
596.	Caroline Southey. b. 1787, d. 1854	687-688
597-601.	George Gordon Byron, Lord Byron. b. 1788, d. 1824	688-694
602.	Sir Aubrey de Vere. b. 1788, d. 1846	694-695
603-604.	Charles Wolfe. b. 1791, d. 1823	695-697
605-618.	Percy Bysshe Shelley. b. 1792, d. 1822	697-717
619.	Hew Ainslie. b. 1792, d. 1878	717
620.	John Keble. b. 1792, d. 1866	718-720
621.	John Clare. b. 1793, d. 1864	720
622.	Felicia Dorothea Hemans. b. 1793, d. 1835	721
623-637.	John Keats. b. 1795, d. 1821	721-744
638.	Jeremiah Joseph Callanan. b. 1795, d. 1839	745
639.	William Sidney Walker. b. 1795, d. 1846	746
640-642.	George Darley. b. 1795, d. 1846	746-749
643-646.	Hartley Coleridge. b. 1796, d. 1849	749-751
647-654.	Thomas Hood. b. 1798, d. 1845	752-762
655.	William Thom. b. 1798, d. 1848	762-764
656.	Sir Henry Taylor. b. 1800, d. 1886	764
657.	Thomas Babington Macaulay, Lord Macaulay. b. 1800. d. 1859	765
658-659.	William Barnes. b. 1801, d. 1886	765-767
660.	Winthrop Mackworth Praed. b. 1802, d. 1839	767-768
661-662.	Sara Coleridge. b. 1802, d. 1850	768-770
663.	Gerald Griffin. b. 1803, d. 1840	770-772
664-665.	James Clarence Mangan. b. 1803, d. 1849	772-776
666-668.	Thomas Lovell Beddoes. b. 1803, d. 1849	777-778
669-672.	Ralph Waldo Emerson. b. 1803, d. 1882	779-785
673.	Richard Henry Horne. b. 1803, d. 1884	785-786
674-675.	Robert Stephen Hawker. b. 1804, d. 1875	786-787
676.	Thomas Wade. b. 1805, d. 1875	787
677.	Francis Mahony. b. 1805, d. 1866	788-790
678-687.	Elizabeth Barrett Browning. b. 1806, d. 1861	790-800
688.	Frederick Tennyson. b. 1807, d. 1898	800
689.	Henry Wadsworth Longfellow. b. 1807, d. 1882	801-803
690.	John Greenleaf Whittier. b. 1807, d. 1892	804

CONTENTS

NUMBER		PAGE
691.	Helen Selina, Lady Dufferin. b. 1807, d. 1867	805-807
692.	Caroline Elizabeth Sarah Norton. b. 1808, d. 1876	807-808
693.	Charles Tennyson Turner. b. 1808, d. 1879	808
694-696.	Edgar Allan Poe. b. 1809, d. 1849	809-814
697-698.	Edward Fitzgerald. b. 1809, d. 1883	814-818
699-709.	Alfred Tennyson, Lord Tennyson. b. 1809, d. 1892	819-847
710.	Richard Monckton Milnes, Lord Houghton. b. 1809, d. 1885	848
711.	Henry Alford. b. 1810, d. 1871	849
712-714.	Sir Samuel Ferguson. b. 1810, d. 1886	849-851
715-730.	Robert Browning. b. 1812, d. 1889	852-867
731.	William Bell Scott. b. 1812, d. 1890	867-872
732-733.	Aubrey De Vere. b. 1814, d. 1902	872-873
734.	George Fox. b. 1815	874
735-738.	Emily Brontë. b. 1818, d. 1848	875-879
739-740.	Charles Kingsley. b. 1819, d. 1875	879-880
741.	Arthur Hugh Clough. b. 1819, d. 1861	880-881
742-743.	Walt Whitman. b. 1819, d. 1892	881-882
744.	John Ruskin. b. 1819, d. 1900	882
745.	Ebenezer Jones. b. 1820, d. 1860	883
746.	Frederick Locker-Lampson. b. 1821, d. 1895	884
747-754.	Matthew Arnold. b. 1822, d. 1888	885-903
755-756.	William Brighty Rands. b. 1823, d. 1880	904-905
757.	William Philpot. b. 1823, d. 1880	906-907
758-759.	William (Johnson) Cory. b. 1823, d. 1892	907-908
760-764.	Coventry Patmore. b. 1823, d. 1896	908-913
765-768.	Sydney Dobell. b. 1824, d. 1874	913-921
769.	William Allingham. b. 1824, d. 1889	921-923
770.	George MacDonald. b. 1824, d. 1905	923
771.	Dante Gabriel Rossetti. b. 1828, d. 1882	923-928
772-776.	George Meredith. b. 1828, d. 1909	929-942
777-778.	Alexander Smith. b. 1829, d. 1867	942-945
779-789.	Christina Georgina Rossetti. b. 1830, d. 1894	946-954
790-793.	Thomas Edward Brown. b. 1830, d. 1897	955-956
794-795.	Edward Robert Bulwer Lytton, Earl of Lytton. b. 1831, d. 1892	957-962
796-799.	James Thomson. b. 1834, d. 1882	963-964
800-802.	William Morris. b. 1834, d. 1896	965-967
803-804.	Roden Berkeley Wriothesley Noel. b. 1834, d. 1894	967-969
805-806.	Thomas Ashe. b. 1836, d. 1889	969-970
807.	Theodore Watts-Dunton. b. 1836, d. 1914	970-972

CONTENTS

NUMBER		PAGE
808-811.	Algernon Charles Swinburne. b. 1837, d. 1909	972-991
812.	William Dean Howells. b. 1837	991
813.	Bret Harte. b. 1839, d. 1902.	992
814-815.	John Todhunter. b. 1839, d. 1916	993-995
816-823.	Wilfrid Scawen Blunt. b. 1840	995-1002
824-826.	Henry Austin Dobson. b. 1840	1002-1004
827.	Henry Clarence Kendall. b. 1841, d. 1882	1004-1006
828-830.	Arthur William Edgar O'Shaughnessy. b. 1844, d. 1881	1006-1010
831.	John Boyle O'Reilly. b. 1844, d. 1890	1010
832-840.	Robert Bridges. b. 1844	1011-1018
841.	Andrew Lang. b. 1844, d. 1912	1018
842-844.	William Ernest Henley. b. 1849, d. 1903	1019-1022
845.	Edmund Gosse. b. 1849	1022-1023
846-848.	Robert Louis Stevenson. b. 1850, d. 1894	1023-1025
849.	T. W. Rolleston. b. 1857	1025-1026
850-851.	John Davidson. b. 1857, d. 1909	1026-1028
852-854.	William Watson. b. 1858	1028-1031
855-856.	Henry Charles Beeching. b. 1859	1031-1033
857.	Bliss Carman. b. 1861	1033-1034
858.	Douglas Hyde. b. 1861	1034-1035
859.	Arthur Christopher Benson. b. 1862	1035-1036
860.	Henry Newbolt. b. 1862	1036-1037
861.	Gilbert Parker. b. 1862	1038
862-864.	William Butler Yeats. b. 1865	1038-1039
865-867.	Rudyard Kipling. b. 1865	1040-1045
868-869.	Richard Le Gallienne. b. 1866	1045-1047
870-871.	Laurence Binyon. b. 1869	1047
872-873.	'A. E.' (George William Russell)	1048-1049
874.	T. Sturge Moore. b. 1870	1049
875.	Francis Thompson. b. 1859, d. 1907	1050-1052
876.	Henry Cust. b. 1861, d. 1917	1053
877.	Katharine Tynan Hinkson. b. 1861	1053-1054
878.	Frances Bannerman	1054-1055
879-880.	Alice Meynell. b. 1850	1055-1056
881.	Dora Sigerson. d. 1918	1056-1057
882.	Margaret L. Woods. b. 1856	1057
883.	Anonymous	1058

1.   *Cuckoo Song*

                                           c. 1250

SUMER is icumen in,
    Lhude sing cuccu!
Groweth sed, and bloweth med,
    And springth the wude nu—
        Sing cuccu!

Awe bleteth after lomb,
    Lhouth after calve cu;
Bulluc sterteth, bucke verteth,
    Murie sing cuccu!

Cuccu, cuccu, well singes thu, cuccu:
    Ne swike thu naver nu;
Sing cuccu, nu, sing cuccu,
    Sing cuccu, sing cuccu, nu!

---

lhude] loud.   awe] ewe.   lhouth] loweth.   sterteth] leaps.
swike] cease.

ANONYMOUS

2. *Alison*

c. 1300

BYTUENE Mershe ant Averil
When spray biginneth to spring,
The lutel foul hath hire wyl
On hyre lud to synge:
Ich libbe in love-longinge
For semlokest of alle thynge,
He may me blisse bringe,
Icham in hire bandoun.
An hendy hap ichabbe y-hent,
Ichot from hevene it is me sent,
From alle wymmen my love is lent
Ant lyht on Alisoun.

On heu hire her is fayr ynoh,
Hire browe broune, hire eye blake;
With lossum chere he on me loh;
With middel smal ant wel y-make;
Bote he me wolle to hire take
For to buen hire owen make,
Long to lyven ichulle forsake
Ant feye fallen adoun.
An hendy hap, etc.

Nihtes when I wende and wake,
For-thi myn wonges waxeth won;

on hyre lud] in her language.　　ich libbe] I live.　　semlokest] seemliest.　　he] she.　　bandoun] thraldom.　　hendy] gracious.
y-hent] seized, enjoyed.　　ichot] I wot.　　lyht] alighted.
hire her] her hair.　　lossum] lovesome.　　loh] laughed.
bote he] unless she.　　buen] be.　　make] mate.　　feye] like to die.
nihtes] at night.　　wende] turn.　　for-thi] on that account.
wonges waxeth won] cheeks grow wan.

ANONYMOUS

Levedi, al for thine sake
Longinge is y-lent me on.
In world his non so wyter mon
That al hire bountè telle con;
Hire swyre is whittore than the swon,
Ant feyrest may in toune.
An hendy hap, etc.

Icham for wowyng al for-wake,
Wery so water in wore;
Lest eny reve me my make
Ichabbe y-yerned yore.
Betere is tholien whyle sore
Then mournen evermore.
Geynest under gore,
Herkne to my roun—
An hendy hap, etc.

3. *Spring-tide*

c. 1300

LENTEN ys come with love to toune,
With blosmen ant with briddes roune,
That al this blisse bryngeth;
Dayes-eyes in this dales,
Notes suete of nyhtegales,
Vch foul song singeth;

2. levedi] lady.   y-lent me on] arrived to me.   so wyter mon] so wise a man.   swyre] neck.   may] maid.   for-wake] worn out with vigils.   so water in wore] as water in a weir.   reve] rob.   y-yerned yore] long been distressed.   tholien] to endure.   geynest under gore] comeliest under woman's apparel.   roun] tale, lay.
3. to toune] in its turn.

3

ANONYMOUS

The threstlecoc him threteth oo,
Away is huere wynter wo,
  When woderove springeth;
This foules singeth ferly fele,
Ant wlyteth on huere winter wele,
  That al the wode ryngeth.

The rose rayleth hire rode,
The leves on the lyhte wode
  Waxen al with wille;
The mone mandeth hire bleo,
The lilie is lossom to seo,
  The fenyl ant the fille;
Wowes this wilde drakes,
Miles murgeth huere makes;
  Ase strem that striketh stille,
Mody meneth; so doth mo
(Ichot ycham on of tho)
  For loue that likes ille.

The mone mandeth hire lyht,
So doth the semly sonne bryht.
  When briddes singeth breme;
Deowes donketh the dounes,
Deores with huere derne rounes
  Domes forte deme;

him threteth oo] is aye chiding them. huere] their. woderove] woodruff. ferly fele] marvellous many. wlyteth] whistle, or look. rayleth hire rode] clothes herself in red. mandeth hire bleo] sends forth her light. lossom to seo] lovesome to see. fille] thyme. wowes] woo. miles] males. murgeth] make merry. makes] mates striketh] flows, trickles. mody meneth] the moody man makes moan. so doth mo] so do many. on of tho] one of them. breme] lustily. deowes] dews. donketh] make dank. deores] dears, lovers. huere derne rounes] their secret tales. domes forte deme] for to give (decide) their decisions.

ANONYMOUS

Wormes woweth under cloude,
Wymmen waxeth wounder proude,
So wel hit wol hem seme,
Yef me shal wonte wille of on,
This wunne weole y wole forgon
Ant wyht in wode be fleme.

4. Blow, Northern Wind

c. 1300

ICHOT a burde in boure bryht,
That fully semly is on syht,
Menskful maiden of myht;
Feir ant fre to fonde;
In al this wurhliche won
A burde of blod ant of bon
Never yete y nuste non
Lussomore in londe.
Blou northerne wynd!
Send thou me my suetyng!
Blou northerne wynd! blou, blou, blou!

With lokkes lefliche ant longe,
With frount ant face feir to fonge,
With murthes monie mote heo monge,
That brid so breme in boure.

3. cloude] clod.   wunne weole] wealth of joy.   y wole forgon]
I will forgo.   wyht] wight.   fleme] banished.
4. Ichot] I know.   burde] maiden.   menskful] worshipful.
feir] fair.   fonde] take, prove.   wurhliche] noble.   won]
multitude.   y nuste] I knew not.   lussomore in londe] lovelier
on earth.   suetyng] sweetheart.   lefliche] lovely.   fonge]
take between hands.   murthes] mirths, joys.   mote heo monge]
may she mingle.   brid] bird.   breme] full of life.

5

ANONYMOUS

With lossom eye grete ant gode,
With browen blysfol under hode,
He that reste him on the Rode,
  That leflych lyf honoure.
    Blou northerne wynd, etc.

Hire lure lumes liht,
Ase a launterne a nyht,
Hire bleo blykyeth so bryht,
  So feyr heo is ant fyn.
A suetly swyre heo hath to holde,
With armes shuldre ase mon wolde,
Ant fingres feyre forte folde,
  God wolde hue were myn!
    Blou northerne wynd, etc.

Heo is coral of godnesse,
Heo is rubie of ryhtfulnesse,
Heo is cristal of clannesse,
  Ant baner of bealtè.
Heo is lilie of largesse,
Heo is parvenke of prouesse,
Heo is solsecle of suetnesse,
  Ant lady of lealtè.

For hire love y carke ant care,
For hire love y droupne ant dare,
For hire love my blisse is bare
  Ant al ich waxe won,

Rode] the Cross.   lure] face.   lumes] beams.   bleo] colour.
suetly swyre] darling neck.   forte] for to.   hue, heo] she.
clannesse] cleanness, purity.   parvenke] periwinkle.   solsecle]
sunflower.   won] wan.

ANONYMOUS

For hire love in slep y slake,
For hire love al nyht ich wake,
For hire love mournynge y make
   More then eny mon.
     Blou northerne wynd!
     Send thou me my suetyng!
     Blou northerne wynd! blou, blou, blou!

5.   *This World's Joy*

c. 1300

WYNTER wakeneth al my care,
  Nou this leves waxeth bare;
Ofte I sike ant mourne sare
  When hit cometh in my thoht
  Of this worldes joie, hou hit goth al to noht.

Nou hit is, and nou hit nys,
Al so hit ner nere, ywys;
That moni mon seith, soth hit ys:
  Al goth bote Godes wille:
  Alle we shule deye, thah us like ylle.

Al that gren me graueth grene,
Nou hit faleweth albydene:
Jesu, help that hit be sene
  Ant shild us from helle!
  For y not whider y shal, ne hou longe her duelle.

5. this leves] these leaves.   sike] sigh.   nys] is not.   al so hit ner nere] as though it had never been.   soth] sooth.   bote] but, except.   thah] though.   faleweth] fadeth.   albydene] altogether.   y not whider] I know not whither.   her duelle] here dwell.

ANONYMOUS

6. *A Hymn to the Virgin*

c. 1300

OF on that is so fayr and bright
    Velut maris stella,
Brighter than the day is light,
    Parens et puella :
Ic crie to the, thou see to me,
Levedy, preye thi Sone for me,
    Tam pia,
That ic mote come to thee
    Maria.

Al this world was for-lore
    Eva peccatrice,
Tyl our Lord was y-bore
    De te genetrice.
With *ave* it went away
Thuster nyth and comz the day
    Salutis ;
The welle springeth ut of the,
    Virtutis.

Levedy, flour of alle thing,
    Rosa sine spina,
Thu bere Jhesu, hevene king,
    Gratia divina :
Of alle thu ber'st the pris,
Levedy, quene of paradys
    Electa :
Mayde milde, moder *es*
    Effecta.

on] one.   levedy] lady.   thuster] dark.   pris] prize.

ANONYMOUS

7. *Of a rose, a lovely rose,*
    Of a rose is al myn song.

c. 1350

LESTENYT, lordynges, both elde and yinge,
How this rose began to sprynge;
Swych a rose to myn lykynge
    In al this word ne knowe I non.

The Aungil came fro hevene tour,
To grete Marye with gret honour,
And seyde sche xuld bere the flour
    That xulde breke the fyndes bond.

The flour sprong in heye Bedlem,
That is bothe bryht and schen:
The rose is Mary hevene qwyn,
    Out of here bosum the blosme sprong.

The ferste braunche is ful of myht,
That sprang on Cyrstemesse nyht,
The sterre schon over Bedlem bryht
    That is bothe brod and long.

The secunde braunche sprong to helle,
The fendys power doun to felle:
Therein myht non sowle dwelle;
    Blyssid be the time the rose sprong!

The thredde braunche is good and swote,
It sprang to hevene crop and rote,
Therein to dwellyn and ben our bote;
    Every day it schewit in prystes hond.

lestenyt] listen.　word] world.　xuld] should.　schen] beautiful.
hevene qwyn] heaven's queen.　bote] salvation.

ANONYMOUS

Prey we to here with gret honour,
Che that bar the blyssid flowr,
Che be our helpe and our socour
   And schyd us fro the fyndes bond.

ROBERT MANNYNG OF BRUNNE
1260-1340

8.   *Praise of Women*

NO thyng ys to man so dere
   As wommanys love in gode manere.
A gode womman is mannys blys,
There her love right and stedfast ys.
There ys no solas under hevene
Of alle that a man may nevene
That shulde a man so moche glew
As a gode womman that loveth true.
Ne derer is none in Goddis hurde
Than a chaste womman with lovely worde.

JOHN BARBOUR
d. 1395

9.   *Freedom*

A! Fredome is a noble thing!
   Fredome mays man to haiff liking;
Fredome all solace to man giffis,
He levys at ese that frely levys!
A noble hart may haiff nane ese,
Na ellys nocht that may him plese,

---

8. nevene] name.   glew] gladden.   hurde] flock.   *9.* liking] liberty.   na ellys nocht] nor aught else.

JOHN BARBOUR

Gyff fredome fail; for fre liking
Is yarnyt our all othir thing.
Na he that ay has levyt fre
May nocht knaw weill the propyrtè,
The angyr, na the wretchyt dome
That is couplyt to foule thyrldome.
Bot gyff he had assayit it,
Than all perquer he suld it wyt;
And suld think fredome mar to prise
Than all the gold in warld that is.
Thus contrar thingis evirmar
Discoweryngis off the tothir ar.

GEOFFREY CHAUCER
1340?-1400

10. *The Love Unfeigned*

O YONGE fresshe folkes, he or she,
In which that love up groweth with your age,
Repeyreth hoom from worldly vanitee,
And of your herte up-casteth the visage
To thilke god that after his image
Yow made, and thinketh al nis but a fayre
This world, that passeth sone as floures fayre.

And loveth him, the which that right for love
Upon a cros, our soules for to beye,
First starf, and roos, and sit in hevene a-bove;
For he nil falsen no wight, dar I seye,
That wol his herte al hoolly on him leye.
And sin he best to love is, and most meke,
What nedeth feyned loves for to seke?

9. yarnyt] yearned for.   perquer] thoroughly, by heart.
10. repeyreth] repair ye.   starf] died.

21

11. Balade

Hyd, Absolon, thy gilte tresses clere;
Ester, ley thou thy meknesse al a-doun;
Hyd, Jonathas, al thy frendly manere;
Penalopee, and Marcia Catoun,
Mak of your wyfhod no comparisoun;
Hyde ye your beautes, Isoude and Eleyne;
My lady cometh, that al this may disteyne.

Thy faire body, lat hit nat appere,
Lavyne; and thou, Lucresse of Rome toun,
And Polixene, that boghten love so dere,
And Cleopatre, with al thy passioun,
Hyde ye your trouthe of love and your renoun;
And thou, Tisbe, that hast of love swich peyne;
My lady cometh, that al this may disteyne.

Herro, Dido, Laudomia, alle y-fere,
And Phyllis, hanging for thy Demophoun,
And Canace, espyed by thy chere,
Ysiphile, betraysed with Jasoun,
Maketh of your trouthe neyther boost ne soun;
Nor Ypermistre or Adriane, ye tweyne;
My lady cometh, that al this may distevne.

12. Merciles Beaute
A Triple Roundel
I. CAPTIVITY

Your eyen two wol slee me sodenly,
I may the beautè of hem not sustene,
So woundeth hit through-out my herte kene.

11. disteyne] bedim.   y-fere] together.

12

GEOFFREY CHAUCER

And but your word wol helen hastily
My hertes wounde, whyl that hit is grene.
Your eyen two wol slee me sodenly,
I may the beautè of hem not sustene.

Upon my trouthe I sey yow feithfully,
That ye ben of my lyf and deeth the quene;
For with my deeth the trouthe shal be sene.
Your eyen two wol slee me sodenly,
I may the beautè of hem not sustene,
So woundeth hit through-out my herte kene.

2. REJECTION

So hath your beautè fro your herte chaced
Pitee, that me ne availeth not to pleyne;
For Daunger halt your mercy in his cheyne.

Giltles my deeth thus han ye me purchaced;
I sey yow sooth, me nedeth not to feyne;
So hath your beautè fro your herte chaced
Pitee, that me ne availeth not to pleyne.

Allas! that nature hath in yow compassed
So greet beautè, that no man may atteyne
To mercy, though he sterve for the peyne.
So hath your beautè fro your herte chaced
Pitee, that me ne availeth not to pleyne;
For Daunger halt your mercy in his cheyne.

3. ESCAPE

Sin I fro Love escaped am so fat,
I never thenk to ben in his prison lene;
Sin I am free, I counte him not a bene.

halt] holdeth.

GEOFFREY CHAUCER

He may answere, and seye this or that;
I do no fors, I speke right as I mene.
Sin I fro Love escaped am so fat,
I never thenk to ben in his prison lene.

Love hath my name y-strike out of his sclat,
And he is strike out of my bokes clene
For ever-mo; ther is non other mene.
Sin I fro Love escaped am so fat,
I never thenk to ben in his prison lene;
Sin I am free, I counte him not a bene.

THOMAS HOCCLEVE

1368-9?-1450?

13. *Lament for Chaucer*

ALLAS! my worthi maister honorable,
This landes verray tresor and richesse!
Deth by thy deth hath harme irreparable
Unto us doon: hir vengeable duresse
Despoiled hath this land of the swetnesse
Of rethorik; for unto Tullius
Was never man so lyk amonges us.

Also who was hier in philosophie
To Aristotle in our tonge but thou?
The steppes of Virgile in poesie
Thou folwedist eeke, men wot wel ynow.
That combre-worlde that the my maister slow—
Wolde I slayn were!—Deth, was to hastyf
To renne on thee and reve the thi lyf . . .

12. sclat] slate.   *13.* hier] heir.   combre-worlde] encumberer of earth.   slow] slew.

14

THOMAS HOCCLEVE

She myghte han taried hir vengeance a while
Til that sum man had egal to the be;
Nay, lat be that! sche knew wel that this yle
May never man forth brynge lyk to the,
And hir office needes do mot she:
God bad hir so, I truste as for the beste;
O maister, maister, God thi soule reste!

JOHN LYDGATE

1370?-1450?

14. *Vox ultima Crucis*

TARYE no lenger; toward thyn heritage
Hast on thy weye, and be of ryght good chere.
Go eche day onward on thy pylgrymage;
Thynke howe short tyme thou hast abyden here.
Thy place is bygged above the sterres clere,
Noon erthly palys wrought in so statly wyse.
Come on, my frend, my brother most entere!
For the I offered my blood in sacryfice.

KING JAMES I OF SCOTLAND

1394-1437

15. *Spring Song of the Birds*

WORSCHIPPE ye that loveris bene this May,
For of your blisse the Kalendis are begonne,
And sing with us, Away, Winter, away!
Cum, Somer, cum, the suete sesoùn and sonne!
Awake for schame! that have your hevynnis wonne,
And amorously lift up your hedis all,
Thank Lufe that list you to his merci call!

14. bygged] built.　　palys] palace.　　*15.* suete] sweet.
Lufe] Love.

ROBERT HENRYSON
1425-1500

16. Robin and Makyne

ROBIN sat on gude green hill,
  Kepand a flock of fe:
Mirry Makyne said him till
  'Robin, thou rew on me:
I haif thee luvit, loud and still,
  Thir yeiris twa or thre;
My dule in dern bot gif thou dill,
  Doutless but dreid I de.'

Robin answerit 'By the Rude
  Na thing of luve I knaw,
But keipis my scheip undir yon wud:
  Lo, quhair they raik on raw.
Quhat has marrit thee in thy mude,
  Makyne, to me thou shaw;
Or quhat is luve, or to be lude?
  Fain wad I leir that law.'

'At luvis lair gif thou will leir
  Tak thair ane A B C;
Be heynd, courtass, and fair of feir,
  Wyse, hardy, and free:
So that no danger do thee deir
  Quhat dule in dern thou dre;
Preiss thee with pain at all poweir
  Be patient and previe.'

kepand] keeping.   fe] sheep, cattle.   him till] to him.
dule in dern] sorrow in secret.   dill] soothe.   but dreid] without
dread, i. e. there is no fear or doubt.   raik on raw] range in
row.   lude] loved.   leir] learn.   lair] lore.   heynd] gentle.
feir] demeanour.   deir] daunt.   dre] endure.   preiss] endeavour.

ROBERT HENRYSON

Robin answerit hir agane,
  'I wat nocht quhat is lufe;
But I haif mervel in certaine
  Quhat makis thee this wanrufe:
The weddir is fair, and I am fain;
  My scheip gois haill aboif;
And we wald pley us in this plane,
  They wald us baith reproif.'

'Robin, tak tent unto my tale,
  And wirk all as I reid,
And thou sall haif my heart all haill,
  Eik and my maiden-heid:
Sen God sendis bute for baill,
  And for murnyng remeid,
In dern with thee bot gif I daill
  Dowtles I am bot deid.'

'Makyne, to-morn this ilka tyde
  And ye will meit me heir,
Peraventure my scheip may gang besyde,
  Quhyle we haif liggit full neir;
But mawgre haif I, and I byde,
  Fra they begin to steir;
Quhat lyis on heart I will nocht hyd;
  Makyn, then mak gude cheir.'

'Robin, thou reivis me roiff and rest;
  I luve bot thee allane.'
'Makyne, adieu! the sone gois west,
  The day is neir-hand gane.'

wanrufe] unrest.   haill] healthy, whole.   aboif] above, up yonder.   and] if.   tak tent] give heed.   reid] advise.   bute for baill] remedy for hurt.   bot gif] but if, unless.   daill] deal. mawgre haif I] I am uneasy.   reivis] robbest.   roiff] quiet.

ROBERT HENRYSON

'Robin, in dule I am so drest
 That luve will be my bane.'
'Ga luve, Makyne, quhair-evir thow list,
 For lemman I luve nane.'
'Robin, I stand in sic a styll,
 I sicht and that full sair.'
'Makyne, I haif been here this quhyle;
 At hame God gif I wair.'
'My huny, Robin, talk ane quhyll,
 Gif thow will do na mair.'
'Makyn, sum uthir man begyle,
 For hamewart I will fair.'

Robin on his wayis went
 As light as leif of tre;
Makyne murnit in hir intent,
 And trowd him nevir to se.
Robin brayd attour the bent:
 Then Makyne cryit on hie,
'Now may thow sing, for I am schent!
 Quhat alis lufe at me?'

Makyne went hame withowttin fail,
 Full wery eftir cowth weip;
Then Robin in a ful fair daill
 Assemblit all his scheip.
Be that sum part of Makynis aill
 Out-throw his hairt cowd creip;
He fallowit hir fast thair till assaill,
 And till her tuke gude keip.

drest] beset.   lemman] mistress.   sicht] sigh.   in hir intent] in her inward thought.   brayd] strode.   bent] coarse grass.   schent] destroyed.   alis] ails.   be that] by the time that.   till] to.   tuke keip] paid attention.

ROBERT HENRYSON

'Abyd, abyd, thow fair Makyne,
  A word for ony thing;
For all my luve, it sall be thyne,
  Withowttin departing.
All haill thy hairt for till haif myne
  Is all my cuvating;
My scheip to-morn, quhyle houris nyne,
  Will neid of no keping.'

'Robin, thow hes hard soung and say,
  In gestis and storeis auld,
The man that will nocht quhen he may
  Sall haif nocht quhen he wald.
I pray to Jesu every day,
  Mot eik thair cairis cauld
That first preissis with thee to play
  Be firth, forrest, or fauld.'

'Makyne, the nicht is soft and dry,
  The weddir is warme and fair,
And the grene woid rycht neir us by
  To walk attour all quhair:
Thair ma na janglour us espy,
  That is to lufe contrair;
Thairin, Makyne, baith ye and I,
  Unsene we ma repair.'

'Robin, that warld is all away,
  And quyt brocht till ane end:
And nevir agane thereto, perfay,
  Sall it be as thow wend;

hard] heard.   gestis] romances.   mot eik] may add to
be] by.   janglour] talebearer.   wend] weened.

For of my pane thow maid it play;
And all in vane I spend:
As thow hes done, sa sall I say,
"Murne on, I think to mend."'

'Makyne, the howp of all my heill,
My hairt on thee is sett;
And evirmair to thee be leill
Quhill I may leif but lett;
Never to faill as utheris feill,
Quhat grace that evir I gett.'
'Robin, with thee I will nocht deill;
Adieu! for thus we mett.'

Makyne went hame blyth anneuche
Attour the holttis hair;
Robin murnit, and Makyne leuche;
Scho sang, he sichit sair:
And so left him baith wo and wreuch,
In dolour and in cair,
Kepand his hird under a huche
Amangis the holttis hair.

17.   *The Bludy Serk*

THIS hinder yeir I hard be tald
Thair was a worthy King;
Dukis, Erlis, and Barronis bald,
He had at his bidding.

16. howp] hope.   but lett] without hindrance.   anneuche] enough.   holttis hair] grey woodlands.   leuche] laughed.   wreuch] peevish.   huche] heuch, cliff.
17. hinder yeir] last year.

ROBERT HENRYSON

The Lord was ancean and ald,
    And sexty yeiris cowth ring;
He had a dochter fair to fald,
    A lusty Lady ying.

Off all fairheid scho bur the flour,
    And eik hir faderis air;
Off lusty laitis and he honour,
    Meik bot and debonair:
Scho wynnit in a bigly bour,
    On fold wes nane so fair,
Princis luvit hir paramour
    In cuntreis our allquhair.

Thair dwelt a lyt besyde the King
    A foull Gyand of ane;
Stollin he has the Lady ying,
    Away with hir is gane,
And kest her in his dungering
    Quhair licht scho micht se nane;
Hungir and cauld and grit thristing
    Scho fand into hir waine.

He wes the laithliest on to luk
    That on the grund mycht gang:
His nailis wes lyk ane hellis cruk,
    Thairwith fyve quarteris lang;

ring] reign.   fald] enfold.   ying] young.   fairheid] beauty. air] heir.   laitis] manners.   bot and] and also.   scho wynnit] she dwelt.   bigly] well-built.   fold] earth.   paramour] lovingly.   our allquhair] all the world over.   a lyt besyde] a little, (i. e. close) beside.   of ane] as any.   kest] cast. dungering] dungeon.   into hir waine] in her lodging.   hellis cruk] hell-claw.

ROBERT HENRYSON

Thair wes nane that he ourtuk,
  In rycht or yit in wrang,
Bot all in schondir he thame schuk,
  The Gyand wes so strang.

He held the Lady day and nycht
  Within his deip dungeoun,
He wald nocht gif of hir a sicht
  For gold nor yit ransoun—
Bot gif the King mycht get a knycht,
  To fecht with his persoun,
To fecht with him beth day and nycht,
  Quhill ane wer dungin doun.

The King gart seik baith fer and neir,
  Beth be se and land,
Off ony knycht gif he mycht heir
  Wald fecht with that Gyand:
A worthy Prince, that had no peir,
  Hes tane the deid on hand
For the luve of the Lady cleir,
  And held full trew cunnand.

That Prince come prowdly to the toun
  Of that Gyand to heir,
And fawcht with him, his awin persoun,
  And tuke him presoneir,
And kest him in his awin dungeoun
  Allane withouten feir,
With hungir, cauld, and confusioun,
  As full weill worthy weir.

quhill] until.   dungin doun] beaten down.   his awin persoun] himself.   withouten feir] without companion.

ROBERT HENRYSON

Syne brak the bour, had hame the bricht
  Unto her fadir fre.
Sa evill wondit wes the Knycht
  That he behuvit to de;
Unlusum was his likame dicht,
  His sark was all bludy;
In all the world was thair a wicht
  So peteouss for to se?

The Lady murnyt and maid grit mane,
  With all her mekill mycht—
'I luvit nevir lufe bot ane,
  That dulfully now is dicht;
God sen my lyfe were fra me tane
  Or I had seen yone sicht,
Or ellis in begging evir to gane
  Furth with yone curtass knycht.'

He said 'Fair lady, now mone I
  De, trestly ye me trow;
Take ye my serk that is bludy,
  And hing it forrow yow;
First think on it, and syne on me,
  Quhen men cumis yow to wow.'
The Lady said 'Be Mary fre,
  Thairto I mak a vow.'

Quhen that scho lukit to the sark
  Scho thocht on the persoun,
And prayit for him with all hir hart
  That lowsit hir of bandoun,

---

the bricht] the fair one.   likame] body.   lowsit hir of bandoun] loosed her from thraldom.

ROBERT HENRYSON

Quhair scho was wont to sit full merk
    Into that deip dungeoun;
And evir quhill scho wes in quert,
    That was hir a lessoun.

Sa weill the Lady luvit the Knycht
    That no man wald scho tak:
Sa suld we do our God of micht
    That did all for us mak;
Quhilk fullily to deid was dicht,
    For sinfull manis sak,
Sa suld we do beth day and nycht,
    With prayaris to him mak.

This King is lyk the Trinitie,
    Baith in hevin and heir;
The manis saule to the Lady,
    The Gyand to Lucefeir,
The Knycht to Chryst, that deit on tre
    And coft our synnis deir;
The pit to Hele with panis fell,
    The Syn to the woweir.

The Lady was wowd, but scho said nay
    With men that wald hir wed;
Sa suld we wryth all sin away
    That in our breist is bred.
I pray to Jesu Chryst verray,
    For ws his blud that bled,
To be our help on domisday
    Quhair lawis ar straitly led.

quert] prison.   coft] bought.   straitly led] strictly carried out.

ROBERT HENRYSON

The saule is Godis dochtir deir,
  And eik his handewerk,
That was betrayit with Lucefeir,
  Quha sittis in hell full merk:
Borrowit with Chrystis angell cleir,
  Hend men, will ye nocht herk?
And for his lufe that bocht us deir
  Think on the BLUDY SERK!

WILLIAM DUNBAR
1465-1520?

18.   *To a Lady*

SWEET rois of vertew and of gentilness,
  Delytsum lily of everie lustynes,
Richest in bontie and in bewtie clear,
And everie vertew that is wenit dear,
Except onlie that ye are mercyless

Into your garth this day I did persew;
There saw I flowris that fresche were of hew;
  Baith quhyte and reid most lusty were to seyne,
  And halesome herbis upon stalkis greene;
Yet leaf nor flowr find could I nane of rew.

I doubt that Merche, with his cauld blastis keyne,
Has slain this gentil herb, that I of mene;
  Quhois piteous death dois to my heart sic paine
  That I would make to plant his root againe,—
So confortand his levis unto me bene.

17. hend] gentle.   18. rois] rose.   wenit] weened, esteemed.
garth] garden-close.   to seyne] to see.   that I of mene] that I complain of, mourn for.

WILLIAM DUNBAR

19. *In Honour of the City of London*

LONDON, thou art of townes *A per se.*
    Soveraign of cities, seemliest in sight,
Of high renoun, riches and royaltie;
    Of lordis, barons, and many a goodly knyght;
    Of most delectable lusty ladies bright;
Of famous prelatis, in habitis clericall;
    Of merchauntis full of substaunce and of myght:
London, thou art the flour of Cities all.

Gladdith anon, thou lusty Troynovaunt,
    Citie that some tyme cleped was New Troy;
In all the erth, imperiall as thou stant,
    Pryncesse of townes, of pleasure and of joy,
    A richer restith under no Christen roy;
For manly power, with craftis naturall,
    Fourmeth none fairer sith the flode of Noy:
London, thou art the flour of Cities all.

Gemme of all joy, jasper of jocunditie,
    Most myghty carbuncle of vertue and valour;
Strong Troy in vigour and in strenuytie;
    Of royall cities rose and geraflour;
    Empress of townes, exalt in honour;
In beawtie beryng the crone imperiall;
    Swete paradise precelling in pleasure;
London, thou art the flour of Cities all.

Above all ryvers thy Ryver hath renowne,
    Whose beryall stremys, pleasaunt and preclare,
Under thy lusty wallys renneth down,
    Where many a swan doth swymme with wyngis fair;

gladdith] rejoice.   Troynovaunt] Troja nova or Trinovantum.
fourmeth] appeareth.   geraflour] gillyflower.

Where many a barge doth saile and row with are;
Where many a ship doth rest with top-royall.
   O, towne of townes! patrone and not compare,
London, thou art the flour of Cities all.

Upon thy lusty Brigge of pylers white
   Been merchauntis full royall to behold;
Upon thy stretis goeth many a semely knyght
   In velvet gownes and in cheynes of gold.
By Julyus Cesar thy Tour founded of old
May be the hous of Mars victoryall,
   Whose artillary with tonge may not be told:
London, thou art the flour of Cities all.

Strong be thy wallis that about thee standis;
   Wise be the people that within thee dwellis;
Fresh is thy ryver with his lusty strandis;
   Blith be thy chirches, wele sownyng be thy bellis;
Rich be thy merchauntis in substaunce that excellis;
Fair be their wives, right lovesom, white and small;
   Clere be thy virgyns, lusty under kellis:
London, thou art the flour of Cities all.

Thy famous Maire, by pryncely governaunce,
   With sword of justice thee ruleth prudently.
No Lord of Parys, Venyce, or Floraunce
   In dignitye or honour goeth to hym nigh.
He is exampler, loode-ster, and guye;
Principall patrone and rose orygynalle,
   Above all Maires as maister most worthy:
London, thou art the flour of Cities all.

are] oar.   small] slender.   kellis] hoods, head-dresses.
guye] guide.

WILLIAM DUNBAR

20. *On the Nativity of Christ*

RORATE *coeli desuper!*
Hevins, distil your balmy schouris!
For now is risen the bricht day-ster,
Fro the rose Mary, flour of flouris:
The cleir Sone, quhom no cloud devouris,
Surmounting Phebus in the Est,
Is cumin of his hevinly touris:
Et nobis Puer natus est.

Archangellis, angellis, and dompnationis,
Tronis, potestatis, and marteiris seir,
And all ye hevinly operationis,
Ster, planeit, firmament, and spheir,
Fire, erd, air, and water cleir,
To Him gife loving, most and lest,
That come in to so meik maneir;
Et nobis Puer natus est.

Synnaris be glad, and penance do,
And thank your Maker hairtfully;
For he that ye micht nocht come to
To you is cumin full humbly
Your soulis with his blood to buy
And loose you of the fiendis arrest—
And only of his own mercy;
Pro nobis Puer natus est.

All clergy do to him inclyne,
And bow unto that bairn benyng,
And do your observance divyne
To him that is of kingis King:

schouris] showers.   cumin] come, entered.   seir] various.
erd] earth.   lest] least.   synnaris] sinners.   benyng] benign.

WILLIAM DUNBAR

Encense his altar, read and sing
In holy kirk, with mind degest,
   Him honouring attour all thing
    Qui nobis Puer natus est.

Celestial foulis in the air,
   Sing with your nottis upon hicht,
In firthis and in forrestis fair
   Be myrthful now at all your mycht;
For passit is your dully nicht,
   Aurora has the cloudis perst,
   The Sone is risen with glaidsum licht,
    Et nobis Puer natus est.

Now spring up flouris fra the rute,
   Revert you upward naturaly,
In honour of the blissit frute
   That raiss up fro the rose Mary;
Lay out your levis lustily,
   Fro deid take life now at the lest
   In wirschip of that Prince worthy
    Qui nobis Puer natus est.

Sing, hevin imperial, most of hicht!
Regions of air mak armony!
All fish in flud and fowl of flicht
   Be mirthful and mak melody!
All *Gloria in excelsis* cry!
Heaven, erd, se, man, bird, and best,—
   He that is crownit abone the sky
    Pro nobis Puer natus est!

attour] over, above.   perst] pierced.   raiss] rose.
best] beast.

21. Lament for the Makers

I THAT in heill was and gladnèss
Am trublit now with great sickness
And feblit with infirmitie:—
Timor Mortis conturbat me.

Our plesance here is all vain glory,
This fals world is but transitory,
The flesh is bruckle, the Feynd is slee:—
Timor Mortis conturbat me.

The state of man does change and vary,
Now sound, now sick, now blyth, now sary,
Now dansand mirry, now like to die:—
Timor Mortis conturbat me.

No state in Erd here standis sicker;
As with the wynd wavis the wicker
So wannis this world's vanitie:—
Timor Mortis conturbat me.

Unto the Death gois all Estatis,
Princis, Prelatis, and Potestatis,
Baith rich and poor of all degree:—
Timor Mortis conturbat me.

He takis the knichtis in to the field
Enarmit under helm and scheild;
Victor he is at all mellie:—
Timor Mortis conturbat me.

heill] health. bruckle] brittle, feeble. slee] sly. dansand] dancing. sicker] sure. wicker] willow. wannis] wanes. mellie] mellay.

WILLIAM DUNBAR

That strong unmerciful tyrand
Takis, on the motheris breast sowkand,
The babe full of benignitie:—
  Timor Mortis conturbat me.

He takis the campion in the stour,
The captain closit in the tour,
The lady in bour full of bewtie:—
  Timor Mortis conturbat me.

He spairis no lord for his piscence,
Na clerk for his intelligence;
His awful straik may no man flee:—
  Timor Mortis conturbat me.

Art-magicianis and astrologgis,
Rethoris, logicianis, and theologgis,
Them helpis no conclusionis slee:—
  Timor Mortis conturbat me.

In medecine the most practicianis,
Leechis, surrigianis, and physicianis,
Themself from Death may not supplee:—
  Timor Mortis conturbat me.

I see that makaris amang the lave
Playis here their padyanis, syne gois to grave;
Sparit is nocht their facultie:—
  Timor Mortis conturbat me.

He has done petuously devour
The noble Chaucer, of makaris flour,
The Monk of Bury, and Gower, all three:—
  Timor Mortis conturbat me.

sowkand] sucking. campion] champion. stour] fight.
piscence] puissance. straik] stroke. supplee] save. makaris] poets. the lave] the leave, the rest. padyanis] pageants.

WILLIAM DUNBAR

The good Sir Hew of Eglintoun,
Ettrick, Heriot, and Wintoun,
He has tane out of this cuntrie :—
Timor Mortis conturbat me.

That scorpion fell has done infeck
Maister John Clerk, and James Afflek,
Fra ballat-making and tragedie :—
Timor Mortis conturbat me.

Holland and Barbour he has berevit;
Alas! that he not with us levit
Sir Mungo Lockart of the Lee :—
Timor Mortis conturbat me.

Clerk of Tranent eke he has tane,
That made the anteris of Gawaine;
Sir Gilbert Hay endit has he :—
Timor Mortis conturbat me.

He has Blind Harry and Sandy Traill
Slain with his schour of mortal hail,
Quhilk Patrick Johnstoun might nought flee :—
Timor Mortis conturbat me.

He has reft Merseir his endite,
That did in luve so lively write,
So short, so quick, of sentence hie :—
Timor Mortis conturbat me.

He has tane Rowll of Aberdene,
And gentill Rowll of Corstorphine;
Two better fallowis did no man see :—
Timor Mortis conturbat me.

anteris] adventures.   schour] shower.   endite] inditing.
fallowis] fellows.

WILLIAM DUNBAR

In Dunfermline he has tane Broun
With Maister Robert Henrysoun;
Sir John the Ross enbrast has he:—
  Timor Mortis conturbat me.

And he has now tane, last of a,
Good gentil Stobo and Quintin Shaw,
Of quhom all wichtis hes pitie:—
  Timor Mortis conturbat me.

Good Maister Walter Kennedy
In point of Death lies verily;
Great ruth it were that so suld be:—
  Timor Mortis conturbat me.

Sen he has all my brether tane,
He will naught let me live alane;
Of force I man his next prey be:—
  Timor Mortis conturbat me.

Since for the Death remeid is none,
Best is that we for Death dispone,
After our death that live may we:—
  Timor Mortis conturbat me.

ANONYMOUS

15th Cent.

22. *May in the Green-Wood*

IN somer when the shawes be sheyne,
  And leves be large and long,
Hit is full merry in feyre foreste
  To here the foulys song.

---

21. wichtis] wights, persons.   man] must.   dispone] make disposition.   *22.* sheyne] bright.

ANONYMOUS

To se the dere draw to the dale
And leve the hilles hee,
And shadow him in the leves grene
Under the green-wode tree.

Hit befell on Whitsontide
Early in a May mornyng,
The Sonne up faire can shyne,
And the briddis mery can syng.

'This is a mery mornyng,' said Litulle Johne,
'Be Hym that dyed on tre;
A more mery man than I am one
Lyves not in Christiantè.

'Pluk up thi hert, my dere mayster,'
Litulle Johne can say,
'And thynk hit is a fulle fayre tyme
In a mornynge of May.'

23. *Carol*
                                        15th Cent.

I SING of a maiden
That is makeles;
King of all kings
To her son she ches.

He came al so still
There his mother was,
As dew in April
That falleth on the grass.

23. makeles] matchless.   ches] chose.

ANONYMOUS

He came al so still
  To his mother's bour,
As dew in April
  That falleth on the flour.

He came al so still
  There his mother lay,
As dew in April
  That falleth on the spray.

Mother and maiden
  Was never none but she;
Well may such a lady
  Goddes mother be.

24. *Quia Amore Langueo*

15th Cent. (?)

IN a valley of this restles mind
  I sought in mountain and in mead,
Trusting a true love for to find.
Upon an hill then took I heed;
A voice I heard (and near I yede)
In great dolour complaining tho:
See, dear soul, how my sides bleed
  Quia amore langueo.

Upon this hill I found a tree,
Under a tree a man sitting;
From head to foot wounded was he;
His hearte blood I saw bleeding:
A seemly man to be a king,
A gracious face to look unto.
I askèd why he had paining;
  [He said,] *Quia amore langueo.*

24. yede] went.

ANONYMOUS

I am true love that false was never;
My sister, man's soul, I loved her thus.
Because we would in no wise dissever
I left my kingdom glorious.
I purveyed her a palace full precious;
She fled, I followed, I loved her so
That I suffered this pain piteous
   Quia amore langueo.

My fair love and my spouse bright!
I saved her from beating, and she hath me bet;
I clothed her in grace and heavenly light;
This bloody shirt she hath on me set;
For longing of love yet would I not let;
Sweete strokes are these: lo!
I have loved her ever as I her het
   Quia amore langueo.

I crowned her with bliss and she me with thorn;
I led her to chamber and she me to die;
I brought her to worship and she me to scorn;
I did her reverence and she me villany.
To love that loveth is no maistry;
Her hate made never my love her foe:
Ask me then no question why—
   Quia amore langueo.

Look unto mine handes, man!
These gloves were given me when I her sought;
They be not white, but red and wan;
Embroidered with blood my spouse them brought.
They will not off; I loose hem nought;

het] promised.

ANONYMOUS

I woo her with hem wherever she go.
These hands for her so friendly fought
   Quia amore langueo.

Marvel not, man, though I sit still.
See, love hath shod me wonder strait:
Buckled my feet, as was her will,
With sharpe nails (well thou may'st wait!)
In my love was never desait;
All my membres I have opened her to;
My body I made her herte's bait
   Quia amore langueo.

In my side I have made her nest;
Look in, how weet a wound is here!
This is her chamber, here shall she rest,
That she and I may sleep in fere.
Here may she wash, if any filth were;
Here is seat for all her woe;
Come when she will, she shall have cheer
   Quia amore langueo.

I will abide till she be ready,
I will her sue if she say nay;
If she be retchless I will be greedy,
If she be dangerous I will her pray;
If she weep, then bide I ne may:
Mine arms ben spread to clip her me to.
Cry once, I come: now, soul, assay
   Quia amore langueo.

Fair love, let us go play:
Apples ben ripe in my gardayne.

bait] resting-place.   weet] wet.   in fere] together.

ANONYMOUS

I shall thee clothe in a new array,
Thy meat shall be milk, honey and wine.
Fair love, let us go dine:
Thy sustenance is in my crippe, lo!
Tarry thou not, my fair spouse mine,
    Quia amore langueo.

If thou be foul, I shall thee make clean;
If thou be sick, I shall thee heal;
If thou mourn ought, I shall thee mene;
Why wilt thou not, fair love, with me deal?
Foundest thou ever love so leal?
What wilt thou, soul, that I shall do?
I may not unkindly thee appeal
    Quia amore langueo.

What shall I do now with my spouse
But abide her of my gentleness,
Till that she look out of her house
Of fleshly affection? love mine she is;
Her bed is made, her bolster is bliss,
Her chamber is chosen; is there none mo.
Look out on me at the window of kindeness
    Quia amore langueo.

My love is in her chamber: hold your peace!
Make ye no noise, but let her sleep.
My babe I would not were in disease,
I may not hear my dear child weep.
With my pap I shall her keep;
Ne marvel ye not though I tend her to:
This wound in my side had ne'er be so deep
    But *Quia amore langueo.*

crippe] scrip.   mene] care for.

ANONYMOUS

Long thou for love never so high,
My love is more than thine may be.
Thou weepest, thou gladdest, I sit thee by:
Yet wouldst thou once, love, look unto me!
Should I always feede thee
With children meat? Nay, love, not so!
I will prove thy love with adversitè
   Quia amore langueo.

Wax not weary, mine own wife!
What mede is aye to live in comfort?
In tribulation I reign more rife
Ofter times than in disport.
In weal and in woe I am aye to support:
Mine own wife, go not me fro!
Thy mede is marked, when thou art mort:
   Quia amore langueo.

25.   *The Nut-Brown Maid*
                                   15th Cent.

He. BE it right or wrong, these men among
        On women do complain ;
Affirming this, how that it is
    A labour spent in vain
To love them wele ; for never a dele
    They love a man again :
For let a man do what he can
    Their favour to attain,
Yet if a new to them pursue,
    Their first true lover than
Laboureth for naught ; for from her thought
    He is a banished man.

25. never a dele] never a bit.   than] then.

ANONYMOUS

She.   *I say not nay, but that all day*
    It is both written and said
  That woman's faith is, as who saith,
    All utterly decayd:
  But nevertheless, right good witnèss
    In this case might be laid
  That they love true and continue:
    Record the Nut-brown Maid,
  Which, when her love came her to prove,
    To her to make his moan,
  Would not depart; for in her heart
    She loved but him alone.

He.   *Then between us let us discuss*
    What was all the manere
  Between them two: we will also
    Tell all the pain in fere
  That she was in. Now I begin,
    So that ye me answere:
  Wherefore all ye that present be,
    I pray you, give an ear.
  I am the Knight. I come by night,
    As secret as I can,
  Saying, Alas! thus standeth the case,
    I am a banished man.

She.   *And I your will for to fulfil*
    In this will not refuse;
  Trusting to show, in wordes few,
    That men have an ill use—
  To their own shame—women to blame,
    And causeless them accuse.

in fere] in company together.

ANONYMOUS

Therefore to you I answer now,
All women to excuse—
Mine own heart dear, with you what cheer?
I pray you, tell anone;
For, in my mind, of all mankind
I love but you alone.

He. It standeth so: a deed is do
Whereof great harm shall grow:
My destiny is for to die
A shameful death, I trow;
Or else to flee. The t' one must be.
None other way I know
But to withdraw as an outlàw,
And take me to my bow.
Wherefore adieu, mine own heart true!
None other rede I can:
For I must to the green-wood go,
Alone, a banished man.

She. O Lord, what is this worldis bliss,
That changeth as the moon!
My summer's day in lusty May
Is darked before the noon.
I hear you say, farewell: Nay, nay,
We dèpart not so soon.
Why say ye so? whither will ye go?
Alas! what have ye done?
All my welfàre to sorrow and care
Should change, if ye were gone:
For, in my mind, of all mankind
I love but you alone.

rede I can] counsel I know.

ANONYMOUS

He. I can believe it shall you grieve,
    And somewhat you distrain;
But afterward, your paines hard
    Within a day or twain
Shall soon aslake; and ye shall take
    Comfort to you again.
Why should ye ought? for, to make thought,
    Your labour were in vain.
And thus I do; and pray you to,
    As hartely as I can:
For I must to the green-wood go,
    Alone, a banished man.

She. Now, sith that ye have showed to me
    The secret of your mind,
I shall be plain to you again,
    Like as ye shall me find.
Sith it is so that ye will go,
    I will not live behind.
Shall never be said the Nut-brown Maid
    Was to her love unkind.
Make you ready, for so am I,
    Although it were anone:
For, in my mind, of all mankind
    I love but you alone.

He. Yet I you rede to take good heed
    What men will think and say:
Of young, of old, it shall be told
    That ye be gone away
Your wanton will for to fulfil,
    In green-wood you to play;

ANONYMOUS

      And that ye might for your delight
        No longer make delay
      Rather than ye should thus for me
        Be called an ill womàn
      Yet would I to the green-wood go,
        Alone, a banished man.

She. Though it be sung of old and young
        That I should be to blame,
      Theirs be the charge that speak so large
        In hurting of my name:
      For I will prove that faithful love
        It is devoid of shame;
      In your distress and heaviness
        To part with you the same:
      And sure all tho that do not so
        True lovers are they none:
      For in my mind, of all mankind
        I love but you alone.

He. I counsel you, Remember how
        It is no maiden's law
      Nothing to doubt, but to run out
        To wood with an outlàw.
      For ye must there in your hand bear
        A bow ready to draw;
      And as a thief thus must you live
        Ever in dread and awe;
      Whereby to you great harm might grow:
        Yet had I liever than
      That I had to the green-wood go,
        Alone, a banished man.

part with] share with.   tho] those.

ANONYMOUS

She. I think not nay but as ye say;
    It is no maiden's lore;
But love may make me for your sake,
    As I have said before,
To come on foot, to hunt and shoot,
    To get us meat and store;
For so that I your company
    May have, I ask no more.
From which to part it maketh my heart
    As cold as any stone;
For, in my mind, of all mankind
    I love but you alone.

He. For an outlàw this is the law,
    That men him take and bind:
Without pitie, hangèd to be,
    And waver with the wind.
If I had need (as God forbede!)
    What socours could ye find?
Forsooth I trow, you and your bow
    For fear would draw behind.
And no mervail; for little avail
    Were in your counsel than:
Wherefore I'll to the green-wood go,
    Alone, a banished man.

She. Right well know ye that women be
    But feeble for to fight;
No womanhede it is, indeed,
    To be bold as a knight:
Yet in such fear if that ye were
    With enemies day and night,

ANONYMOUS

    I would withstand, with bow in hand,
      To grieve them as I might,
    And you to save; as women have
      From death men many one:
    For, in my mind, of all mankind
      I love but you alone.

He. Yet take good hede; for ever I drede
      That ye could not sustain
    The thorny ways, the deep vallèys,
      The snow, the frost, the rain,
    The cold, the heat; for dry or wete,
      We must lodge on the plain;
    And, us above, no other roof
      But a brake bush or twain:
    Which soon should grieve you, I believe;
      And ye would gladly than
    That I had to the green-wood go,
      Alone, a banished man.

She. Sith I have here been partynere
      With you of joy and bliss,
    I must alsò part of your woe
      Endure, as reason is:
    Yet I am sure of one pleasùre,
      And shortly it is this—
    That where ye be, me seemeth, pardé,
      I could not fare amiss.
    Without more speech I you beseech
      That we were shortly gone;
    For, in my mind, of all mankind
      I love but you alone.

ANONYMOUS

He. If ye go thyder, ye must consider,
    When ye have lust to dine,
There shall no meat be for to gete,
    Nether bere, ale, ne wine,
Ne shetès clean, to lie between,
    Made of thread and twine;
None other house, but leaves and boughs,
    To cover your head and mine.
Lo, mine heart sweet, this ill diète
    Should make you pale and wan:
Wherefore I'll to the green-wood go,
    Alone, a banished man.

She. Among the wild deer such an archère,
    As men say that ye be,
Ne may not fail of good vitayle
    Where is so great plentè:
And water clear of the rivere
    Shall be full sweet to me;
With which in hele I shall right wele
    Endure, as ye shall see;
And, or we go, a bed or two
    I can provide anone;
For, in my mind, of all mankind
    I love but you alone.

He. Lo yet, before, ye must do more,
    If ye will go with me:
As, cut your hair up by your ear,
    Your kirtle by the knee;
With bow in hand for to withstand
    Your enemies, if need be:

hele] health.

ANONYMOUS

And this same night, before daylight,
  To woodward will I flee.
If that ye will all this fulfil,
  Do it shortly as ye can:
Else will I to the green-wood go,
  Alone, a banished man.

She. I shall as now do more for you
  Than 'longeth to womanhede;
To short my hair, a bow to bear,
  To shoot in time of need.
O my sweet mother! before all other
  For you I have most drede!
But now, adieu! I must ensue
  Where fortune doth me lead.
All this make ye: Now let us flee;
  The day cometh fast upon:
For, in my mind, of all mankind
  I love but you alone.

He. Nay, nay, not so; ye shall not go,
  And I shall tell you why—
Your appetite is to be light
  Of love, I well espy:
For, right as ye have said to me,
  In likewise hardily
Ye would answere whosoever it were,
  In way of company:
It is said of old, Soon hot, soon cold;
  And so is a woman:
Wherefore I to the wood will go,
  Alone, a banished man.

ANONYMOUS

She. If ye take heed, it is no need
    Such words to say to me;
For oft ye prayed, and long assayed,
    Or I loved you, pardè:
And though that I of ancestry
    A baron's daughter be,
Yet have you proved how I you loved,
    A squire of low degree;
And ever shall, whatso befall
    To die therefore anone;
For, in my mind, of all mankind
    I love but you alone.

He. A baron's child to be beguiled,
    It were a cursèd deed!
To be felàw with an outlaw—
    Almighty God forbede!
Yet better were the poor squyere
    Alone to forest yede
Than ye shall say another day
    That by my cursèd rede
Ye were betrayed. Wherefore, good maid,
    The best rede that I can,
Is, that I to the green-wood go,
    Alone, a banished man.

She. Whatever befall, I never shall
    Of this thing be upbraid:
But if ye go, and leave me so,
    Then have ye me betrayed.
Remember you wele, how that ye dele;
    For if ye, as ye said,

yede] went.

ANONYMOUS

    Be so unkind to leave behind
      Your love, the Nut-brown Maid,
    Trust me truly that I shall die
      Soon after ye be gone:
    For, in my mind, of all mankind
      I love but you alone.

He. If that ye went, ye should repent;
      For in the forest now
    I have purveyed me of a maid
      Whom I love more than you:
    Another more fair than ever ye were
      I dare it well avow;
    And of you both each should be wroth
      With other, as I trow:
    It were mine ease to live in peace;
      So will I, if I can:
    Wherefore I to the wood will go,
      Alone, a banished man.

She. Though in the wood I understood
      Ye had a paramour,
    All this may nought remove my thought,
      But that I will be your':
    And she shall find me soft and kind
      And courteis every hour;
    Glad to fulfil all that she will
      Command me, to my power:
    For had ye, lo, an hundred mo,
      Yet would I be that one:
    For, in my mind, of all mankind
      I love but you alone.

ANONYMOUS

He. Mine own dear love, I see the prove
    That ye be kind and true;
  Of maid, of wife, in all my life,
    The best that ever I knew.
  Be merry and glad; be no more sad;
    The case is changèd new;
  For it were ruth that for your truth
    Ye should have cause to rue.
  Be not dismayed, whatsoever I said
    To you when I began:
  I will not to the green-wood go;
    I am no banished man.

She. These tidings be more glad to me
    Than to be made a queen,
  If I were sure they should endure;
    But it is often seen
  When men will break promise they speak
    The wordis on the splene.
  Ye shape some wile me to beguile,
    And steal from me, I ween:
  Then were the case worse than it was,
    And I more wo-begone:
  For, in my mind, of all mankind
    I love but you alone.

He. Ye shall not nede further to drede:
    I will not disparàge
  You (God defend), sith you descend
    Of so great a linàge.
  Now understand: to Westmoreland,
    Which is my heritage,

on the splene] that is, in haste.

ANONYMOUS

I will you bring; and with a ring,
  By way of marriàge
I will you take, and lady make,
  As shortly as I can:
Thus have you won an Earles son,
  And not a banished man.

Here may ye see that women be
  In love meek, kind, and stable ;
Let never man reprove them than,
  Or call them variable ;
But rather pray God that we may
  To them be comfortable ;
Which sometime proveth such as He loveth,
  If they be charitable.
For sith men would that women should
  Be meek to them each one ;
Much more ought they to God obey,
  And serve but Him alone.

26. *As ye came from the Holy Land*

16th Cent.

AS ye came from the holy land
  Of Walsinghame,
Met you not with my true love
  By the way as you came?

How should I know your true love,
  That have met many a one
As I came from the holy land,
  That have come, that have gone?

51

ANONYMOUS

She is neither white nor brown,
    But as the heavens fair;
There is none hath her form divine
    In the earth or the air.

Such a one did I meet, good sir,
    Such an angelic face,
Who like a nymph, like a queen, did appear
    In her gait, in her grace.

She hath left me here alone
    All alone, as unknown,
Who sometime did me lead with herself,
    And me loved as her own.

What's the cause that she leaves you alone
    And a new way doth take,
That sometime did love you as her own,
    And her joy did you make?

I have loved her all my youth,
    But now am old, as you see:
Love likes not the falling fruit,
    Nor the withered tree.

Know that Love is a careless child,
    And forgets promise past:
He is blind, he is deaf when he list,
    And in faith never fast.

His desire is a dureless content,
    And a trustless joy;
He is won with a world of despair,
    And is lost with a toy.

ANONYMOUS

Of womenkind such indeed is the love,
  Or the word love abusèd,
Under which many childish desires
  And conceits are excusèd.

But true love is a durable fire,
  In the mind ever burning,
Never sick, never dead, never cold,
  From tself never turning.

27. *The Lover in Winter Plaineth for the Spring*
                           16th Cent. (?)

O WESTERN wind, when wilt thou blow
  That the small rain down can rain?
Christ, that my love were in my arms
  And I in my bed again!

28. *Balow*
                                16th Cent.

BALOW, my babe, lie still and sleep!
  It grieves me sore to see thee weep.
Wouldst thou be quiet I'se be glad,
Thy mourning makes my sorrow sad:
Balow my boy, thy mother's joy,
Thy father breeds me great annoy—
      Balow, la-low!

When he began to court my love,
And with his sugred words me move,
His faynings false and flattering cheer
To me that time did not appear:

ANONYMOUS

But now I see most cruellye
He cares ne for my babe nor me—
    Balow, la-low!

Lie still, my darling, sleep awhile,
And when thou wak'st thou'le sweetly smile:
But smile not as thy father did,
To cozen maids: nay, God forbid!
But yet I fear thou wilt go near
Thy father's heart and face to bear—
    Balow, la-low!

I cannot choose but ever will
Be loving to thy father. still;
Where'er he go, where'er he ride,
My love with him doth still abide;
In weal or woe, where'er he go,
My heart shall ne'er depart him fro—
    Balow, la-low!

But do not, do not, pretty mine,
To faynings false thy heart incline!
Be loyal to thy lover true,
And never change her for a new:
If good or fair, of her have care
For women's banning's wondrous sare—
    Balow, la-low!

Bairn, by thy face I will beware;
Like Sirens' words, I'll come not near;
My babe and I together will live;
He'll comfort me when cares do grieve.
My babe and I right soft will lie,
And ne'er respect man's crueltye—
    Balow, la-low!

ANONYMOUS

    Farewell, farewell, the falsest youth
    That ever kist a woman's mouth!
    I wish all maids be warn'd by me
    Never to trust man's curtesye;
    For if we do but chance to bow,
    They'll use us then they care not how—
        Balow, la-low!

29. *The Old Cloak*
16th Cent. (?)

THIS winter's weather it waxeth cold,
    And frost it freezeth on every hill,
And Boreas blows his blast so bold
    That all our cattle are like to spill.
Bell, my wife, she loves no strife;
    She said unto me quietlye,
Rise up, and save cow Crumbock's life!
    Man, put thine old cloak about thee!

He. O Bell my wife, why dost thou flyte?
    Thou kens my cloak is very thin:
It is so bare and over worn,
    A crickè thereon cannot renn.
Then I'll no longer borrow nor lend;
    For once I'll new apparell'd be;
To-morrow I'll to town and spend;
    For I'll have a new cloak about me.

She. Cow Crumbock is a very good cow:
    She has been always true to the pail;
She has helped us to butter and cheese, I trow,
    And other things she will not fail.

29. flyte] scold.

ANONYMOUS

    I would be loth to see her pine.
      Good husband, counsel take of me:
    It is not for us to go so fine—
      Man, take thine old cloak about thee!

He. My cloak it was a very good cloak,
      It hath been always true to the wear;
    But now it is not worth a groat:
      I have had it four and forty year'.
    Sometime it was of cloth in grain:
      'Tis now but a sigh clout, as you may see:
    It will neither hold out wind nor rain;
      And I'll have a new cloak about me.

She. It is four and forty years ago
      Sine the one of us the other did ken;
    And we have had, betwixt us two,
      Of children either nine or ten:
    We have brought them up to women and men:
      In the fear of God I trow they be.
    And why wilt thou thyself misken?
      Man, take thine old cloak about thee!

He. O Bell my wife, why dost thou flyte?
      Now is now, and then was then:
    Seek now all the world throughout,
      Thou kens not clowns from gentlemen:
    They are clad in black, green, yellow and blue,
      So far above their own degree.
    Once in my life I'll take a view;
      For I'll have a new cloak about me.

cloth in grain] scarlet cloth.   sigh clout] a rag for straining.

ANONYMOUS

She. King Stephen was a worthy peer;
　　His breeches cost him but a crown;
　He held them sixpence all too dear,
　　Therefore he called the tailor 'lown.'
　He was a king and wore the crown,
　　And thou'se but of a low degree:
　It's pride that puts this country down:
　　Man, take thy old cloak about thee!

He. Bell my wife, she loves not strife,
　　Yet she will lead me, if she can;
　And to maintain an easy life
　　I oft must yield, though I'm good-man.
　It's not for a man with a woman to threap,
　　Unless he first give o'er the plea:
　As we began, so will we keep,
　　And I'll take my old cloak about me.

JOHN SKELTON
1460?-1529

30. *To Mistress Margery Wentworth*

WITH margerain gentle,
　　The flower of goodlihead,
Embroidered the mantle
　　Is of your maidenhead.
Plainly I cannot glose;
　　Ye be, as I divine,
The pretty primrose,
　　The goodly columbine.

29. threap] argue.　　*30.* margerain] marjoram.

Benign, courteous, and meek,
　With wordes well devised;
In you, who list to seek,
　Be virtues well comprised.
With margerain gentle,
　The flower of goodlihead,
Embroidered the mantle
　Is of your maidenhead.

31. *To Mistress Margaret Hussey*

MERRY Margaret
　　As midsummer flower,
Gentle as falcon
Or hawk of the tower:
With solace and gladness,
Much mirth and no madness,
All good and no badness;
　　So joyously,
　　So maidenly,
　　So womanly
　　Her demeaning
　　In every thing,
　　Far, far passing
　　That I can indite,
　　Or suffice to write
Of Merry Margaret
As midsummer flower,
Gentle as falcon
Or hawk of the tower.

JOHN SKELTON

As patient and still
And as full of good will
As fair Isaphill,
Coliander,
Sweet pomander,
Good Cassander;
Steadfast of thought,
Well made, well wrought.
Far may be sought,
Ere that ye can find
So courteous, so kind
As merry Margaret,
This midsummer flower.
Gentle as falcon
Or hawk of the tower.

STEPHEN HAWES
d. 1523

32. *The True Knight*

FOR knighthood is not in the feats of warre,
As for to fight in quarrel right or wrong,
But in a cause which truth can not defarre:
He ought himself for to make sure and strong,
Justice to keep mixt with mercy among:
And no quarrell a knight ought to take
But for a truth, or for the common's sake.

31. Isaphill] Hypsipyle.   coliander] coriander seed, an aromatic.
pomander] a ball of perfume.   Cassander] Cassandra.
32. defarre] undo.

STEPHEN HAWES

33. *An Epitaph*

O MORTAL folk, you may behold and see
   How I lie here, sometime a mighty knight;
The end of joy and all prosperitee
   Is death at last, thorough his course and might:
   After the day there cometh the dark night,
     For though the daye be never so long,
     At last the bells ringeth to evensong.

SIR THOMAS WYATT
1503-1542

34. *Forget not yet*

The Lover Beseecheth his Mistress not to Forget his Steadfast Faith and True Intent

FORGET not yet the tried intent
   Of such a truth as I have meant;
My great travail so gladly spent,
   Forget not yet!

Forget not yet when first began
The weary life ye know, since whan
The suit, the service, none tell can;
   Forget not yet!

Forget not yet the great assays,
The cruel wrong, the scornful ways,
The painful patience in delays,
   Forget not yet!

Forget not! O, forget not this!—
How long ago hath been, and is,
The mind that never meant amiss—
   Forget not yet!

Forget not then thine own approved,
The which so long hath thee so loved,
Whose steadfast faith yet never moved:
Forget not this!

35. *The Appeal*

An Earnest Suit to his Unkind Mistress, not to Forsake him

AND wilt thou leave me thus!
  Say nay, say nay, for shame!
—To save thee from the blame
Of all my grief and grame.
And wilt thou leave me thus?
  Say nay! say nay!

And wilt thou leave me thus,
That hath loved thee so long
In wealth and woe among:
And is thy heart so strong
As for to leave me thus?
  Say nay! say nay!

And wilt thou leave me thus,
That hath given thee my heart
Never for to depart
Neither for pain nor smart:
And wilt thou leave me thus?
  Say nay! say nay!

35. grame] sorrow.

And wilt thou leave me thus,
And have no more pitye
Of him that loveth thee?
Alas, thy cruelty!
And wilt thou leave me thus?
Say nay! say nay!

36. *A Revocation*

WHAT should I say?
 —Since Faith is dead,
And Truth away
 From you is fled?
 Should I be led
  With doubleness?
  Nay! nay! mistress.

I promised you,
 And you promised me,
To be as true
 As I would be.
 But since I see
  Your double heart,
  Farewell my part!

Thought for to take
 'Tis not my mind;
But to forsake
 One so unkind;
 And as I find
  So will I trust.
  Farewell, unjust!

SIR THOMAS WYATT

> Can ye say nay
> But that you said
> That I alway
> Should be obeyed?
> And—thus betrayed
> Or that I wist!
> Farewell, unkist!

37. *Vixi Puellis Nuper Idoneus* . . .

THEY flee from me that sometime did me seek,
 With naked foot stalking within my chamber:
Once have I seen them gentle, tame, and meek,
 That now are wild, and do not once remember
 That sometime they have put themselves in danger
To take bread at my hand; and now they range,
Busily seeking in continual change.

Thanked be fortune, it hath been otherwise
 Twenty times better; but once especial—
In thin array: after a pleasant guise,
 When her loose gown did from her shoulders fall,
 And she me caught in her arms long and small,
And therewithal so sweetly did me kiss,
And softly said, '*Dear heart, how like you this?*'

It was no dream; for I lay broad awaking:
 But all is turn'd now, through my gentleness,
Into a bitter fashion of forsaking;
 And I have leave to go of her goodness;
 And she also to use new-fangleness.
But since that I unkindly so am servèd,
'*How like you this?*'—what hath she now deservèd?

38. *To His Lute*

MY lute, awake! perform the last
  Labour that thou and I shall waste,
And end that I have now begun;
For when this song is said and past,
  My lute, be still, for I have done.

As to be heard where ear is none,
As lead to grave in marble stone,
  My song may pierce her heart as soon:
Should we then sing, or sigh, or moan?
  No, no, my lute! for I have done.

The rocks do not so cruelly
Repulse the waves continually,
  As she my suit and affection;
So that I am past remedy:
  Whereby my lute and I have done.

Proud of the spoil that thou hast got
Of simple hearts thorough Love's shot,
  By whom, unkind, thou hast them won;
Think not he hath his bow forgot,
  Although my lute and I have done.

Vengeance shall fall on thy disdain,
That makest but game of earnest pain:
  Trow not alone under the sun
Unquit to cause thy lover's plain,
  Although my lute and I have done.

SIR THOMAS WYATT

May chance thee lie wither'd and old
The winter nights that are so cold,
  Plaining in vain unto the moon:
Thy wishes then dare not be told:
  Care then who list! for I have done.

And then may chance thee to repent
The time that thou has lost and spent
  To cause thy lover's sigh and swoon:
Then shalt thou know beauty but lent,
  And wish and want as I have done.

Now cease, my lute! this is the last
Labour that thou and I shall waste,
  And ended is that we begun:
Now is this song both sung and past—
  My lute, be still, for I have done.

HENRY HOWARD, EARL OF SURREY
1516-47

39. *Description of Spring*

Wherein each thing renews, save only the Lover

THE soote season, that bud and bloom forth brings,
  With green hath clad the hill and eke the vale:
The nightingale with feathers new she sings;
The turtle to her make hath told her tale.
Summer is come, for every spray now springs:
The hart hath hung his old head on the pale;
The buck in brake his winter coat he flings;
The fishes flete with new repairèd scale.

39. make] mate.

The adder all her slough away she slings;
The swift swallow pursueth the flies smale;
The busy bee her honey now she mings;
Winter is worn that was the flowers' bale.

And thus I see among these pleasant things
Each care decays, and yet my sorrow springs.

40. *Complaint of the Absence of Her Lover being upon the Sea*

O HAPPY dames! that may embrace
    The fruit of your delight,
Help to bewail the woful case
    And eke the heavy plight
Of me, that wonted to rejoice
The fortune of my pleasant choice:
Good ladies, help to fill my mourning voice.

In ship, freight with rememberance
    Of thoughts and pleasures past,
He sails that hath in governance
    My life while it will last:
With scalding sighs, for lack of gale,
Furthering his hope, that is his sail,
Toward me, the swete port of his avail.

Alas! how oft in dreams I see
    Those eyes that were my food;
Which sometime so delighted me,
    That yet they do me good:

39. mings] mingles, mixes.

Wherewith I wake with his return
Whose absent flame did make me burn:
But when I find the lack, Lord! how I mourn!

When other lovers in arms across
  Rejoice their chief delight,
Drownèd in tears, to mourn my loss
  I stand the bitter night
In my window where I may see
Before the winds how the clouds flee:
Lo! what a mariner love hath made me!

And in green waves when the salt flood
  Doth rise by rage of wind,
A thousand fancies in that mood
  Assail my restless mind.
Alas! now drencheth my sweet foe,
That with the spoil of my heart did go,
And left me; but alas! why did he so?

And when the seas wax calm again
  To chase fro me annoy,
My doubtful hope doth cause me plain;
  So dread cuts off my joy.
Thus is my wealth mingled with woe
And of each thought a doubt doth grow;
—Now he comes! Will he come? Alas! no, no.

41.   *The Means to attain Happy Life*

MARTIAL, the things that do attain
  The happy life be these, I find:—
The richesse left, not got with pain;
  The fruitful ground, the quiet mind;

40. drencheth] i.e. is drenched or drowned.

HENRY HOWARD, EARL OF SURREY

 The equal friend; no grudge, no strife;
  No charge of rule, nor governance;
 Without disease, the healthful life;
  The household of continuance;

 The mean diet, no delicate fare;
  True wisdom join'd with simpleness;
 The night dischargèd of all care,
  Where wine the wit may not oppress.

 The faithful wife, without debate;
  Such sleeps as may beguile the night:
 Contented with thine own estate
  Ne wish for death, ne fear his might.

NICHOLAS GRIMALD
1519-62

42.   A True Love

WHAT sweet relief the showers to thirsty plants we see,
What dear delight the blooms to bees, my true love is to me!
As fresh and lusty Ver foul Winter doth exceed—
As morning bright, with scarlet sky, doth pass the evening's weed—
As mellow pears above the crabs esteemèd be—
So doth my love surmount them all, whom yet I hap to see!
The oak shall olives bear, the lamb the lion fray,
The owl shall match the nightingale in tuning of her lay,

42. fray] affright.

NICHOLAS GRIMALD

Or I my love let slip out of mine entire heart,
So deep reposèd in my breast is she for her desart!
For many blessèd gifts, O happy, happy land!
Where Mars and Pallas strive to make their glory most
   to stand!
Yet, land, more is thy bliss that, in this cruel age,
A Venus' imp thou hast brought forth, so steadfast and
   so sage.
Among the Muses Nine a tenth if Jove would make,
And to the Graces Three a fourth, her would Apollo take.
Let some for honour hunt, and hoard the massy gold:
With her so I may live and die, my weal cannot be told.

ALEXANDER SCOTT
1520?-158-

43.   *A Bequest of His Heart*

HENCE, heart, with her that must depart,
   And hald thee with thy soverane!
For I had liever want ane heart,
   Nor have the heart that dois me pain.
   Therefore, go, with thy luve remain,
And let me leif thus unmolest;
   And see that thou come not again,
But bide with her thou luvis best.

Sen she that I have servit lang
   Is to depart so suddenly,
Address thee now, for thou sall gang
   And bear thy lady company.

43. hald] keep.   sen] since.

ALEXANDER SCOTT

Fra she be gone, heartless am I,
For quhy? thou art with her possest.
   Therefore, my heart, go hence in high,
And bide with her thou luvis best.

Though this belappit body here
   Be bound to servitude and thrall,
My faithful heart is free entier
   And mind to serve my lady at all.
   Would God that I were perigall
Under that redolent rose to rest!
   Yet at the least, my heart, thou sall
Abide with her thou luvis best.

Sen in your garth the lily quhyte
   May not remain amang the laif,
Adieu the flower of whole delite!
   Adieu the succour that may me saif!
   Adieu the fragrant balme suaif,
And lamp of ladies lustiest!
   My faithful heart she shall it haif
To bide with her it luvis best.

Deploir, ye ladies cleir of hue,
   Her absence, sen she must depart!
And, specially, ye luveris true
   That wounded bene with Luvis dart.
   For some of you sall want ane heart
As well as I; therefore at last
   Do go with mine, with mind inwart,
And bide with her thou luvis best!

belappit] downtrodden.   perigall] made equal to, privileged.
garth] garden-close.   laif] rest.   with mind inwart] with inner mind, i. e. in spirit.

ALEXANDER SCOTT

44.   *A Rondel of Love*

LO, quhat it is to love
   Learn ye that list to prove,
By me, I say, that no ways may
   The ground of grief remove,
But still decay both nicht and day:
   Lo, quhat it is to love!

Love is ane fervent fire
   Kindlit without desire,
Short pleasure, long displeasure,
   Repentance is the hire;
Ane pure tressour without measour;
   Love is ane fervent fire.

To love and to be wise,
   To rage with good advice;
Now thus, now than, so gois the game,
   Incertain is the dice;
There is no man, I say, that can
   Both love and to be wise.

Flee always from the snare,
   Learn at me to beware;
It is ane pain, and double trane
   Of endless woe and care;
For to refrain that danger plain,
   Flee always from the snare.

ROBERT WEVER
c. 1550

45. *In Youth is Pleasure*

IN a harbour grene aslepe whereas I lay,
  The byrdes sang swete in the middes of the day,
I dreamèd fast of mirth and play:
    In youth is pleasure, in youth is pleasure.

Methought I walked still to and fro,
And from her company I could not go—
But when I waked it was not so:
    In youth is pleasure, in youth is pleasure.

Therefore my hart is surely pyght
Of her alone to have a sight
Which is my joy and hartes delight:
    In youth is pleasure, in youth is pleasure.

RICHARD EDWARDES
1523-66

46. *Amantium Irae*

IN going to my naked bed as one that would have slept,
  I heard a wife sing to her child, that long before had wept;
She sighèd sore and sang full sweet, to bring the babe to rest,
That would not cease but crièd still, in sucking at her breast.
She was full weary of her watch, and grievèd with her child,
She rockèd it and rated it, till that on her it smiled.
Then did she say, Now have I found this proverb true to prove,
The falling out of faithful friends renewing is of love.

Then took I paper, pen, and ink, this proverb for to write,
In register for to remain of such a worthy wight:
As she proceeded thus in song unto her little brat,
Much matter utter'd she of weight, in place whereas she sat:

RICHARD EDWARDES

And provèd plain there was no beast, nor creature bearing life,
Could well be known to live in love without discord and strife:
Then kissèd she her little babe, and sware by God above,
The falling out of faithful friends renewing is of love.

She said that neither king nor prince nor lord could live aright,
Until their puissance they did prove, their manhood and their might.
When manhood shall be matched so that fear can take no place,
Then weary works make warriors each other to embrace,
And left their force that failèd them, which did consume the rout,
That might before have lived their time, their strength and nature out:
Then did she sing as one that thought no man could her reprove,
The falling out of faithful friends renewing is of love.

She said she saw no fish nor fowl, nor beast within her haunt,
That met a stranger in their kind, but could give it a taunt:
Since flesh might not endure, but rest must wrath succeed,
And force the fight to fall to play in pasture where they feed,
So noble nature can well end the work she hath begun,
And bridle well that will not cease her tragedy in some:
Thus in song she oft rehearsed, as did her well behove,
The falling out of faithful friends renewing is of love.

I marvel much pardy (quoth she) for to behold the rout,
To see man, woman, boy and beast, to toss the world about:
Some kneel, some crouch, some beck, some check, and some can smoothly smile,
And some embrace others in arm, and there think many a wile,
Some stand aloof at cap and knee, some humble and some stout,
Yet are they never friends in deed until they once fall out:
Thus ended she her song and said, before she did remove,
The falling out of faithful friends renewing is of love.

GEORGE GASCOIGNE
1525?-77

47. *A Lover's Lullaby*

SING lullaby, as women do,
    Wherewith they bring their babes to rest;
And lullaby can I sing too,
    As womanly as can the best.
With lullaby they still the child;
And if I be not much beguiled,
Full many a wanton babe have I,
Which must be still'd with lullaby.

First lullaby my youthful years,
    It is now time to go to bed:
For crookèd age and hoary hairs
    Have won the haven within my head.
With lullaby, then, youth be still;
With lullaby content thy will;
Since courage quails and comes behind,
Go sleep, and so beguile thy mind!

Next lullaby my gazing eyes,
    Which wonted were to glance apace;
For every glass may now suffice
    To show the furrows in thy face.
With lullaby then wink awhile;
With lullaby your looks beguile;
Let no fair face, nor beauty bright,
Entice you eft with vain delight.

And lullaby my wanton will;
    Let reason's rule now reign thy thought;
Since all too late I find by skill
    How dear I have thy fancies bought;

GEORGE GASCOIGNE

With lullaby now take thine ease,
With lullaby thy doubts appease;
For trust to this, if thou be still,
My body shall obey thy will.

Thus lullaby my youth, mine eyes,
  My will, my ware, and all that was:
I can no more delays devise;
  But welcome pain, let pleasure pass.
With lullaby now take your leave;
With lullaby your dreams deceive;
And when you rise with waking eye,
Remember then this lullaby.

ALEXANDER MONTGOMERIE
1540?-1610?

48. *The Night is Near Gone*

HEY! now the day dawis;
  The jolly cock crawis;
Now shroudis the shawis
  Thro' Nature anon.
The thissel-cock cryis
On lovers wha lyis:
Now skaillis the skyis;
  The nicht is neir gone.

The fieldis ouerflowis
  With gowans that growis,
Quhair lilies like low is
  As red as the rone.

48. shroudis] dress themselves.   shawis] woods.   skaillis] clears.   gowans] daisies.   low] flame.   rone] rowan.

ALEXANDER MONTGOMERIE

The turtle that true is,
With notes that renewis,
Her pairty pursuis:
　The nicht is neir gone.
Now hairtis with hindis
Conform to their kindis,
Hie tursis their tyndis
　On ground quhair they grone.
Now hurchonis, with hairis,
Aye passis in pairis;
Quhilk duly declaris
　The nicht is neir gone.

The season excellis
Through sweetness that smellis;
Now Cupid compellis
　Our hairtis echone
On Venus wha waikis,
To muse on our maikis,
Syne sing for their saikis—
　'The nicht is neir gone!'

All courageous knichtis
Aganis the day dichtis
The breist-plate that bright is
　To fight with their fone.
The stonèd steed stampis
Through courage, and crampis,
Syne on the land lampis:
　The nicht is neir gone.

pairty] partner, mate.　　tursis] carry.　　tyndis] antlers.
grone] groan, bell.　hurchonis] hedgehogs, 'urchins.'　maikis]
mates.　fone] foes.　stonèd steed] stallion.　crampis] prances.
lampis] gallops.

ALEXANDER MONTGOMERIE

The freikis on feildis
That wight wapins weildis
With shyning bright shieldis
  At Titan in trone;
Stiff speiris in reistis
Ouer corseris crestis
Are broke on their breistis:
  The nicht is neir gone.

So hard are their hittis,
Some sweyis, some sittis,
And some perforce flittis
  On ground quhile they grone.
Syne groomis that gay is
On blonkis that brayis
With swordis assayis:—
  The nicht is neir gone.

WILLIAM STEVENSON
1530?-1575

49. *Jolly Good Ale and Old*

I CANNOT eat but little meat,
  My stomach is not good;
But sure I think that I can drink
  With him that wears a hood.
Though I go bare, take ye no care,
  I nothing am a-cold;
I stuff my skin so full within
  Of jolly good ale and old.
    Back and side go bare, go bare;
    Both foot and hand go cold;

48. freikis] men, warriors.   wight wapins] stout weapons. at Titan] over against Titan (the sun), or read 'as.'   flittis] are cast.   blonkis] white palfreys.

WILLIAM STEVENSON

    But, belly, God send thee good ale enough,
    Whether it be new or old.

I love no roast but a nut-brown toast,
    And a crab laid in the fire;
A little bread shall do me stead;
    Much bread I not desire.
No frost nor snow, no wind, I trow,
    Can hurt me if I wold;
I am so wrapp'd and thoroughly lapp'd
    Of jolly good ale and old.
      Back and side go bare, go bare, &c.

And Tib, my wife, that as her life
    Loveth well good ale to seek,
Full oft drinks she till ye may see
    The tears run down her cheek :
Then doth she trowl to me the bowl
    Even as a maltworm should,
And saith, 'Sweetheart, I took my part
    Of this jolly good ale and old.'
      Back and side go bare, go bare, &c.

Now let them drink till they nod and wink,
    Even as good fellows should do;
They shall not miss to have the bliss
    Good ale doth bring men to;
And all poor souls that have scour'd bowls
    Or have them lustily troll'd,
God save the lives of them and their wives,
    Whether they be young or old.
      Back and side go bare, go bare;
      Both foot and hand go cold;
      But, belly, God send thee good ale enough,
      Whether it be new or old.

ANONYMOUS (SCOTTISH)
16th Cent.

50. *When Flora had O'erfret the Firth*

QUHEN Flora had o'erfret the firth
  In May of every moneth queen;
Quhen merle and mavis singis with mirth
  Sweet melling in the shawis sheen;
Quhen all luvaris rejoicit bene
And most desirous of their prey,
    I heard a lusty luvar mene
  —'I luve, but I dare nocht assay!'

'Strong are the pains I daily prove,
  But yet with patience I sustene,
I am so fetterit with the luve
    Only of my lady sheen,
  Quhilk for her beauty micht be queen,
Nature so craftily alway
    Has done depaint that sweet serene:
  —Quhom I luve I dare nocht assay.

'She is so bricht of hyd and hue,
  I luve but her alone, I ween;
Is none her luve that may eschew,
    That blinkis of that dulce amene;
  So comely cleir are her twa een
That she mae luvaris dois affray
    Than ever of Greece did fair Helene:
  —Quhom I luve I dare nocht assay!'

o'erfret] adorned.   shawis] woods.   sheen] beautiful.   mene] mourn.   hyd] skin.   blinkis] gets a glimpse.   dulce amene] gentle and pleasant one.   mae] more.

ANONYMOUS (SCOTTISH)

51. *Lusty May*
16th Cent.

O LUSTY May, with Flora queen!
 The balmy dropis from Phoebus sheen
 Preluciand beams before the day:
By that Diana growis green
 Through gladness of this lusty May.

Then Esperus, that is so bricht,
Til woful hairtis castis his light,
 With bankis that bloomis on every brae;
And schouris are shed forth of their sicht
 Through gladness of this lusty May.

Birdis on bewis of every birth,
Rejoicing notis makand their mirth
 Richt plesantly upon the spray,
With flourishingis o'er field and firth
 Through gladness of this lusty May.

All luvaris that are in care
To their ladies they do repair
 In fresh morningis before the day,
And are in mirth ay mair and mair
 Through gladness of this lusty May.

52. *My Heart is High Above*
16th Cent.

MY heart is high above, my body is full of bliss,
 For I am set in luve as well as I would wiss
I luve my lady pure and she luvis me again,
I am her serviture, she is my soverane;

51. sheen] bright.   til] into.   schouris] showers.   bewis] boughs.   birth] kind.   *52.* wiss] wish.

ANONYMOUS

She is my very heart, I am her howp and heill,
She is my joy invart, I am her luvar leal;
I am her bond and thrall, she is at my command;
I am perpetual her man, both foot and hand;
The thing that may her please my body sall fulfil;
Quhatever her disease, it does my body ill.
My bird, my bonny ane, my tender babe venust,
My luve, my life alane, my liking and my lust!
We interchange our hairtis in others armis soft,
Spriteless we twa depairtis, usand our luvis oft.
We mourn when licht day dawis, we plain the nicht is short,
We curse the cock that crawis, that hinderis our disport.
I glowffin up aghast, quhen I her miss on nicht,
And in my oxter fast I find the bowster richt;
Then languor on me lies like Morpheus the mair,
Quhilk causes me uprise and to my sweet repair.
And then is all the sorrow forth of remembrance
That ever I had a-forrow in luvis observance.
Thus never I do rest, so lusty a life I lead,
Quhen that I list to test the well of womanheid.
Luvaris in pain, I pray God send you sic remeid
As I have nicht and day, you to defend from deid!
Therefore be ever true unto your ladies free,
And they will on you rue as mine has done on me.

heill] health.   invart] inward.   venust] delightful.   glowffin] blink on awaking.   oxter] armpit.   a-forrow] aforetime.

NUMBERS
FROM
ELIZABETHAN MISCELLANIES & SONG-BOOKS
BY UNNAMED OR UNCERTAIN AUTHORS

53.   *A Praise of His Lady*

Tottel's Miscellany, 1557

GIVE place, you ladies, and begone!
　　Boast not yourselves at all!
For here at hand approacheth one
　　Whose face will stain you all.

The virtue of her lively looks
　　Excels the precious stone;
I wish to have none other books
　　To read or look upon.

In each of her two crystal eyes
　　Smileth a naked boy;
It would you all in heart suffice
　　To see that lamp of joy.

I think Nature hath lost the mould
　　Where she her shape did take;
Or else I doubt if Nature could
　　So fair a creature make.

She may be well compared
　　Unto the Phœnix kind,
Whose like was never seen or heard,
　　That any man can find.

ANONYMOUS

In life she is Diana chaste,
  In troth Penelopey;
In word and eke in deed steadfast.
  —What will you more we say?

If all the world were sought so far,
  Who could find such a wight?
Her beauty twinkleth like a star
  Within the frosty night.

Her rosial colour comes and goes
  With such a comely grace,
More ruddier, too, than doth the rose,
  Within her lively face.

At Bacchus' feast none shall her meet,
  Ne at no wanton play,
Nor gazing in an open street,
  Nor gadding as a stray.

The modest mirth that she doth use
  Is mix'd with shamefastness;
All vice she doth wholly refuse,
  And hateth idleness.

O Lord! it is a world to see
  How virtue can repair,
And deck in her such honesty,
  Whom Nature made so fair.

Truly she doth so far exceed
  Our women nowadays,
As doth the jeliflower a weed;
  And more a thousand ways.

ANONYMOUS

How might I do to get a graff
  Of this unspotted tree?
—For all the rest are plain but chaff,
  Which seem good corn to be.

This gift alone I shall her give;
  When death doth what he can,
Her honest fame shall ever live
  Within the mouth of man.

     ? by *John Heywood*

54. *To Her Sea-faring Lover*
       Tottel's Miscellany, 1557

SHALL I thus ever long, and be no whit the neare?
 And shall I still complain to thee, the which me will not hear?
Alas! say nay! say nay! and be no more so dumb,
But open thou thy manly mouth and say that thou wilt come:
Whereby my heart may think, although I see not thee,
That thou wilt come—thy word so sware—if thou a live man be.
The roaring hugy waves they threaten my poor ghost,
And toss thee up and down the seas in danger to be lost.
Shall they not make me fear that they have swallowed thee?
—But as thou art most sure alive, so wilt thou come to me.
Whereby I shall go see thy ship ride on the strand,
And think and say *Lo where he comes* and *Sure here will he land:*

54. neare] nearer.

ANONYMOUS

And then I shall lift up to thee my little hand,
And thou shalt think thine heart in ease, in health to see
    me stand.
And if thou come indeed (as Christ thee send to do!)
Those arms which miss thee now shall then embrace [and
    hold] thee too:
Each vein to every joint the lively blood shall spread
Which now for want of thy glad sight doth show full
    pale and dead.
But if thou slip thy troth, and do not come at all,
As minutes in the clock do strike so call for death I shall:
To please both thy false heart and rid myself from woe,
That rather had to die in troth than live forsaken so!

55. *The Faithless Shepherdess*

William Byrd's *Songs of Sundry Natures*, 1589

WHILE that the sun with his beams hot
    Scorchèd the fruits in vale and mountain,
Philon the shepherd, late forgot,
    Sitting beside a crystal fountain
        In shadow of a green oak tree,
        Upon his pipe this song play'd he:
Adieu, Love, adieu, Love, untrue Love!
Untrue Love, untrue Love, adieu, Love!
Your mind is light, soon lost for new love.

So long as I was in your sight
    I was your heart, your soul, your treasure;
And evermore you sobb'd and sigh'd
    Burning in flames beyond all measure:
        —Three days endured your love to me,
        And it was lost in other three!

ANONYMOUS

Adieu, Love, adieu, Love, untrue Love!
Untrue Love, untrue Love, adieu, Love!
Your mind is light, soon lost for new love.

Another shepherd you did see,
  To whom your heart was soon enchainèd;
Full soon your love was leapt from me,
Full soon my place he had obtainèd.
  Soon came a third your love to win,
  And we were out and he was in.
Adieu, Love, adieu, Love, untrue Love!
Untrue Love, untrue Love, adieu, Love!
Your mind is light, soon lost for new love.

Sure you have made me passing glad
  That you your mind so soon removèd,
Before that I the leisure had
  To choose you for my best belovèd:
    For all my love was pass'd and done
    Two days before it was begun.
Adieu, Love, adieu, Love, untrue Love!
Untrue Love, untrue Love, adieu, Love!
Your mind is light, soon lost for new love.

56. *Crabbed Age and Youth*
                       The Passionate Pilgrim, 1599

CRABBÈD Age and Youth
  Cannot live together:
Youth is full of pleasance,
Age is full of care;
Youth like summer morn,
Age like winter weather;

ANONYMOUS

Youth like summer brave,
Age like winter bare.
Youth is full of sport,
Age's breath is short;
Youth is nimble, Age is lame;
Youth is hot and bold,
Age is weak and cold;
Youth is wild, and Age is tame.
Age, I do abhor thee;
Youth, I do adore thee;
O, my Love, my Love is young!
Age, I do defy thee:
O, sweet shepherd, hie thee!
For methinks thou stay'st too long.
     ? by *William Shakespeare*

57.   *Phyllida's Love-Call*
       England's Helicon, 1600

Phyllida. CORYDON, arise, my Corydon!
    Titan shineth clear.
Corydon. Who is it that calleth Corydon?
   Who is it that I hear?
Phyl. Phyllida, thy true love, calleth thee,
  Arise then, arise then,
   Arise and keep thy flock with me!
Cor. Phyllida, my true love, is it she?
  I come then, I come then,
   I come and keep my flock with thee.

Phyl. Here are cherries ripe for my Corydon;
  Eat them for my sake.
Cor. Here's my oaten pipe, my lovely one,
  Sport for thee to make.

ANONYMOUS

Phyl. Here are threads, my true love, fine as silk,
  To knit thee, to knit thee,
   A pair of stockings white as milk.
Cor. Here are reeds, my true love, fine and neat,
  To make thee, to make thee,
   A bonnet to withstand the heat.

Phyl. I will gather flowers, my Corydon,
  To set in thy cap.
Cor. I will gather pears, my lovely one,
  To put in thy lap.
Phyl. I will buy my true love garters gay,
  For Sundays, for Sundays,
   To wear about his legs so tall.
Cor. I will buy my true love yellow say,
  For Sundays, for Sundays,
   To wear about her middle small.

Phyl. When my Corydon sits on a hill
  Making melody—
Cor. When my lovely one goes to her wheel,
  Singing cheerily—
Phyl. Sure methinks my true love doth excel
  For sweetness, for sweetness,
   Our Pan, that old Arcadian knight.
Cor. And methinks my true love bears the bell
  For clearness, for clearness,
   Beyond the nymphs that be so bright.

Phyl. Had my Corydon, my Corydon,
  Been, alack! her swain—
Cor. Had my lovely one, my lovely one,
  Been in Ida plain—

say] *soie*, silk.

ANONYMOUS

Phyl. Cynthia Endymion had refused,
    Preferring, preferring,
      My Corydon to play withal.
Cor. The Queen of Love had been excused
    Bequeathing, bequeathing,
      My Phyllida the golden ball.
Phyl. Yonder comes my mother, Corydon!
    Whither shall I fly?
Cor. Under yonder beech, my lovely one,
    While she passeth by.
Phyl. Say to her thy true love was not here;
    Remember, remember,
      To-morrow is another day.
Cor. Doubt me not, my true love, do not fear;
    Farewell then, farewell then!
      Heaven keep our loves alway!

58.   *A Pedlar*

                    John Dowland's *Second Book of Songs or Airs*, 1600

FINE knacks for ladies! cheap, choice, brave, and new,
    Good pennyworths—but money cannot move:
I keep a fair but for the Fair to view—
A beggar may be liberal of love.
Though all my wares be trash, the heart is true.
           The heart is true.

Great gifts are guiles and look for gifts again;
    My trifles come as treasures from my mind:
It is a precious jewel to be plain;
    Sometimes in shell the orient'st pearls we find:—
Of others take a sheaf, of me a grain!
           Of me a grain!

ANONYMOUS

59.   *Hey nonny no!*
                                Christ Church MS.

HEY nonny no!
  Men are fools that wish to die!
Is't not fine to dance and sing
When the bells of death do ring?
Is't not fine to swim in wine,
And turn upon the toe,
And sing hey nonny no!
When the winds blow and the seas flow?
Hey nonny no!

60.   *Preparations*
                                Christ Church MS.

YET if His Majesty, our sovereign lord,
  Should of his own accord
Friendly himself invite,
And say 'I'll be your guest to-morrow night,'
How should we stir ourselves, call and command
All hands to work! 'Let no man idle stand!

'Set me fine Spanish tables in the hall;
See they be fitted all;
Let there be room to eat
And order taken that there want no meat.
See every sconce and candlestick made bright,
That without tapers they may give a light.

'Look to the presence: are the carpets spread,
The dazie o'er the head,
The cushions in the chairs,
And all the candles lighted on the stairs?
Perfume the chambers, and in any case
Let each man give attendance in his place!'

ANONYMOUS

Thus, if a king were coming, would we do;
And 'twere good reason too;
For 'tis a duteous thing
To show all honour to an earthly king,
And after all our travail and our cost,
So he be pleased, to think no labour lost.

But at the coming of the King of Heaven
All's set at six and seven;
We wallow in our sin,
Christ cannot find a chamber in the inn.
We entertain Him always like a stranger,
And, as at first, still lodge Him in the manger.

61. *The New Jerusalem*

Song of Mary the Mother of Christ (London: E. Allde), 1601

HIERUSALEM, my happy home,
  When shall I come to thee?
When shall my sorrows have an end,
  Thy joys when shall I see?

O happy harbour of the Saints!
  O sweet and pleasant soil!
In thee no sorrow may be found,
  No grief, no care, no toil.

There lust and lucre cannot dwell,
  There envy bears no sway;
There is no hunger, heat, nor cold,
  But pleasure every way.

Thy walls are made of precious stones,
  Thy bulwarks diamonds square;
Thy gates are of right orient pearl,
  Exceeding rich and rare.

ANONYMOUS

Thy turrets and thy pinnacles
  With carbuncles do shine;
Thy very streets are paved with gold,
  Surpassing clear and fine.

Ah, my sweet home, Hierusalem,
  Would God I were in thee!
Would God my woes were at an end,
  Thy joys that I might see!

Thy gardens and thy gallant walks
  Continually are green;
There grows such sweet and pleasant flowers
  As nowhere else are seen.

Quite through the streets, with silver sound,
  The flood of Life doth flow;
Upon whose banks on every side
  The wood of Life doth grow.

There trees for evermore bear fruit,
  And evermore do spring;
There evermore the angels sit,
  And evermore do sing.

Our Lady sings *Magnificat*
  With tones surpassing sweet;
And all the virgins bear their part,
  Sitting about her feet.

Hierusalem, my happy home,
  Would God I were in thee!
Would God my woes were at an end,
  Thy joys that I might see!

ANONYMOUS

62.   *Icarus*

Robert Jones's *Second Book of Songs and Airs*, 1601

LOVE wing'd my Hopes and taught me how to fly
  Far from base earth, but not to mount too high:
    For true pleasure
    Lives in measure,
    Which if men forsake,
Blinded they into folly run and grief for pleasure take.

But my vain Hopes, proud of their new-taught flight,
Enamour'd sought to woo the sun's fair light,
    Whose rich brightness
    Moved their lightness
    To aspire so high
That all scorch'd and consumed with fire now drown'd in
  woe they lie.

And none but Love their woeful hap did rue,
For Love did know that their desires were true;
    Though fate frownèd,
    And now drownèd
    They in sorrow dwell,
It was the purest light of heav'n for whose fair love they fell.

63.   *Madrigal*

Davison's *Poetical Rhapsody*, 1602

MY Love in her attire doth show her wit,
  It doth so well become her;
For every season she hath dressings fit,
  For Winter, Spring, and Summer.
    No beauty she doth miss
      When all her robes are on:
    But Beauty's self she is
      When all her robes are gone.

ANONYMOUS

64. How can the Heart forget her?

Davison's *Poetical Rhapsody*, 1602

AT her fair hands how have I grace entreated
   With prayers oft repeated!
Yet still my love is thwarted:
Heart, let her go, for she'll not be converted—
    Say, shall she go?
     O no, no, no, no, no!
She is most fair, though she be marble-hearted.

How often have my sighs declared my anguish,
Wherein I daily languish!
Yet still she doth procure it:
Heart, let her go, for I can not endure it—
    Say, shall she go?
     O no, no, no, no, no!
She gave the wound, and she alone must cure it.

But shall I still a true affection owe her,
Which prayers, sighs, tears do show her,
And shall she still disdain me?
Heart, let her go, if they no grace can gain me—
    Say, shall she go?
     O no, no, no, no, no!
She made me hers, and hers she will retain me.

But if the love that hath and still doth burn me
No love at length return me,
Out of my thoughts I'll set her:
Heart, let her go, O heart I pray thee, let her!
    Say, shall she go?
     O no, no, no, no, no!
Fix'd in the heart, how can the heart forget her?

? *F.* or *W. Davison*

ANONYMOUS

65.   *Tears*

John Dowland's *Third and Last
Book of Songs or Airs*, 1603

WEEP you no more, sad fountains;
 What need you flow so fast?
Look how the snowy mountains
 Heaven's sun doth gently waste!
But my Sun's heavenly eyes
 View not your weeping,
 That now lies sleeping
Softly, now softly lies
 Sleeping.

Sleep is a reconciling,
 A rest that peace begets;
Doth not the sun rise smiling
 When fair at even he sets?
Rest you then, rest, sad eyes!
 Melt not in weeping,
 While she lies sleeping
Softly, now softly lies
 Sleeping.

66.   *My Lady's Tears*

John Dowland's *Third and Last
Book of Songs or Airs*, 1603

I SAW my Lady weep,
 And Sorrow proud to be advancèd so
In those fair eyes where all perfections keep.
 Her face was full of woe;
But such a woe (believe me) as wins more hearts
Than Mirth can do with her enticing parts.

ANONYMOUS

Sorrow was there made fair,
And Passion wise; Tears a delightful thing;
Silence beyond all speech, a wisdom rare:
   She made her sighs to sing,
And all things with so sweet a sadness move
As made my heart at once both grieve and love.

   O fairer than aught else
The world can show, leave off in time to grieve!
Enough, enough: your joyful look excels:
   Tears kill the heart, believe.
O strive not to be excellent in woe,
Which only breeds your beauty's overthrow.

67.   *Sister, Awake!*

Thomas Bateson's *First Set of*
English Madrigals, 1604

SISTER, awake! close not your eyes!
   The day her light discloses,
And the bright morning doth arise
   Out of her bed of roses.

See the clear sun, the world's bright eye,
   In at our window peeping:
Lo, how he blusheth to espy
   Us idle wenches sleeping!

Therefore awake! make haste, I say,
   And let us, without staying,
All in our gowns of green so gay
   Into the Park a-maying!

ANONYMOUS

68.   *Devotion*
Captain Tobias Hume's *The First
Part of Airs, &c.*, 1605

FAIN would I change that note
   To which fond Love hath charm'd me
Long, long to sing by rote,
Fancying that that harm'd me:
Yet when this thought doth come,
'Love is the perfect sum
   Of all delight,'
I have no other choice
Either for pen or voice
   To sing or write.

O Love! they wrong thee much
That say thy sweet is bitter,
When thy rich fruit is such
As nothing can be sweeter.
Fair house of joy and bliss,
Where truest pleasure is,
   I do adore thee:
I know thee what thou art,
I serve thee with my heart,
   And fall before thee.

69.   *Since First I saw your Face*
Thomas Ford's *Music of
Sundry Kinds*, 1607

SINCE first I saw your face I resolved to honour and renown ye;
If now I be disdainèd I wish my heart had never known ye.
What? I that loved and you that liked, shall we begin to wrangle?
No, no, no, my heart is fast, and cannot disentangle.

ANONYMOUS

If I admire or praise you too much, that fault you may
    forgive me;
Or if my hands had stray'd but a touch, then justly might
    you leave me.
I ask'd you leave, you bade me love; is't now a time to
    chide me?
No, no, no, I'll love you still what fortune e'er betide me.

The Sun, whose beams most glorious are, rejecteth no
    beholder,
And your sweet beauty past compare made my poor eyes
    the bolder:
Where beauty moves and wit delights and signs of kind-
    ness bind me,
There, O there! where'er I go I'll leave my heart behind
    me!

70. *There is a Lady sweet and kind*

Thomas Ford's Music of
Sundry Kinds, 1607

THERE is a Lady sweet and kind,
    Was never face so pleased my mind;
I did but see her passing by,
And yet I love her till I die.

Her gesture, motion, and her smiles,
Her wit, her voice my heart beguiles,
Beguiles my heart, I know not why,
And yet I love her till I die.

Cupid is wingèd and doth range,
Her country so my love doth change:
But change she earth, or change she sky,
Yet will I love her till I die.

ANONYMOUS

71. *Love not me for comely grace*

John Wilbye's *Second Set of Madrigals*, 1609

LOVE not me for comely grace,
    For my pleasing eye or face,
Nor for any outward part,
No, nor for a constant heart:
    For these may fail or turn to ill,
    So thou and I shall sever:
Keep, therefore, a true woman's eye,
And love me still but know not why—
    So hast thou the same reason still
    To doat upon me ever!

72. *The Wakening*

John Attye's *First Book of Airs*, 1622

ON a time the amorous Silvy
    Said to her shepherd, 'Sweet, how do ye?
Kiss me this once and then God be with ye,
    My sweetest dear!
Kiss me this once and then God be with ye,
For now the morning draweth near.'

With that, her fairest bosom showing,
Op'ning her lips, rich perfumes blowing,
She said, 'Now kiss me and be going,
    My sweetest dear!
Kiss me this once and then be going,
For now the morning draweth near.'

With that the shepherd waked from sleeping,
And spying where the day was peeping,
He said, 'Now take my soul in keeping,
    My sweetest dear!
Kiss me and take my soul in keeping,
Since I must go, now day is near.'

NICHOLAS BRETON
1542-1626

73.   *Phillida and Coridon*

IN the merry month of May,
  In a morn by break of day,
Forth I walk'd by the wood-side
When as May was in his pride:
There I spièd all alone
Phillida and Coridon.
Much ado there was, God wot!
He would love and she would not.
She said, Never man was true;
He said, None was false to you.
He said, He had loved her long;
She said, Love should have no wrong.
Coridon would kiss her then;
She said, Maids must kiss no men
Till they did for good and all;
Then she made the shepherd call
All the heavens to witness truth
Never loved a truer youth.
Thus with many a pretty oath,
Yea and nay, and faith and troth,
Such as silly shepherds use
When they will not Love abuse,
Love, which had been long deluded,
Was with kisses sweet concluded;
And Phillida, with garlands gay,
Was made the Lady of the May.

NICHOLAS BRETON?

74.   *A Cradle Song*
The Arbor of Amorous Devices, 1593-4

COME little babe, come silly soul,
 Thy father's shame, thy mother's grief,
Born as I doubt to all our dole,
And to thyself unhappy chief:
    Sing lullaby, and lap it warm,
    Poor soul that thinks no creature harm.

Thou little think'st and less dost know
The cause of this thy mother's moan;
Thou want'st the wit to wail her woe,
And I myself am all alone:
    Why dost thou weep? why dost thou wail?
    And know'st not yet what thou dost ail.

Come, little wretch—ah, silly heart!
Mine only joy, what can I more?
If there be any wrong thy smart,
That may the destinies implore:
    'Twas I, I say, against my will,
    I wail the time, but be thou still.

And dost thou smile? O, thy sweet face!
Would God Himself He might thee see!—
No doubt thou wouldst soon purchase grace,
I know right well, for thee and me:
    But come to mother, babe, and play,
    For father false is fled away.

Sweet boy, if it by fortune chance
Thy father home again to send,

NICHOLAS BRETON?

If death do strike me with his lance,
Yet mayst thou me to him commend:
  If any ask thy mother's name,
  Tell how by love she purchased blame.
Then will his gentle heart soon yield:
I know him of a noble mind:
Although a lion in the field,
A lamb in town thou shalt him find:
  Ask blessing, babe, be not afraid,
  His sugar'd words hath me betray'd.
Then mayst thou joy and be right glad;
Although in woe I seem to moan,
Thy father is no rascal lad,
A noble youth of blood and bone:
  His glancing looks, if he once smile,
  Right honest women may beguile.
Come, little boy, and rock asleep;
Sing lullaby and be thou still;
I, that can do naught else but weep,
Will sit by thee and wail my fill:
  God bless my babe, and lullaby
  From this thy father's quality.

SIR WALTER RALEIGH
1552-1618

The Silent Lover

75.
    i

PASSIONS are liken'd best to floods and streams:
  The shallow murmur, but the deep are dumb;
So, when affection yields discourse, it seems
  The bottom is but shallow whence they come.
They that are rich in words, in words discover
That they are poor in that which makes a lover.

SIR WALTER RALEIGH

76.   *ii*

WRONG not, sweet empress of my heart,
  The merit of true passion,
With thinking that he feels no smart,
  That sues for no compassion.

Silence in love bewrays more woe
  Than words, though ne'er so witty:
A beggar that is dumb, you know,
  May challenge double pity.

Then wrong not, dearest to my heart,
  My true, though secret passion;
He smarteth most that hides his smart,
  And sues for no compassion.

77.   *His Pilgrimage*

GIVE me my scallop-shell of quiet,
  My staff of faith to walk upon,
My scrip of joy, immortal diet,
  My bottle of salvation,
My gown of glory, hope's true gage;
And thus I'll take my pilgrimage.

Blood must be my body's balmer;
  No other balm will there be given;
Whilst my soul, like quiet palmer,
  Travelleth towards the land of heaven;
Over the silver mountains,
Where spring the nectar fountains;
    There will I kiss
    The bowl of bliss;

SIR WALTER RALEIGH

And drink mine everlasting fill
Upon every milken hill.
My soul will be a-dry before;
But, after, it will thirst no more.

78. *The Conclusion*

EVEN such is Time, that takes in trust
Our youth, our joys, our all we have,
And pays us but with earth and dust;
Who in the dark and silent grave,
When we have wander'd all our ways,
Shuts up the story of our days;
But from this earth, this grave, this dust,
My God shall raise me up, I trust.

EDMUND SPENSER
1552–1599

79. *Whilst it is prime*

FRESH Spring, the herald of loves mighty king,
In whose cote-armour richly are displayd
All sorts of flowers, the which on earth do spring,
In goodly colours gloriously arrayd—
Goe to my love, where she is carelesse layd,
Yet in her winters bowre not well awake;
Tell her the joyous time wil not be staid,
Unlesse she doe him by the forelock take;
Bid her therefore her selfe soone ready make,
To wayt on Love amongst his lovely crew;
Where every one, that misseth then her make,
Shall be by him amearst with penance dew.
    Make hast, therefore, sweet love, whilest it is prime;
    For none can call againe the passèd time.

79. make] mate.

EDMUND SPENSER

80.   *A Ditty*

In praise of Eliza, Queen of the Shepherds

SEE where she sits upon the grassie greene,
    (O seemely sight!)
Yclad in Scarlot, like a mayden Queene,
    And ermines white:
Upon her head a Cremosin coronet
With Damaske roses and Daffadillies set:
    Bay leaves betweene,
    And primroses greene,
Embellish the sweete Violet.

Tell me, have ye seene her angelick face
    Like Phœbe fayre?
Her heavenly haveour, her princely grace,
    Can you well compare?
The Redde rose medled with the White yfere,
In either cheeke depeincten lively chere:
    Her modest eye,
    Her Majestie,
Where have you seene the like but there?

I see Calliope speede her to the place,
    Where my Goddesse shines;
And after her the other Muses trace
    With their Violines.
Bene they not Bay braunches which they do beare,
All for Elisa in her hand to weare?
    So sweetely they play,
    And sing all the way,
That it a heaven is to heare.

medled] mixed.   yfere] together.

EDMUND SPENSER

Lo, how finely the Graces can it foote
    To the Instrument:
They dauncen deffly, and singen soote,
    In their meriment.
Wants not a fourth Grace to make the daunce even?
Let that rowme to my Lady be yeven.
    She shal be a Grace,
    To fyll the fourth place,
And reigne with the rest in heaven.

Bring hether the Pincke and purple Cullambine,
    With Gelliflowres;
Bring Coronations, and Sops-in-wine
    Worne of Paramoures:
Strowe me the ground with Daffadowndillies,
And Cowslips, and Kingcups, and lovèd Lillies:
    The pretie Pawnce,
    And the Chevisaunce,
Shall match with the fayre flowre Delice.

Now ryse up, Elisa, deckèd as thou art
    In royall aray;
And now ye daintie Damsells may depart
    Eche one her way.
I feare I have troubled your troupes to longe:
Let dame Elisa thanke you for her song:
    And if you come hether
    When Damsines I gether,
I will part them all you among.

    soote] sweet.   coronations] carnations.   sops-in-wine] striped pinks.   pawnce] pansy.   chevisaunce] wallflower.   flowre delice] iris.

EDMUND SPENSER

81. *Prothalamion*

CALME was the day, and through the trembling ayre
Sweete-breathing Zephyrus did softly play
A gentle spirit, that lightly did delay
Hot Titans beames, which then did glyster fayre;
When I, (whom sullein care,
Through discontent of my long fruitlesse stay
In Princes Court, and expectation vayne
Of idle hopes, which still doe fly away,
Like empty shaddowes, did afflict my brayne,)
Walkt forth to ease my payne
Along the shoare of silver streaming Themmes;
Whose rutty Bancke, the which his River hemmes,
Was paynted all with variable flowers,
And all the meades adornd with daintie gemmes
Fit to decke maydens bowres,
And crowne their Paramours
Against the Brydale day, which is not long:
    Sweete Themmes! runne softly, till I end my Song.

There, in a Meadow, by the Rivers side,
A Flocke of Nymphes I chauncèd to espy,
All lovely Daughters of the Flood thereby,
With goodly greenish locks, all loose untyde,
As each had bene a Bryde;
And each one had a little wicker basket,
Made of fine twigs, entraylèd curiously,
In which they gathered flowers to fill their flasket.
And with fine Fingers cropt full featéously
The tender stalkes on hye.
Of every sort, which in that Meadow grew,
They gathered some; the Violet, pallid blew,

EDMUND SPENSER

The little Dazie, that at evening closes,
The virgin Lillie, and the Primrose trew,
With store of vermeil Roses,
To decke their Bridegromes posies
Against the Brydale day, which was not long :
    Sweete Themmes! runne softly, till I end my Song.

With that I saw two Swannes of goodly hewe
Come softly swimming downe along the Lee;
Two fairer Birds I yet did never see;
The snow, which doth the top of Pindus strew,
Did never whiter shew;
Nor Jove himselfe, when he a Swan would be,
For love of Leda, whiter did appeare;
Yet Leda was (they say) as white as he,
Yet not so white as these, nor nothing neare;
So purely white they were,
That even the gentle streame, the which them bare,
Seem'd foule to them, and bad his billowes spare
To wet their silken feathers, least they might
Soyle their fayre plumes with water not so fayre,
And marre their beauties bright,
That shone as heavens light,
Against their Brydale day, which was not long :
    Sweete Themmes! runne softly, till I end my Song.

Eftsoones the Nymphes, which now had Flowers their fill,
Ran all in haste to see that silver brood,
As they came floating on the Christal Flood;
Whom when they sawe, they stood amazèd still,
Their wondring eyes to fill;
Them seem'd they never saw a sight so fayre,
Of Fowles, so lovely, that they sure did deeme
Them heavenly borne, or to be that same payre

EDMUND SPENSER

Which through the Skie draw Venus silver Teeme;
For sure they did not seeme
To be begot of any earthly Seede,
But rather Angels, or of Angels breede;
Yet were they bred of Somers-heat, they say,
In sweetest Season, when each Flower and weede
The earth did fresh aray;
So fresh they seem'd as day,
Even as their Brydale day, which was not long:
 Sweete Themmes! runne softly, till I end my Song.

Then forth they all out of their baskets drew
Great store of Flowers, the honour of the field,
That to the sense did fragrant odours yield,
All which upon those goodly Birds they threw
And all the Waves did strew,
That like old Peneus Waters they did seeme,
When downe along by pleasant Tempes shore,
Scattred with Flowres, through Thessaly they streeme,
That they appeare, through Lillies plenteous store,
Like a Brydes Chamber flore.
Two of those Nymphes, meane while, two Garlands bound
Of freshest Flowres which in that Mead they found,
The which presenting all in trim Array,
Their snowie Foreheads therewithall they crownd,
Whil'st one did sing this Lay,
Prepar'd against that Day,
Against their Brydale day, which was not long:
 Sweete Themmes! runne softly, till I end my Song.

'Ye gentle Birdes! the worlds faire ornament,
And heavens glorie, whom this happie hower
Doth leade unto your lovers blisfull bower,
Joy may you have, and gentle hearts content

EDMUND SPENSER

Of your loves couplement;
And let faire Venus, that is Queene of love,
With her heart-quelling Sonne upon you smile,
Whose smile, they say, hath vertue to remove
All Loves dislike, and friendships faultie guile
For ever to assoile.
Let endlesse Peace your steadfast hearts accord,
And blessèd Plentie wait upon your bord;
And let your bed with pleasures chast abound,
That fruitfull issue may to you afford,
Which may your foes confound,
And make your joyes redound
Upon your Brydale day, which is not long:
    Sweete Themmes! runne softlie, till I end my Song.'

So ended she; and all the rest around
To her redoubled that her undersong,
Which said their brydale daye should not be long:
And gentle Eccho from the neighbour ground
Their accents did resound.
So forth those joyous Birdes did passe along,
Adowne the Lee, that to them murmurde low,
As he would speake, but that he lackt a tong,
Yet did by signes his glad affection show,
Making his streame run slow.
And all the foule which in his flood did dwell
Gan flock about these twaine, that did excell
The rest, so far as Cynthia doth shend
The lesser starres. So they, enrangèd well,
Did on those two attend,
And their best service lend
Against their wedding day, which was not long:
    Sweete Themmes! runne softly, till I end my Song.

EDMUND SPENSER

At length they all to mery London came,
To mery London, my most kyndly Nurse,
That to me gave this Lifes first native sourse,
Though from another place I take my name,
An house of aunrient fame:
There when they came, whereas those bricky towres
The which on Themmes brode agèd backe doe ryde,
Where now the studious Lawyers have their bowers,
There whylome wont the Templer Knights to byde,
Till they decayd through pride:
Next whereunto there standes a stately place,
Where oft I gaynèd giftes and goodly grace
Of that great Lord, which therein wont to dwell,
Whose want too well now feeles my freendles case;
But ah! here fits not well
Olde woes, but joyes, to tell
Against the Brydale daye, which is not long:
 Sweete Themmes! runne softly, till I end my Song.

Yet therein now doth lodge a noble Peer,
Great Englands glory, and the Worlds wide wonder,
Whose dreadfull name late through all Spaine did thunder,
And Hercules two pillors standing neere
Did make to quake and feare:
Faire branch of Honor, flower of Chevalrie!
That fillest England with thy triumphes fame,
Joy have thou of thy noble victorie,
And endlesse happinesse of thine owne name
That promiseth the same;
That through thy prowesse, and victorious armes,
Thy country may be freed from forraine harmes;
And great Elisaes glorious name may ring
Through al the world, fil'd with thy wide Alarmes,

Which some brave muse may sing
To ages following,
Upon the Brydale day, which is not long:
   Sweete Themmes! runne softly till I end my Song.

From those high Towers this noble Lord issuing,
Like Radiant Hesper, when his golden hayre
In th' Ocean billowes he hath bathèd fayre,
Descended to the Rivers open vewing,
With a great traine ensuing.
Above the rest were goodly to bee seene
Two gentle Knights of lovely face and feature,
Beseeming well the bower of anie Queene,
With gifts of wit, and ornaments of nature,
Fit for so goodly stature,
That like the twins of Jove they seem'd in sight,
Which decke the Bauldricke of the Heavens bright;
They two, forth pacing to the Rivers side,
Received those two faire Brides, their Loves delight;
Which, at th' appointed tyde,
Each one did make his Bryde
Against their Brydale day, which is not long:
   Sweete Themmes! runne softly, till I end my Song.

82. *Epithalamion*

YE learnèd sisters, which have oftentimes
   Beene to me ayding, others to adorne,
Whom ye thought worthy of your gracefull rymes,
That even the greatest did not greatly scorne
To heare theyr names sung in your simple layes,
But joyèd in theyr praise;
And when ye list your owne mishaps to mourne,

EDMUND SPENSER

Which death, or love, or fortunes wreck did rayse,
Your string could soone to sadder tenor turne,
And teach the woods and waters to lament
Your dolefull dreriment:
Now lay those sorrowfull complaints aside;
And, having all your heads with girlands crownd,
Helpe me mine owne loves prayses to resound;
Ne let the same of any be envide:
So Orpheus did for his owne bride!
So I unto my selfe alone will sing;
The woods shall to me answer, and my Eccho ring.

Early, before the worlds light-giving lampe
His golden beame upon the hils doth spred,
Having disperst the nights unchearefull dampe,
Doe ye awake; and, with fresh lusty-hed,
Go to the bowre of my belovèd love,
My truest turtle dove;
Bid her awake; for Hymen is awake,
And long since ready forth his maske to move.
With his bright Tead that flames with many a flake,
And many a bachelor to waite on him,
In theyr fresh garments trim.
Bid her awake therefore, and soone her dight,
For lo! the wishèd day is come at last,
That shall, for all the paynes and sorrowes past,
Pay to her usury of long delight:
And, whylest she doth her dight,
Doe ye to her of joy and solace sing,
That all the woods may answer, and your eccho ring.

Bring with you all the Nymphes that you can heare
Both of the rivers and the forrests greene,

tead] torch.

EDMUND SPENSER

And of the sea that neighbours to her neare:
Al with gay girlands goodly wel beseene.
And let them also with them bring in hand
Another gay girland
For my fayre love, of lillyes and of roses,
Bound truelove wize, with a blew silke riband.
And let them make great store of bridale poses,
And let them eeke bring store of other flowers,
To deck the bridale bowers.
And let the ground whereas her foot shall tread,
For feare the stones her tender foot should wrong,
Be strewed with fragrant flowers all along,
And diapred lyke the discolored mead.
Which done, doe at her chamber dore awayt,
For she will waken strayt;
The whiles doe ye this song unto her sing,
The woods shall to you answer, and your Eccho ring.

Ye Nymphes of Mulla, which with carefull heed
The silver scaly trouts doe tend full well,
And greedy pikes which use therein to feed;
(Those trouts and pikes all others doo excell;)
And ye likewise, which keepe the rushy lake,
Where none doo fishes take;
Bynd up the locks the which hang scatterd light,
And in his waters, which your mirror make,
Behold your faces as the christall bright,
That when you come whereas my love doth lie,
No blemish she may spie.
And eke, ye lightfoot mayds, which keepe the deere,
That on the hoary mountayne used to towre;
And the wylde wolves, which seeke them to devoure,
With your steele darts doo chace from comming neer;
Be also present heere,

EDMUND SPENSER

To helpe to decke her, and to help to sing,
That all the woods may answer, and your eccho ring.

Wake now, my love, awake! for it is time;
The Rosy Morne long since left Tithones bed,
All ready to her silver coche to clyme;
And Phœbus gins to shew his glorious hed.
Hark! how the cheerefull birds do chaunt theyr laies
And carroll of Loves praise.
The merry Larke hir mattins sings aloft;
The Thrush replyes; the Mavis descant playes;
The Ouzell shrills; the Ruddock warbles soft;
So goodly all agree, with sweet consent,
To this dayes merriment.
Ah! my deere love, why doe ye sleepe thus long?
When meeter were that ye should now awake,
T' awayt the comming of your joyous make,
And hearken to the birds love-learnèd song,
The deawy leaves among!
Nor they of joy and pleasance to you sing,
That all the woods them answer, and theyr eccho ring.

My love is now awake out of her dreames,
And her fayre eyes, like stars that dimmèd were
With darksome cloud, now shew theyr goodly beams
More bright then Hesperus his head doth rere.
Come now, ye damzels, daughters of delight,
Helpe quickly her to dight:
But first come ye fayre houres, which were begot
In Joves sweet paradice of Day and Night;
Which doe the seasons of the yeare allot,
And al, that ever in this world is fayre,
Doe make and still repayre:

ruddock] redbreast.

EDMUND SPENSER

And ye three handmayds of the Cyprian Queene,
The which doe still adorne her beauties pride,
Helpe to addorne my beautifullest bride:
And, as ye her array, still throw betweene
Some graces to be seene;
And, as ye use to Venus, to her sing,
The whiles the woods shal answer, and your eccho ring.

Now is my love all ready forth to come:
Let all the virgins therefore well awayt:
And ye fresh boyes, that tend upon her groome,
Prepare your selves; for he is comming strayt.
Set all your things in seemely good aray,
Fit for so joyfull day:
The joyfulst day that ever sunne did see.
Faire Sun! shew forth thy favourable ray,
And let thy lifull heat not fervent be,
For feare of burning her sunshyny face,
Her beauty to disgrace.
O fayrest Phœbus! father of the Muse!
If ever I did honour thee aright,
Or sing the thing that mote thy mind delight,
Doe not thy servants simple boone refuse;
But let this day, let this one day, be myne;
Let all the rest be thine.
Then I thy soverayne prayses loud wil sing,
That all the woods shal answer, and theyr eccho ring.

Harke! how the Minstrils gin to shrill aloud
Their merry Musick that resounds from far,
The pipe, the tabor, and the trembling Croud,
That well agree withouten breach or jar.

croud] violin.

EDMUND SPENSER

But, most of all, the Damzels doe delite
When they their tymbrels smyte,
And thereunto doe daunce and carrol sweet,
That all the sences they doe ravish quite;
The whyles the boyes run up and downe the street,
Crying aloud with strong confusèd noyce,
As if it were one voyce,
Hymen, iö Hymen, Hymen, they do shout;
That even to the heavens theyr shouting shrill
Doth reach, and all the firmament doth fill;
To which the people standing all about,
As in approvance, doe thereto applaud,
And loud advaunce her laud;
And evermore they Hymen, Hymen sing,
That al the woods them answer, and theyr eccho ring.

Loe! where she comes along with portly pace,
Lyke Phœbe, from her chamber of the East,
Arysing forth to run her mighty race,
Clad all in white, that seemes a virgin best.
So well it her beseemes, that ye would weene
Some angell she had beene.
Her long loose yellow locks lyke golden wyre,
Sprinckled with perle, and perling flowres atweene,
Doe lyke a golden mantle her attyre;
And, being crownèd with a girland greene,
Seeme lyke some mayden Queene.
Her modest eyes, abashèd to behold
So many gazers as on her do stare,
Upon the lowly ground affixèd are;
Ne dare lift up her countenance too bold,
But blush to heare her prayses sung so loud,
So farre from being proud.

EDMUND SPENSER

Nathlesse doe ye still loud her prayses sing,
That all the woods may answer, and your eccho ring.

Tell me, ye merchants daughters, did ye see
So fayre a creature in your towne before;
So sweet, so lovely, and so mild as she,
Adornd with beautyes grace and vertues store?
Her goodly eyes lyke Saphyres shining bright,
Her forehead yvory white,
Her cheekes lyke apples which the sun hath rudded,
Her lips lyke cherryes charming men to byte.
Her brest like to a bowle of creame uncrudded,
Her paps lyke lyllies budded,
Her snowie necke lyke to a marble towre;
And all her body like a pallace fayre,
Ascending up, with many a stately stayre,
To honors seat and chastities sweet bowre.
Why stand ye still ye virgins in amaze,
Upon her so to gaze,
Whiles ye forget your former lay to sing,
To which the woods did answer, and your eccho ring?

But if ye saw that which no eyes can see,
The inward beauty of her lively spright,
Garnisht with heavenly guifts of high degree,
Much more then would ye wonder at that sight,
And stand astonisht lyke to those which red
Medusaes mazeful hed.
There dwels sweet love, and constant chastity,
Unspotted fayth, and comely womanhood,
Regard of honour, and mild modesty;
There vertue raynes as Queene in royal throne,
And giveth lawes alone,
The which the base affections doe obay,

EDMUND SPENSER

And yeeld theyr services unto her will;
Ne thought of thing uncomely ever may
Thereto approch to tempt her mind to ill.
Had ye once seene these her celestial threasures,
And unrevealèd pleasures,
Then would ye wonder, and her prayses sing,
That al the woods should answer, and your echo ring.

Open the temple gates unto my love,
Open them wide that she may enter in,
And all the postes adorne as doth behove,
And all the pillours deck with girlands trim,
For to receyve this Saynt with honour dew,
That commeth in to you.
With trembling steps, and humble reverence,
She commeth in, before th' Almighties view;
Of her ye virgins learne obedience,
When so ye come into those holy places,
To humble your proud faces:
Bring her up to th' high altar, that she may
The sacred ceremonies there partake,
The which do endlesse matrimony make;
And let the roring Organs loudly play
The praises of the Lord in lively notes;
The whiles, with hollow throates,
The Choristers the joyous Antheme sing,
That al the woods may answere, and their eccho ring.

Behold, whiles she before the altar stands,
Hearing the holy priest that to her speakes,
And blesseth her with his two happy hands,
How the red roses flush up in her cheekes,
And the pure snow, with goodly vermill stayne
Like crimsin dyde in grayne:

EDMUND SPENSER

That even th' Angels, which continually
About the sacred Altare doe remaine,
Forget their service and about her fly,
Ofte peeping in her face, that seems more fayre,
The more they on it stare.
But her sad eyes, still fastened on the ground,
Are governèd with goodly modesty,
That suffers not one looke to glaunce awry,
Which may let in a little thought unsownd.
Why blush ye, love, to give to me your hand,
The pledge of all our band!
Sing, ye sweet Angels, Alleluya sing,
That all the woods may answere, and your eccho ring.

Now al is done: bring home the bride againe;
Bring home the triumph of our victory:
Bring home with you the glory of her gaine;
With joyance bring her and with jollity.
Never had man more joyfull day then this,
Whom heaven would heape with blis,
Make feast therefore now all this live-long day;
This day for ever to me holy is.
Poure out the wine without restraint or stay,
Poure not by cups, but by the belly full,
Poure out to all that wull,
And sprinkle all the postes and wals with wine,
That they may sweat, and drunken be withall.
Crowne ye God Bacchus with a coronall,
And Hymen also crowne with wreathes of vine;
And let the Graces daunce unto the rest,
For they can doo it best:
The whiles the maydens doe theyr carroll sing,
To which the woods shall answer, and theyr eccho ring.

EDMUND SPENSER

Ring ye the bels, ye yong men of the towne,
And leave your wonted labors for this day:
This day is holy; doe ye write it downe,
That ye for ever it remember may.
This day the sunne is in his chiefest hight,
With Barnaby the bright,
From whence declining daily by degrees,
He somewhat loseth of his heat and light,
When once the Crab behind his back he sees.
But for this time it ill ordainèd was,
To chose the longest day in all the yeare,
And shortest night, when longest fitter weare:
Yet never day so long, but late would passe.
Ring ye the bels, to make it weare away,
And bonefiers make all day;
And daunce about them, and about them sing,
That all the woods may answer, and your eccho

Ah! when will this long weary day have end,
And lende me leave to come unto my love?
How slowly do the houres theyr numbers spend
How slowly does sad Time his feathers move?
Hast thee, O fayrest Planet, to thy home,
Within the Westerne fome:
Thy tyrèd steedes long since have need of rest.
Long though it be, at last I see it gloome,
And the bright evening-star with golden creast
Appeare out of the East.
Fayre childe of beauty! glorious lampe of love!
That all the host of heaven in rankes doost lead,
And guydest lovers through the nights sad dread,
How chearefully thou lookest from above,
And seemst to laugh atweene thy twinkling light,
As joying in the sight

EDMUND SPENSER

Of these glad many, which for joy doe sing,
That all the woods them answer, and their echo ring!
Now ceasse, ye damsels, your delights fore-past;
Enough it is that all the day was youres:
Now day is doen, and night is nighing fast,
Now bring the Bryde into the brydall boures.
The night is come, now soon her disaray,
And in her bed her lay;
Lay her in lillies and in violets,
And silken courteins over her display,
And odourd sheetes, and Arras coverlets.
Behold how goodly my faire love does ly,
In proud humility!
Like unto Maia, when as Jove her took
In Tempe, lying on the flowry gras,
Twixt sleepe and wake, after she weary was,
With bathing in the Acidalian brooke.
Now it is night, ye damsels may be gon,
And leave my love alone,
And leave likewise your former lay to sing:
The woods no more shall answere, nor your echo ring.

Now welcome, night! thou night so long expected,
That long daies labour doest at last defray,
And all my cares, which cruell Love collected,
Hast sumd in one, and cancellèd for aye:
Spread thy broad wing over my love and me,
That no man may us see;
And in thy sable mantle us enwrap,
From feare of perrill and foule horror free.
Let no false treason seeke us to entrap,
Nor any dread disquiet once annoy
The safety of our joy;

122

EDMUND SPENSER

But let the night be calme, and quietsome,
Without tempestuous storms or sad afray:
Lyke as when Jove with fayre Alcmena lay,
When he begot the great Tirynthian groome:
Or lyke as when he with thy selfe did lie
And begot Majesty.
And let the mayds and yong men cease to sing;
Ne let the woods them answer nor theyr eccho ring.

Let no lamenting cryes, nor dolefull teares,
Be heard all night within, nor yet without:
Ne let false whispers, breeding hidden feares,
Breake gentle sleepe with misconceivèd dout.
Let no deluding dreames, nor dreadfull sights,
Make sudden sad affrights;
Ne let house-fyres, nor lightnings helpelesse harmes,
Ne let the Pouke, nor other evill sprights,
Ne let mischivous witches with theyr charmes,
Ne let hob Goblins, names whose sence we see not,
Fray us with things that be not:
Let not the shriech Oule nor the Storke be heard,
Nor the night Raven, that still deadly yels;
Nor damnèd ghosts, cald up with mighty spels,
Nor griesly vultures, make us once affeard:
Ne let th' unpleasant Quyre of Frogs still croking
Make us to wish theyr choking.
Let none of these theyr drery accents sing;
Ne let the woods them answer, nor theyr eccho ring.

But let stil Silence trew night-watches keepe,
That sacred Peace may in assurance rayne,
And tymely Sleep, when it is tyme to sleepe,
May poure his limbs forth on your pleasant playne;
The whiles an hundred little wingèd loves,

EDMUND SPENSER

Like divers-fethered doves,
Shall fly and flutter round about your bed,
And in the secret darke, that none reproves,
Their prety stealthes shal worke, and snares shal spread
To filch away sweet snatches of delight,
Conceald through covert night.
Ye sonnes of Venus, play your sports at will!
For greedy pleasure, carelesse of your toyes,
Thinks more upon her paradise of joyes,
Then what ye do, albe it good or ill.
All night therefore attend your merry play,
For it will soone be day:
Now none doth hinder you, that say or sing;
Ne will the woods now answer, nor your Eccho ring.

Who is the same, which at my window peepes?
Or whose is that faire face that shines so bright?
Is it not Cinthia, she that never sleepes,
But walkes about high heaven al the night?
O! fayrest goddesse, do thou not envy
My love with me to spy:
For thou likewise didst love, though now unthought,
And for a fleece of wooll, which privily
The Latmian shepherd once unto thee brought,
His pleasures with thee wrought.
Therefore to us be favorable now;
And sith of wemens labours thou hast charge,
And generation goodly dost enlarge,
Encline thy will t'effect our wishfull vow,
And the chast wombe informe with timely seed
That may our comfort breed:
Till which we cease our hopefull hap to sing;
Ne let the woods us answere, nor our Eccho ring.

EDMUND SPENSER

And thou, great Juno! which with awful might
The lawes of wedlock still dost patronize;
And the religion of the faith first plight
With sacred rites hast taught to solemnize;
And eeke for comfort often callèd art
Of women in their smart;
Eternally bind thou this lovely band,
And all thy blessings unto us impart.
And thou, glad Genius! in whose gentle hand
The bridale bowre and geniall bed remaine,
Without blemish or staine;
And the sweet pleasures of theyr loves delight
With secret ayde doest succour and supply,
Till they bring forth the fruitfull progeny;
Send us the timely fruit of this same night.
And thou, fayre Hebe! and thou, Hymen free!
Grant that it may so be.
Til which we cease your further prayse to sing;
Ne any woods shall answer, nor your Eccho ring.

And ye high heavens, the temple of the gods,
In which a thousand torches flaming bright
Doe burne, that to us wretched earthly clods
In dreadful darknesse lend desirèd light
And all ye powers which in the same remayne,
More then we men can fayne!
Poure out your blessing on us plentiously,
And happy influence upon us raine,
That we may raise a large posterity,
Which from the earth, which they may long possesse
With lasting happinesse,
Up to your haughty pallaces may mount;
And, for the guerdon of theyr glorious merit,

EDMUND SPENSER

May heavenly tabernacles there inherit,
Of blessèd Saints for to increase the count.
So let us rest, sweet love, in hope of this,
And cease till then our tymely joyes to sing:
The woods no more us answer, nor our eccho ring!

Song! made in lieu of many ornaments,
With which my love should duly have been deet,
Which cutting off through hasty accidents,
Ye would not stay your dew time to expect,
But promist both to recompens;
Be unto her a goodly ornament,
And for short time an endlesse moniment.

83. From 'Daphnaïda'
An Elegy

SHE fell away in her first ages spring,
  Whil'st yet her leafe was greene, and fresh her rinde,
And whil'st her braunch faire blossomes foorth did bring,
She fell away against all course of kinde.
For age to dye is right, but youth is wrong;
She fel away like fruit blowne downe with winde.
Weepe, Shepheard! weepe, to make my undersong.

Yet fell she not as one enforst to dye,
Ne dyde with dread and grudging discontent,
But as one toyld with travaile downe doth lye,
So lay she downe, as if to sleepe she went,
And closde her eyes with carelesse quietnesse;
The whiles soft death away her spirit hent,
And soule assoyld from sinfull fleshlinesse.

EDMUND SPENSER

How happie was I when I saw her leade
The Shepheards daughters dauncing in a rownd!
How trimly would she trace and softly tread
The tender grasse, with rosie garland crownd!
And when she list advance her heavenly voyce,
Both Nymphes and Muses nigh she made astownd,
And flocks and shepheards caused to rejoyce.

But now, ye Shepheard lasses! who shall lead
Your wandring troupes, or sing your virelayes?
Or who shall dight your bowres, sith she is dead
That was the Lady of your holy-dayes?
Let now your blisse be turnèd into bale,
And into plaints convert your joyous playes,
And with the same fill every hill and dale.

For I will walke this wandring pilgrimage,
Throughout the world from one to other end,
And in affliction wast my better age:
My bread shall be the anguish of my mind,
My drink the teares which fro mine eyes do raine,
My bed the ground that hardest I may finde;
So will I wilfully increase my paine.

Ne sleepe (the harbenger of wearie wights)
Shall ever lodge upon mine ey-lids more;
Ne shall with rest refresh my fainting sprights,
Nor failing force to former strength restore:
But I will wake and sorrow all the night
With Philumene, my fortune to deplore;
With Philumene, the partner of my plight.

And ever as I see the starres to fall,
And under ground to goe to give them light

EDMUND SPENSER

Which dwell in darknes, I to minde will call
How my fair Starre (that shinde on me so bright)
Fell sodainly and faded under ground;
Since whose departure, day is turnd to night,
And night without a Venus starre is found.

And she, my love that was, my Saint that is,
When she beholds from her celestiall throne
(In which shee joyeth in eternall blis)
My bitter penance, will my case bemone,
And pitie me that living thus doo die;
For heavenly spirits have compassion
On mortall men, and rue their miserie.

So when I have with sorowe satisfide
Th' importune fates, which vengeance on me seeke,
And th' heavens with long languor pacifide,
She, for pure pitie of my sufferance meeke,
Will send for me; for which I daylie long:
And will till then my painful penance eeke.
Weep, Shepheard! weep, to make my undersong!

84.   *Easter*

MOST glorious Lord of Lyfe! that, on this day,
   Didst make Thy triumph over death and sin;
And, having harrowd hell, didst bring away
Captivity thence captive, us to win:
This joyous day, deare Lord, with joy begin;
And grant that we, for whom thou diddest dye,
Being with Thy deare blood clene washt from sin,
May live for ever in felicity!

EDMUND SPENSER

And that Thy love we weighing worthily,
May likewise love Thee for the same againe;
And for Thy sake, that all lyke deare didst buy,
With love may one another entertayne!
  So let us love, deare Love, lyke as we ought,
  —Love is the lesson which the Lord us taught.

JOHN LYLY
1553-1606

85.   *Cards and Kisses*

CUPID and my Campaspe play'd
  At cards for kisses—Cupid paid:
He stakes his quiver, bow, and arrows,
His mother's doves, and team of sparrows;
Loses them too; then down he throws
The coral of his lips, the rose
Growing on 's cheek (but none knows how);
With these, the crystal of his brow,
And then the dimple of his chin:
All these did my Campaspe win.
At last he set her both his eyes—
She won, and Cupid blind did rise.
  O Love! has she done this for thee?
  What shall, alas! become of me?

86.   *Spring's Welcome*

WHAT bird so sings, yet so does wail?
  O 'tis the ravish'd nightingale.
Jug, jug, jug, jug, tereu! she cries,
And still her woes at midnight rise.

JOHN LYLY

Brave prick-song! Who is't now we hear?
None but the lark so shrill and clear;
Now at heaven's gate she claps her wings,
The morn not waking till she sings.
Hark, hark, with what a pretty throat
Poor robin redbreast tunes his note!
Hark how the jolly cuckoos sing
Cuckoo! to welcome in the spring!
Cuckoo! to welcome in the spring!

ANTHONY MUNDAY
1553-1633

87. *Beauty Bathing*

BEAUTY sat bathing by a spring,
   Where fairest shades did hide her;
The winds blew calm, the birds did sing,
   The cool streams ran beside her.
My wanton thoughts enticed mine eye
To see what was forbidden:
But better memory said Fie;
   So vain desire was chidden—
      Hey nonny nonny O!
      Hey nonny nonny!

Into a slumber then I fell,
   And fond imagination
Seemèd to see, but could not tell,
   Her feature or her fashion:
But ev'n as babes in dreams do smile,
   And sometimes fall a-weeping,
So I awaked as wise that while
   As when I fell a-sleeping.

SIR PHILIP SIDNEY

1554-86

88. *The Bargain*

MY true love hath my heart, and I have his,
   By just exchange one for another given:
I hold his dear, and mine he cannot miss,
   There never was a better bargain driven:
     My true love hath my heart, and I have his.

His heart in me keeps him and me in one,
   My heart in him his thoughts and senses guides:
He loves my heart, for once it was his own,
   I cherish his because in me it bides:
     My true love hath my heart, and I have his.

89. *Song*

WHO hath his fancy pleasèd
   With fruits of happy sight,
Let here his eyes be raisèd
   On Nature's sweetest light;
A light which doth dissever
   And yet unite the eyes,
A light which, dying never,
   Is cause the looker dies.

She never dies, but lasteth
   In life of lover's heart;
He ever dies that wasteth
   In love his chiefest part:
Thus is her life still guarded
   In never-dying faith;
Thus is his death rewarded,
   Since she lives in his death.

SIR PHILIP SIDNEY

Look then, and die! The pleasure
  Doth answer well the pain :
Small loss of mortal treasure,
  Who may immortal gain!
Immortal be her graces,
  Immortal is her mind;
They, fit for heavenly places—
  This, heaven in it doth bind.

But eyes these beauties see not,
  Nor sense that grace descries;
Yet eyes deprivèd be not
  From sight of her fair eyes—
Which, as of inward glory
  They are the outward seal,
So may they live still sorry,
  Which die not in that weal.

But who hath fancies pleasèd
  With fruits of happy sight,
Let here his eyes be raisèd
  On Nature's sweetest light!

90. *Voices at the Window*

WHO is it that, this dark night,
  Underneath my window plaineth?
It is one who from thy sight
  Being, ah, exiled, disdaineth
Every other vulgar light.
Why, alas, and are you he?
  Be not yet those fancies changèd?
Dear, when you find change in me,
  Though from me you be estrangèd,
Let my change to ruin be.

SIR PHILIP SIDNEY

Well, in absence this will die:
  Leave to see, and leave to wonder.
Absence sure will help, if I
  Can learn how myself to sunder
From what in my heart doth lie.

But time will these thoughts remove;
  Time doth work what no man knoweth.
Time doth as the subject prove:
  With time still the affection groweth
In the faithful turtle-dove.

What if you new beauties see?
  Will not they stir new affection?
I will think they pictures be
  (Image-like, of saints' perfection)
Poorly counterfeiting thee.

But your reason's purest light
  Bids you leave such minds to nourish.
Dear, do reason no such spite!
  Never doth thy beauty flourish
More than in my reason's sight.

91. *Philomela*

THE Nightingale, as soon as April bringeth
  Unto her rested sense a perfect waking,
While late-bare Earth, proud of new clothing, springeth,
  Sings out her woes, a thorn her song-book making;
    And mournfully bewailing,
    Her throat in tunes expresseth
    What grief her breast oppresseth,
For Tereus' force on her chaste will prevailing.

90. leave] cease.

SIR PHILIP SIDNEY

O Philomela fair, O take some gladness
That here is juster cause of plaintful sadness!
Thine earth now springs, mine fadeth;
Thy thorn without, my thorn my heart invadeth.

Alas! she hath no other cause of anguish
  But Tereus' love, on her by strong hand wroken;
Wherein she suffering, all her spirits languish,
  Full womanlike complains her will was broken
    But I, who, daily craving,
    Cannot have to content me,
    Have more cause to lament me,
Since wanting is more woe than too much having.

O Philomela fair, O take some gladness
That here is juster cause of plaintful sadness!
Thine earth now springs, mine fadeth;
Thy thorn without, my thorn my heart invadeth.

92.   The Highway

HIGHWAY, since you my chief Parnassus be,
  And that my Muse, to some ears not unsweet,
Tempers her words to trampling horses' feet
More oft than to a chamber-melody,—
Now blessèd you bear onward blessèd me
To her, where I my heart, safe-left, shall meet;
My Muse and I must you of duty greet
With thanks and wishes, wishing thankfully;
Be you still fair, honour'd by public heed;
By no encroachment wrong'd, nor time forgot;
Nor blamed for blood, nor shamed for sinful deed;
And that you know I envy you no lot
  Of highest wish, I wish you so much bliss,
  Hundreds of years you Stella's feet may kiss!

SIR PHILIP SIDNEY

93.   *His Lady's Cruelty*

WITH how sad steps, O moon, thou climb'st the skies!
   How silently, and with how wan a face!
What! may it be that even in heavenly place
That busy archer his sharp arrows tries?
Sure, if that long-with-love-acquainted eyes
Can judge of love, thou feel'st a lover's case:
I read it in thy looks; thy languish'd grace
To me, that feel the like, thy state descries.
Then, even of fellowship, O Moon, tell me,
Is constant love deem'd there but want of wit?
Are beauties there as proud as here they be?
Do they above love to be loved, and yet
   Those lovers scorn whom that love doth possess?
   Do they call 'virtue' there—ungratefulness?

94.   *Sleep*

COME, Sleep; O Sleep! the certain knot of peace.
   The baiting-place of wit, the balm of woe,
The poor man's wealth, the prisoner's release,
Th' indifferent judge between the high and low;
With shield of proof shield me from out the prease
Of those fierce darts Despair at me doth throw:
O make in me those civil wars to cease;
I will good tribute pay, if thou do so.
Take thou of me smooth pillows, sweetest bed,
A chamber deaf to noise and blind of light,
A rosy garland and a weary head;
And if these things, as being thine by right,
   Move not thy heavy grace, thou shalt in me,
   Livelier than elsewhere, Stella's image see.

94. prease] press.

SIR PHILIP SIDNEY

95. *Splendidis longum valedico Nugis*

LEAVE me, O Love, which reachest but to dust,
  And thou, my mind, aspire to higher things!
Grow rich in that which never taketh rust:
Whatever fades, but fading pleasure brings.
Draw in thy beams, and humble all thy might
To that sweet yoke where lasting freedoms be;
Which breaks the clouds and opens forth the light
That doth both shine and give us sight to see.
O take fast hold! let that light be thy guide
In this small course which birth draws out to death,
And think how evil becometh him to slide
Who seeketh Heaven, and comes of heavenly breath.
  Then farewell, world! thy uttermost I see:
  Eternal Love, maintain thy life in me!

FULKE GREVILLE, LORD BROOKE
1554–1628

96. *Myra*

I, WITH whose colours Myra dress'd her head,
  I, that ware posies of her own hand-making,
I, that mine own name in the chimneys read
  By Myra finely wrought ere I was waking:
Must I look on, in hope time coming may
With change bring back my turn again to play?

I, that on Sunday at the church-stile found
  A garland sweet with true-love-knots in flowers,
Which I to wear about mine arms was bound
  That each of us might know that all was ours:
Must I lead now an idle life in wishes,
And follow Cupid for his loaves and fishes?

96. chimneys] *cheminées*, chimney-screens of tapestry work.

LORD BROOKE

I, that did wear the ring her mother left,
  I, for whose love she gloried to be blamèd,
I, with whose eyes her eyes committed theft,
  I, who did make her blush when I was namèd:
Must I lose ring, flowers, blush, theft, and go naked,
Watching with sighs till dead love be awakèd?

Was it for this that I might Myra see
  Washing the water with her beauty's white?
Yet would she never write her love to me.
  Thinks wit of change when thoughts are in delight?
Mad girls may safely love as they may leave;
No man can *print* a kiss: lines may deceive.

THOMAS LODGE
1556?-1625

97. *Rosalind's Madrigal*

LOVE in my bosom like a bee
    Doth suck his sweet:
Now with his wings he plays with me,
    Now with his feet.
Within mine eyes he makes his nest,
His bed amidst my tender breast;
My kisses are his daily feast,
And yet he robs me of my rest:
    Ah! wanton, will ye?

And if I sleep, then percheth he
    With pretty flight,
And makes his pillow of my knee
    The livelong night.

96. deceive] betray.

Strike I my lute, he tunes the string;
He music plays if so I sing;
He lends me every lovely thing,
Yet cruel he my heart doth sting:
    Whist, wanton, still ye!
Else I with roses every day
    Will whip you hence,
And bind you, when you long to play,
    For your offence.
I'll shut mine eyes to keep you in;
I'll make you fast it for your sin;
I'll count your power not worth a pin.
—Alas! what hereby shall I win
    If he gainsay me?

What if I beat the wanton boy
    With many a rod?
He will repay me with annoy,
    Because a god.
Then sit thou safely on my knee;
Then let thy bower my bosom be;
Lurk in mine eyes, I like of thee;
O Cupid, so thou pity me,
    Spare not, but play thee!

98. *Phillis* I

MY Phillis hath the morning sun
    At first to look upon her;
And Phillis hath morn-waking birds
    Her risings still to honour.
My Phillis hath prime-feather'd flowers,
    That smile when she treads on them;

THOMAS LODGE

And Phillis hath a gallant flock,
　That leaps since she doth own them.
But Phillis hath too hard a heart,
　Alas that she should have it!
It yields no mercy to desert,
　Nor grace to those that crave it.

99.　　　　*Phillis* 2

LOVE guards the roses of thy lips
　And flies about them like a bee;
If I approach he forward skips,
　And if I kiss he stingeth me.

Love in thine eyes doth build his bower,
　And sleeps within their pretty shine;
And if I look the boy will lower,
　And from their orbs shoot shafts divine.

Love works thy heart within his fire,
　And in my tears doth firm the same;
And if I tempt it will retire,
　And of my plaints doth make a game.

Love, let me cull her choicest flowers;
　And pity me, and calm her eye;
Make soft her heart, dissolve her lowers
　Then will I praise thy deity.

But if thou do not, Love, I'll truly serve her
In spite of thee, and by firm faith deserve her.

THOMAS LODGE

100. Rosaline

LIKE to the clear in highest sphere
  Where all imperial glory shines,
Of selfsame colour is her hair
  Whether unfolded or in twines:
    Heigh ho, fair Rosaline!
Her eyes are sapphires set in snow,
  Resembling heaven by every wink;
The gods do fear whenas they glow,
  And I do tremble when I think
    Heigh ho, would she were mine!

Her cheeks are like the blushing cloud
  That beautifies Aurora's face,
Or like the silver crimson shroud
  That Phœbus' smiling looks doth grace.
    Heigh ho, fair Rosaline!
Her lips are like two budded roses
  Whom ranks of lilies neighbour nigh,
Within whose bounds she balm encloses
  Apt to entice a deity:
    Heigh ho, would she were mine!

Her neck like to a stately tower
  Where Love himself imprison'd lies,
To watch for glances every hour
  From her divine and sacred eyes:
    Heigh ho, fair Rosaline!
Her paps are centres of delight,
  Her breasts are orbs of heavenly frame,
Where Nature moulds the dew of light
  To feed perfection with the same:
    Heigh ho, would she were mine!

THOMAS LODGE

With orient pearl, with ruby red,
  With marble white, with sapphire blue,
Her body every way is fed,
    Yet soft to touch and sweet in view:
      Heigh ho, fair Rosaline!
Nature herself her shape admires;
  The gods are wounded in her sight;
And Love forsakes his heavenly fires
    And at her eyes his brand doth light:
      Heigh ho, would she were mine!

Then muse not, Nymphs, though I bemoan
  The absence of fair Rosaline,
Since for a fair there's fairer none,
    Nor for her virtues so divine:
      Heigh ho, fair Rosaline!
Heigh ho, my heart! would God that she were mine!

GEORGE PEELE
1558?–97

101. *Fair and Fair*

Œnone. FAIR and fair, and twice so fair,
    As fair as any may be;
  The fairest shepherd on our green,
    A love for any lady.
Paris. Fair and fair, and twice so fair,
    As fair as any may be;
  Thy love is fair for thee alone
    And for no other lady.
Œnone. My love is fair, my love is gay,
    As fresh as bin the flowers in May
  And of my love my roundelay,
    My merry, merry, merry roundelay,

     Concludes with Cupid's curse,—
   'They that do change old love for new
    Pray gods they change for worse!'
Ambo Simul. They that do change old love for new,
    Pray gods they change for worse!

Œnone. Fair and fair, etc.
Paris. Fair and fair, etc.
  Thy love is fair, etc.
Œnone. My love can pipe, my love can sing,
  My love can many a pretty thing,
  And of his lovely praises ring
  My merry, merry, merry roundelays
   Amen to Cupid's curse,—
  'They that do change,' etc.
Paris. They that do change, etc.
Ambo. Fair and fair, etc.

102. *A Farewell to Arms*
   (TO QUEEN ELIZABETH)

HIS golden locks Time hath to silver turn'd;
 O Time too swift, O swiftness never ceasing!
His youth 'gainst time and age hath ever spurn'd,
 But spurn'd in vain; youth waneth by increasing:
Beauty, strength, youth, are flowers but fading seen;
Duty, faith, love, are roots, and ever green.

His helmet now shall make a hive for bees;
 And, lovers' sonnets turn'd to holy psalms,
A man-at-arms must now serve on his knees,
 And feed on prayers, which are Age his alms:
But though from court to cottage he depart,
His Saint is sure of his unspotted heart.

GEORGE PEELE

And when he saddest sits in homely cell,
  He'll teach his swains this carol for a song,—
'Blest be the hearts that wish my sovereign well,
  Curst be the souls that think her any wrong.'
Goddess, allow this agèd man his right
To be your beadsman now that was your knight.

ROBERT GREENE
1560-92

103.   *Samela*

LIKE to Diana in her summer weed,
  Girt with a crimson robe of brightest dye,
    Goes fair Samela.
Whiter than be the flocks that straggling feed
  When wash'd by Arethusa faint they lie,
    Is fair Samela.
As fair Aurora in her morning grey,
  Deck'd with the ruddy glister of her love
    Is fair Samela;
Like lovely Thetis on a calmèd day
  Whenas her brightness Neptune's fancy move,
    Shines fair Samela.

Her tresses gold, her eyes like glassy streams,
  Her teeth are pearl, the breasts are ivory
    Of fair Samela;
Her cheeks like rose and lily yield forth gleams;
  Her brows bright arches framed of ebony.
    Thus fair Samela
Passeth fair Venus in her bravest hue,
  And Juno in the show of majesty
    (For she's Samela!),

Pallas in wit,—all three, if you well view,
For beauty, wit, and matchless dignity,
   Yield to Samela.

104.   *Fawnia*

AH! were she pitiful as she is fair,
  Or but as mild as she is seeming so,
Then were my hopes greater than my despair,
Then all the world were heaven, nothing woe.
Ah! were her heart relenting as her hand,
That seems to melt even with the mildest touch,
Then knew I where to seat me in a land
Under wide heavens, but yet there is not such.
So as she shows she seems the budding rose,
Yet sweeter far than is an earthly flower;
Sovran of beauty, like the spray she grows;
Compass'd she is with thorns and canker'd flower.
  Yet were she willing to be pluck'd and worn,
  She would be gather'd, though she grew on thorn.

Ah! when she sings, all music else be still,
For none must be compared to her note;
Ne'er breathed such glee from Philomela's bill,
Nor from the morning-singer's swelling throat.
Ah! when she riseth from her blissful bed
She comforts all the world as doth the sun,
And at her sight the night's foul vapour's fled;
When she is set the gladsome day is done.
  O glorious sun, imagine me the west,
  Shine in my arms, and set thou in my breast!

ROBERT GREENE

105. *Sephestia's Lullaby*

WEEP not, my wanton, smile upon my knee;
  When thou art old there's grief enough for thee.
    Mother's wag, pretty boy,
    Father's sorrow, father's joy;
    When thy father first did see
    Such a boy by him and me,
    He was glad, I was woe;
    Fortune changèd made him so,
    When he left his pretty boy,
    Last his sorrow, first his joy.
Weep not, my wanton, smile upon my knee;
When thou art old there's grief enough for thee.
    Streaming tears that never stint,
    Like pearl-drops from a flint,
    Fell by course from his eyes,
    That one another's place supplies;
    Thus he grieved in every part,
    Tears of blood fell from his heart,
    When he left his pretty boy,
    Father's sorrow, father's joy.
Weep not, my wanton, smile upon my knee;
When thou art old there's grief enough for thee.
    The wanton smiled, father wept,
    Mother cried, baby leapt;
    More he crow'd, more we cried,
    Nature could not sorrow hide:
    He must go, he must kiss
    Child and mother, baby bliss,
    For he left his pretty boy,
    Father's sorrow, father's joy.
Weep not, my wanton, smile upon my knee,
When thou art old there's grief enough for thee.

ALEXANDER HUME
1560-1609

106. *A Summer Day*

O PERFECT Light, which shaid away
    The darkness from the light,
And set a ruler o'er the day,
    Another o'er the night—

Thy glory, when the day forth flies,
    More vively doth appear
Than at mid day unto our eyes
    The shining sun is clear.

The shadow of the earth anon
    Removes and drawis by,
While in the East, when it is gone,
    Appears a clearer sky.

Which soon perceive the little larks,
    The lapwing and the snipe,
And tune their songs, like Nature's clerks,
    O'er meadow, muir, and stripe.

Our hemisphere is polisht clean,
    And lighten'd more and more,
While everything is clearly seen
    Which seemit dim before:

Except the glistering astres bright,
    Which all the night were clear,
Offuskit with a greater light
    No longer do appear.

shaid] parted.   stripe] rill.   offuskit] darkened.

ALEXANDER HUME

The golden globe incontinent
 Sets up his shining head,
And o'er the earth and firmament
 Displays his beams abread.

For joy the birds with boulden throats
 Against his visage sheen
Take up their kindly musick notes
 In woods and gardens green.

The dew upon the tender crops,
 Like pearlis white and round,
Or like to melted silver drops,
 Refreshis all the ground.

The misty reek, the clouds of rain,
 From tops of mountains skails,
Clear are the highest hills and plain,
 The vapours take the vales.

The ample heaven of fabrick sure
 In cleanness does surpass
The crystal and the silver pure,
 Or clearest polisht glass.

The time so tranquil is and still
 That nowhere shall ye find,
Save on a high and barren hill,
 An air of peeping wind.

All trees and simples, great and small,
 That balmy leaf do bear,
Than they were painted on a wall
 No more they move or steir.

boulden] swollen. sheen] bright. skails] clears. simples] herbs.

ALEXANDER HUME

Calm is the deep and purple sea,
    Yea, smoother than the sand;
The waves that weltering wont to be
    Are stable like the land.

So silent is the cessile air
    That every cry and call
The hills and dales and forest fair
    Again repeats them all.

The flourishes and fragrant flowers,
    Through Phoebus' fostering heat,
Refresht with dew and silver showers
    Cast up an odour sweet.

The cloggit busy humming bees,
    That never think to drone,
On flowers and flourishes of trees
    Collect their liquor brown.

The Sun, most like a speedy post
    With ardent course ascends;
The beauty of the heavenly host
    Up to our zenith tends.

The burning beams down from his face
    So fervently can beat,
That man and beast now seek a place
    To save them from the heat.

The herds beneath some leafy tree
    Amidst the flowers they lie;
The stable ships upon the sea
    Tend up their sails to dry.

cessile] yielding, ceasing.   flourishes] blossoms.

ALEXANDER HUME

With gilded eyes and open wings
   The cock his courage shows;
With claps of joy his breast he dings,
   And twenty times he crows.

The dove with whistling wings so blue
   The winds can fast collect;
Her purple pens turn many a hue
   Against the sun direct.

Now noon is went; gone is midday,
   The heat doth slake at last;
The sun descends down West away,
   For three of clock is past.

The rayons of the sun we see
   Diminish in their strength;
The shade of every tower and tree
   Extendit is in length.

Great is the calm, for everywhere
   The wind is setting down;
The reek throws right up in the air
   From every tower and town.

The gloming comes; the day is spent;
   The sun goes out of sight;
And painted is the occident
   With purple sanguine bright.

Our west horizon circular
   From time the sun be set
Is all with rubies, as it were,
   Or roses red o'erfret.

ALEXANDER HUME

What pleasure were to walk and see,
  Endlong a river clear,
The perfect form of every tree
  Within the deep appear.
O then it were a seemly thing,
  While all is still and calm,
The praise of God to play and sing
  With cornet and with shalm!
All labourers draw home at even,
  And can to other say,
Thanks to the gracious God of heaven,
  Which sent this summer day.

GEORGE CHAPMAN
1560-1634

107. *Bridal Song*

O COME, soft rest of cares! come, Night!
  Come, naked Virtue's only tire,
The reapèd harvest of the light
  Bound up in sheaves of sacred fire.
    Love calls to war:
      Sighs his alarms,
    Lips his swords are,
      The field his arms.
Come, Night, and lay thy velvet hand
  On glorious Day's outfacing face;
And all thy crownèd flames command
  For torches to our nuptial grace.
    Love calls to war:
      Sighs his alarms,
    Lips his swords are,
      The field his arms.

ROBERT SOUTHWELL
1561-95

108   Times go by Turns

THE loppèd tree in time may grow again,
   Most naked plants renew both fruit and flower;
The sorest wight may find release of pain,
The driest soil suck in some moist'ning shower;
Times go by turns and chances change by course,
From foul to fair, from better hap to worse.

The sea of Fortune doth not ever flow,
She draws her favours to the lowest ebb;
Her tides hath equal times to come and go,
Her loom doth weave the fine and coarsest web;
No joy so great but runneth to an end,
No hap so hard but may in fine amend.

Not always fall of leaf nor ever spring,
No endless night yet not eternal day;
The saddest birds a season find to sing,
The roughest storm a calm may soon allay:
Thus with succeeding turns God tempereth all,
That man may hope to rise, yet fear to fall.

A chance may win that by mischance was lost;
The net that holds no great, takes little fish;
In some things all, in all things none are crost,
Few all they need, but none have all they wish;
Unmeddled joys here to no man befall:
Who least, hath some; who most, hath never all.

unmeddled] unmixed.

109. *The Burning Babe*

AS I in hoary winter's night
    Stood shivering in the snow,
Surprised I was with sudden heat
    Which made my heart to. glow;
And lifting up a fearful eye
    To view what fire was near,
A pretty babe all burning bright
    Did in the air appear;
Who, scorchèd with excessive heat,
    Such floods of tears did shed,
As though His floods should quench His flames,
    Which with His tears were bred:
'Alas!' quoth He, 'but newly born
    In fiery heats I fry,
Yet none approach to warm their hearts
    Or feel my fire but I!
'My faultless breast the furnace is;
    The fuel, wounding thorns;
Love is the fire, and sighs the smoke;
    The ashes, shames and scorns;
The fuel Justice layeth on,
    And Mercy blows the coals,
The metal in this furnace wrought
    Are men's defilèd souls:
For which, as now on fire I am
    To work them to their good,
So will I melt into a bath,
    To wash them in my blood.'
With this He vanish'd out of sight
    And swiftly shrunk away,
And straight I callèd unto mind
    That it was Christmas Day.

HENRY CONSTABLE
1562?-1613?

110. On the Death of Sir Philip Sidney

GIVE pardon, blessèd soul, to my bold cries,
    If they, importune, interrupt thy song,
Which now with joyful notes thou sing'st among
The angel-quiristers of th' heavenly skies.
Give pardon eke, sweet soul, to my slow eyes,
That since I saw thee now it is so long,
And yet the tears that unto thee belong
To thee as yet they did not sacrifice.
I did not know that thou wert dead before;
I did not feel the grief I did sustain;
The greater stroke astonisheth the more;
Astonishment takes from us sense of pain;
    I stood amazed when others' tears begun,
    And now begin to weep when they have done.

SAMUEL DANIEL
1562-1619

111. Love is a Sickness

LOVE is a sickness full of woes,
    All remedies refusing;
A plant that with most cutting grows,
    Most barren with best using.
        Why so?
More we enjoy it, more it dies;
If not enjoy'd, it sighing cries—
        Heigh ho!

Love is a torment of the mind,
    A tempest everlasting;
And Jove hath made it of a kind
    Not well, nor full nor fasting.
        Why so?

SAMUEL DANIEL

More we enjoy it, more it dies;
If not enjoy'd, it sighing cries—
Heigh ho!

112. *Ulysses and the Siren*

Siren. COME, worthy Greek! Ulysses, come,
    Possess these shores with me:
The winds and seas are troublesome,
    And here we may be free.
Here may we sit and view their toil
    That travail in the deep,
And joy the day in mirth the while,
    And spend the night in sleep.

Ulysses. Fair Nymph, if fame or honour were
    To be attain'd with ease,
Then would I come and rest me there,
    And leave such toils as these.
But here it dwells, and here must I
    With danger seek it forth:
To spend the time luxuriously
    Becomes not men of worth.

Siren. Ulysses, O be not deceived
    With that unreal name;
This honour is a thing conceived,
    And rests on others' fame:
Begotten only to molest
    Our peace, and to beguile
The best thing of our life—our rest,
    And give us up to toil.

Ulysses. Delicious Nymph, suppose there were
    No honour nor report,
Yet manliness would scorn to wear
    The time in idle sport:
For toil doth give a better touch
    To make us feel our joy,
And ease finds tediousness as much
    As labour yields annoy.

Siren. Then pleasure likewise seems the shore
    Whereto tends all your toil,
Which you forgo to make it more,
    And perish oft the while.
Who may disport them diversely
    Find never tedious day,
And ease may have variety
    As well as action may.

Ulysses. But natures of the noblest frame
    These toils and dangers please;
And they take comfort in the same
    As much as you in ease;
And with the thought of actions past
    Are recreated still:
When Pleasure leaves a touch at last
    To show that it was ill.

Siren. That doth *Opinion* only cause
    That's out of *Custom* bred,
Which makes us many other laws
    Than ever *Nature* did.
No widows wail for our delights,
    Our sports are without blood;
The world we see by warlike wights
    Receives more hurt than good.

SAMUEL DANIEL

Ulysses. But yet the state of things require
 These motions of unrest:
 And these great Spirits of high desire
 Seem born to turn them best:
 To purge the mischiefs that increase
 And all good order mar :
 For oft we see a wicked peace
 To be well changed for war.
Siren. Well, well, Ulysses, then I see
 I shall not have thee here :
 And therefore I will come to thee,
 And take my fortune there.
 I must be won, that cannot win,
 Yet lost were I not won;
 For beauty hath created been
 T' undo, or be undone.

113. *Beauty, Time, and Love*
   SONNETS. I

FAIR is my Love and cruel as she 's fair;
 Her brow-shades frown, although her eyes are sunny.
Her smiles are lightning, though her pride despair,
And her disdains are gall, her favours honey:
A modest maid, deck'd with a blush of honour,
Whose feet do tread green paths of youth and love;
The wonder of all eyes that look upon her,
Sacred on earth, design'd a Saint above.
Chastity and Beauty, which were deadly foes,
Live reconcilèd friends within her brow;
And had she Pity to conjoin with those,
Then who had heard the plaints I utter now?
 For had she not been fair, and thus unkind,
 My Muse had slept, and none had known my mind.

SAMUEL DANIEL

II

My spotless love hovers with purest wings,
About the temple of the proudest frame,
Where blaze those lights, fairest of earthly things,
Which clear our clouded world with brightest flame.
My ambitious thoughts, confinèd in her face,
Affect no honour but what she can give;
My hopes do rest in limits of her grace;
I weigh no comfort unless she relieve.
For she, that can my heart imparadise,
Holds in her fairest hand what dearest is;
My Fortune's wheel's the circle of her eyes,
Whose rolling grace deign once a turn of bliss.
   All my life's sweet consists in her alone;
   So much I love the most Unloving one.

III

And yet I cannot reprehend the flight
Or blame th' attempt presuming so to soar;
The mounting venture for a high delight
Did make the honour of the fall the more.
For who gets wealth, that puts not from the shore?
Danger hath honour, great designs their fame;
Glory doth follow, courage goes before;
And though th' event oft answers not the same—
Suffice that high attempts have never shame.
The mean observer, whom base safety keeps,
Lives without honour, dies without a name,
And in eternal darkness ever sleeps.—
   And therefore, *Delia*, 'tis to me no blot
   To have attempted, tho' attain'd thee not.

SAMUEL DANIEL

IV

When men shall find thy flow'r, thy glory, pass,
And thou with careful brow, sitting alone,
Receivèd hast this message from thy glass,
That tells the truth and says that *All is gone;*
Fresh shalt thou see in me the wounds thou mad'st,
Though spent thy flame, in me the heat remaining:
I that have loved thee thus before thou fad'st—
My faith shall wax, when thou art in thy waning.
The world shall find this miracle in me,
That fire can burn when all the matter's spent:
Then what my faith hath been thyself shalt see,
And that thou wast unkind thou may'st repent.—
   Thou may'st repent that thou hast scorn'd my tears,
   When Winter snows upon thy sable hairs.

V

Beauty, sweet Love, is like the morning dew,
Whose short refresh upon the tender green
Cheers for a time, but till the sun doth show,
And straight 'tis gone as it had never been.
Soon doth it fade that makes the fairest flourish,
Short is the glory of the blushing rose;
The hue which thou so carefully dost nourish;
Yet which at length thou must be forced to lose.
When thou, surcharged with burthen of thy years,
Shalt bend thy wrinkles homeward to the earth;
And that, in Beauty's Lease expired, appears
The Date of Age, the Calends of our Death—
   But ah, no more!—this must not be foretold,
   For women grieve to think they must be old.

SAMUEL DANIEL

VI

I must not grieve my Love, whose eyes would read
Lines of delight, whereon her youth might smile;
Flowers have time before they come to seed,
And she is young, and now must sport the while.
And sport, Sweet Maid, in season of these years,
And learn to gather flowers before they wither;
And where the sweetest blossom first appears,
Let Love and Youth conduct thy pleasures thither.
Lighten forth smiles to clear the clouded air,
And calm the tempest which my sighs do raise;
Pity and smiles do best become the fair;
Pity and smiles must only yield thee praise.
    Make me to say when all my griefs are gone,
    Happy the heart that sighed for such a one!

VII

Let others sing of Knights and Paladines
In agèd accents and untimely words,
Paint shadows in imaginary lines,
Which well the reach of their high wit records:
But I must sing of thee, and those fair eyes
Authentic shall my verse in time to come;
When yet th' unborn shall say, *Lo, where she lies!*
Whose beauty made him speak, that else was dumb!
These are the arcs, the trophies I erect,
That fortify thy name against old age;
And these thy sacred virtues must protect
Against the Dark, and Time's consuming rage.
    Though th' error of my youth in them appear,
    Suffice, they show I lived, and loved thee dear.

MARK ALEXANDER BOYD
1563-1601

114. Sonet

FRA bank to bank, fra wood to wood I rin,
  Ourhailit with my feeble fantasie;
  Like til a leaf that fallis from a tree,
Or til a reed ourblawin with the win.

Twa gods guides me: the ane of tham is blin,
  Yea and a bairn brocht up in vanitie;
  The next a wife ingenrit of the sea,
And lichter nor a dauphin with her fin.

Unhappy is the man for evermair
  That tills the sand and sawis in the air;
  But twice unhappier is he, I lairn,
That feidis in his hairt a mad desire,
And follows on a woman throw the fire,
  Led by a blind and teachit by a bairn.

JOSHUA SYLVESTER
1563-1618

115. Ubique

WERE I as base as is the lowly plain,
  And you, my Love, as high as heaven above,
Yet should the thoughts of me, your humble swain,
Ascend to heaven in honour of my love.
Were I as high as heaven above the plain,
And you, my Love, as humble and as low
As are the deepest bottoms of the main,
Wheresoe'er you were, with you my love should go.

JOSHUA SYLVESTER

Were you the earth, dear Love, and I the skies,
My love should shine on you like to the Sun,
And look upon you with ten thousand eyes,
Till heaven wax'd blind, and till the world were done.
Wheresoe'er I am,—below, or else above you—
Wheresoe'er you are, my heart shall truly love you.

MICHAEL DRAYTON
1563-1631

116.   To His Coy Love

I PRAY thee, leave, love me no more,
  Call home the heart you gave me!
I but in vain that saint adore
  That can but will not save me.
These poor half-kisses kill me quite—
  Was ever man thus servèd?
Amidst an ocean of delight
  For pleasure to be starvèd?

Show me no more those snowy breasts
  With azure riverets branchèd,
Where, whilst mine eye with plenty feasts,
  Yet is my thirst not stanchèd;
O Tantalus, thy pains ne'er tell!
  By me thou art prevented:
'Tis nothing to be plagued in Hell,
  But thus in Heaven tormented.

Clip me no more in those dear arms,
  Nor thy life's comfort call me,
O these are but too powerful charms,
  And do but more enthral me!

MICHAEL DRAYTON

But see how patient I am grown
In all this coil about thee :
Come, nice thing, let my heart alone,
I cannot live without thee !

117. *The Parting*

SINCE there 's no help, come let us kiss and part—
  Nay, I have done, you get no more of me ;
And I am glad, yea, glad with all my heart,
That thus so cleanly I myself can free.
Shake hands for ever, cancel all our vows,
And when we meet at any time again,
Be it not seen in either of our brows
That we one jot of former love retain.
Now at the last gasp of Love's latest breath,
When, his pulse failing, Passion speechless lies,
When Faith is kneeling by his bed of death,
And Innocence is closing up his eyes,
  —Now if thou wouldst, when all have given him over,
  From death to life thou might'st him yet recover.

118. *Sirena*

NEAR to the silver *Trent*
  SIRENA dwelleth ;
She to whom Nature lent
  All that excelleth ;
By which the Muses late
  And the neat Graces
Have for their greater state
  Taken their places ;
Twisting an anadem
  Wherewith to crown her,

MICHAEL DRAYTON

As it belong'd to them
  Most to renown her.
    On thy bank,
    In a rank,
    Let thy swans sing her,
    And with their music
      Along let them bring her.
Tagus and *Pactolus*
  Are to thee debtor,
Nor for their gold to us
  Are they the better:
Henceforth of all the rest
  Be thou the River
Which, as the daintiest,
  Puts them down ever.
For as my precious one
  O'er thee doth travel,
She to pearl paragon
  Turneth thy gravel.
      On thy bank . . .
Our mournful Philomel,
  That rarest tuner,
Henceforth in Aperil
  Shall wake the sooner,
And to her shall complain
  From the thick cover,
Redoubling every strain
  Over and over:
For when my Love too long
  Her chamber keepeth,
As though it suffer'd wrong,
  The Morning weepeth.
      On thy bank . . .

MICHAEL DRAYTON

Oft have I seen the Sun,
    To do her honour,
Fix himself at his noon
    To look upon her;
And hath gilt every grove,
    Every hill near her,
With his flames from above
    Striving to cheer her:
And when she from his sight
    Hath herself turnèd,
He, as it had been night,
    In clouds hath mournèd.
        On thy bank . . .

The verdant meads are seen,
    When she doth view them,
In fresh and gallant green
    Straight to renew them;
And every little grass
    Broad itself spreadeth,
Proud that this bonny lass
    Upon it treadeth:
Nor flower is so sweet
    In this large cincture,
But it upon her feet
    Leaveth some tincture.
        On thy bank . . .

The fishes in the flood,
    When she doth angle,
For the hook strive a-good
    Them to entangle;
And leaping on the land,
    From the clear water,

MICHAEL DRAYTON

Their scales upon the sand
    Lavishly scatter;
Therewith to pave the mould
    Whereon she passes,
So herself to behold
    As in her glasses.
          On thy bank . . .
When she looks out by night,
    The stars stand gazing,
Like comets to our sight
    Fearfully blazing;
As wond'ring at her eyes
    With their much brightness,
Which so amaze the skies,
    Dimming their lightness.
The raging tempests are calm
    When she speaketh,
Such most delightsome balm
    From her lips breaketh.
          On thy bank . . .
In all our *Brittany*
    There's not a fairer,
Nor can you fit any
    Should you compare her.
Angels her eyelids keep,
    All hearts surprising;
Which look whilst she doth sleep
    Like the sun's rising:
She alone of her kind
    Knoweth true measure,
And her unmatchèd mind
    Is heaven's treasure.
          On thy bank . . .

MICHAEL DRAYTON

Fair *Dove* and *Darwen* clear,
   Boast ye your beauties,
To *Trent* your mistress here
   Yet pay your duties:
My Love was higher born
   Tow'rds the full fountains,
Yet she doth moorland scorn
   And the *Peak* mountains;
Nor would she none should dream
   Where she abideth,
Humble as is the stream
   Which by her slideth.
        On thy bank . . .

Yet my poor rustic Muse
   Nothing can move her,
Nor the means I can use,
   Though her true lover:
Many a long winter's night
   Have I waked for her,
Yet this my piteous plight
   Nothing can stir her.
All thy sands, silver *Trent*,
   Down to the *Humber*,
The sighs that I have spent
   Never can number.
      On thy bank,
      In a rank,
      Let thy swans sing her,
    And with their music
      Along let them bring her.

MICHAEL DRAYTON

119.   *Agincourt*

FAIR stood the wind for France
  When we our sails advance,
  Nor now to prove our chance
    Longer will tarry;
  But putting to the main,
  At Caux, the mouth of Seine,
  With all his martial train
    Landed King Harry.

And taking many a fort,
Furnish'd in warlike sort,
Marcheth tow'rds Agincourt
  In happy hour;
Skirmishing day by day
With those that stopp'd his way,
Where the French gen'ral lay
  With all his power.

Which, in his height of pride,
King Henry to deride,
His ransom to provide
  Unto him sending;
Which he neglects the while
As from a nation vile,
Yet with an angry smile
  Their fall portending.

And turning to his men,
Quoth our brave Henry then,
'Though they to one be ten
  Be not amazèd:

MICHAEL DRAYTON

Yet have we well begun;
Battles so bravely won
Have ever to the sun
    By fame been raisèd.

'And for myself (quoth he)
This my full rest shall be:
England ne'er mourn for me
    Nor more esteem me:
Victor I will remain
Or on this earth lie slain,
Never shall she sustain
    Loss to redeem me.

'Poitiers and Cressy tell,
When most their pride did swell,
Under our swords they fell:
    No less our skill is
Than when our grandsire great,
Claiming the regal seat,
By many a warlike feat
    Lopp'd the French lilies.'

The Duke of York so dread
The eager vaward led;
With the main Henry sped
    Among his henchmen.
Excester had the rear,
A braver man not there;
O Lord, how hot they were
    On the false Frenchmen!

They now to fight are gone,
Armour on armour shone,
Drum now to drum did groan,
    To hear was wonder;

That with the cries they make
The very earth did shake:
Trumpet to trumpet spake,
    Thunder to thunder.

Well it thine age became,
O noble Erpingham,
Which didst the signal aim
    To our hid forces!
When from a meadow by,
Like a storm suddenly
The English archery
    Stuck the French horses.

With Spanish yew so strong,
Arrows a cloth-yard long
That like to serpents stung,
    Piercing the weather;
None from his fellow starts,
But playing manly parts,
And like true English hearts
    Stuck close together.

When down their bows they threw,
And forth their bilbos drew,
And on the French they flew,
    Not one was tardy;
Arms were from shoulders sent,
Scalps to the teeth were rent,
Down the French peasants went—
    Our men were hardy.

This while our noble king,
His broadsword brandishing,

---

bilbos] swords, from Bilboa.

MICHAEL DRAYTON

Down the French host did ding
    As to o'erwhelm it;
And many a deep wound lent,
His arms with blood besprent,
And many a cruel dent
    Bruisèd his helmet.

Gloster, that duke so good,
Next of the royal blood,
For famous England stood
    With his brave brother;
Clarence, in steel so bright,
Though but a maiden knight,
Yet in that furious fight
    Scarce such another.

Warwick in blood did wade,
Oxford the foe invade,
And cruel slaughter made
    Still as they ran up;
Suffolk his axe did ply,
Beaumont and Willoughby
Bare them right doughtily,
    Ferrers and Fanhope.

Upon Saint Crispin's Day
Fought was this noble fray,
Which fame did not delay
    To England to carry.
O when shall English men
With such acts fill a pen?
Or England breed again
    Such a King Harry?

MICHAEL DRAYTON

120.   *To the Virginian Voyage*

YOU brave heroic minds
  Worthy your country's name,
  That honour still pursue;
  Go and subdue!
Whilst loitering hinds
  Lurk here at home with shame.

Britons, you stay too long:
  Quickly aboard bestow you,
    And with a merry gale
    Swell your stretch'd sail
With vows as strong
  As the winds that blow you.

Your course securely steer,
  West and by south forth keep!
    Rocks, lee-shores, nor shoals
    When Eolus scowls
You need not fear;
  So absolute the deep.

And cheerfully at sea
  Success you still entice
    To get the pearl and gold,
    And ours to hold
Virginia,
  Earth's only paradise.

Where nature hath in store
  Fowl, venison, and fish,
    And the fruitfull'st soil
    Without your toil
Three harvests more,
  All greater than your wish.

MICHAEL DRAYTON

And the ambitious vine
   Crowns with his purple mass
      The cedar reaching high
      To kiss the sky,
The cypress, pine,
   And useful sassafras.

To whom the Golden Age
   Still nature's laws doth give,
      No other cares attend,
      But them to defend
From winter's rage,
   That long there doth not live.

When as the luscious smell
   Of that delicious land
      Above the seas that flows
      The clear wind throws,
Your hearts to swell
   Approaching the dear strand;

In kenning of the shore
   (Thanks to God first given)
      O you the happiest men,
      Be frolic then!
Let cannons roar,
   Frighting the wide heaven.

And in regions far,
   Such heroes bring ye forth
      As those from whom we came;
      And plant our name
Under that star
   Not known unto our North.

MICHAEL DRAYTON

   And as there plenty grows
     Of laurel everywhere—
       Apollo's sacred tree—
       You it may see
   A poet's brows
     To crown, that may sing there.

   Thy *Voyages* attend,
     Industrious Hakluyt,
       Whose reading shall inflame
       Men to seek fame,
   And much commend
     To after times thy wit.

CHRISTOPHER MARLOWE
1564-93

121. *The Passionate Shepherd to His Love*

COME live with me and be my Love,
   And we will all the pleasures prove
That hills and valleys, dales and fields,
Or woods or steepy mountain yields.

And we will sit upon the rocks,
And see the shepherds feed their flocks
By shallow rivers, to whose falls
Melodious birds sing madrigals.

And I will make thee beds of roses
And a thousand fragrant posies;
A cap of flowers, and a kirtle
Embroider'd all with leaves of myrtle.

CHRISTOPHER MARLOWE

A gown made of the finest wool
Which from our pretty lambs we pull;
Fair-linèd slippers for the cold,
With buckles of the purest gold.

A belt of straw and ivy-buds
With coral clasps and amber studs:
And if these pleasures may thee move,
Come live with me and be my Love.

The shepherd swains shall dance and sing
For thy delight each May morning:
If these delights thy mind may move,
Then live with me and be my Love.

122.   *Her Reply*

(WRITTEN BY SIR WALTER RALEIGH)

IF all the world and love were young,
And truth in every shepherd's tongue,
These pretty pleasures might me move
To live with thee and be thy Love.

But Time drives flocks from field to fold;
When rivers rage and rocks grow cold;
And Philomel becometh dumb;
The rest complains of cares to come.

The flowers do fade, and wanton fields
To wayward Winter reckoning yields:
A honey tongue, a heart of gall,
Is fancy's spring, but sorrow's fall.

(SIR WALTER RALEIGH)

Thy gowns, thy shoes, thy beds of roses,
Thy cap, thy kirtle, and thy posies,
Soon break, soon wither—soon forgotten,
In folly ripe, in reason rotten.

Thy belt of straw and ivy-buds,
Thy coral clasps and amber studs,—
All these in me no means can move
To come to thee and be thy Love.

But could youth last, and love still breed,
Had joys no date, nor age no need,
Then these delights my mind might move
To live with thee and be thy Love.

WILLIAM SHAKESPEARE
1564-1616

123. *Silvia*

WHO is Silvia? What is she?
  That all our swains commend her?
Holy, fair, and wise is she;
  The heaven such grace did lend her,
  That she might admirèd be.

Is she kind as she is fair?
  For beauty lives with kindness:
Love doth to her eyes repair,
  To help him of his blindness;
  And, being help'd, inhabits there.

Then to Silvia let us sing,
  That Silvia is excelling;
She excels each mortal thing
  Upon the dull earth dwelling:
  To her let us garlands bring.

WILLIAM SHAKESPEARE

124.   *The Blossom*

ON a day—alack the day!—
    Love, whose month is ever May,
Spied a blossom passing fair
Playing in the wanton air:
Through the velvet leaves the wind
All unseen 'gan passage find;
That the lover, sick to death,
Wish'd himself the heaven's breath.
Air, quoth he, thy cheeks may blow;
Air, would I might triumph so!
But, alack, my hand is sworn
Ne'er to pluck thee from thy thorn:
Vow, alack, for youth unmeet;
Youth so apt to pluck a sweet!
Do not call it sin in me
That I am forsworn for thee;
Thou for whom e'en Jove would swear
Juno but an Ethiop were;
And deny himself for Jove,
Turning mortal for thy love.

Spring and Winter

125.   i

WHEN daisies pied and violets blue,
    And lady-smocks all silver-white,
And cuckoo-buds of yellow hue
    Do paint the meadows with delight,
The cuckoo then, on every tree,
Mocks married men; for thus sings he,
            Cuckoo!

Cuckoo, cuckoo!—O word of fear,
Unpleasing to a married ear!

When shepherds pipe on oaten straws,
   And merry larks are ploughmen's clocks,
When turtles tread, and rooks, and daws,
   And maidens bleach their summer smocks
The cuckoo then, on every tree,
Mocks married men; for thus sings he,
        Cuckoo!
Cuckoo, cuckoo!—O word of fear,
Unpleasing to a married ear!

126.   *ii*

WHEN icicles hang by the wall,
   And Dick the shepherd blows his nail,
And Tom bears logs into the hall,
   And milk comes frozen home in pail,
When blood is nipp'd, and ways be foul,
Then nightly sings the staring owl,
        To-whit!
To-who!—a merry note,
While greasy Joan doth keel the pot.

When all aloud the wind doth blow,
   And coughing drowns the parson's saw,
And birds sit brooding in the snow,
   And Marian's nose looks red and raw,
When roasted crabs hiss in the bowl,
Then nightly sings the staring owl,
        To-whit!
To-who!—a merry note,
While greasy Joan doth keel the pot.

126. keel] skim.

WILLIAM SHAKESPEARE

Fairy Land

127.
         i

OVER hill, over dale,
    Thorough bush, thorough brier,
Over park, over pale,
    Thorough flood, thorough fire,
I do wander everywhere,
Swifter than the moonè's sphere;
And I serve the fairy queen,
To dew her orbs upon the green:
The cowslips tall her pensioners be;
In their gold coats spots you see;
Those be rubies, fairy favours,
In those freckles live their savours:
I must go seek some dew-drops here,
And hang a pearl in every cowslip's ear.

128.
         ii

YOU spotted snakes with double tongue,
    Thorny hedgehogs, be not seen;
Newts and blind-worms, do no wrong;
    Come not near our fairy queen.
        Philomel, with melody,
        Sing in our sweet lullaby;
    Lulla, lulla, lullaby; lulla, lulla, lullaby!
        Never harm,
        Nor spell nor charm,
    Come our lovely lady nigh;
    So, good night, with lullaby.

Weaving spiders, come not here;
    Hence, you long-legg'd spinners, hence!

WILLIAM SHAKESPEARE

Beetles black, approach not near ;
Worm nor snail, do no offence.

    Philomel, with melody,
    Sing in our sweet lullaby;
Lulla, lulla, lullaby ; lulla, lulla, lullaby !
      Never harm.
    Nor spell nor charm,
    Come our lovely lady nigh ;
    So, good night, with lullaby.

129.   *iii*

COME unto these yellow sands,
    And then take hands :
Court'sied when you have, and kiss'd,—
    The wild waves whist,—
Foot it featly here and there ;
And, sweet sprites, the burthen bear.
      Hark, hark !
      Bow, wow,
    The watch-dogs bark :
      Bow, wow.
    Hark, hark ! I hear
The strain of strutting chanticleer
Cry, Cock-a-diddle-dow !

130.   *iv*

WHERE the bee sucks, there suck I:
    In a cowslip's bell I lie ;
There I couch when owls do cry.
On the bat's back I do fly
After summer merrily :
    Merrily, merrily, shall I live now,
    Under the blossom that hangs on the bough.

WILLIAM SHAKESPEARE

131.   *v*

  FULL fathom five thy father lies;
    Of his bones are coral made;
  Those are pearls that were his eyes:
    Nothing of him that doth fade,
  But doth suffer a sea-change
  Into something rich and strange.
  Sea-nymphs hourly ring his knell:
          Ding-dong.
    Hark! now I hear them—
          Ding-dong, bell!

132.   *Love*

  TELL me where is Fancy bred,
    Or in the heart or in the head?
  How begot, how nourishèd?
      Reply, reply.
  It is engender'd in the eyes,
  With gazing fed; and Fancy dies
  In the cradle where it lies.
      Let us all ring Fancy's knell:
        I'll begin it,—Ding, dong, bell.
All. Ding, dong, bell.

133.   *Sweet-and-Twenty*

  O MISTRESS mine, where are you roaming?
    O, stay and hear! your true love's coming,
  That can sing both high and low:
  Trip no further, pretty sweeting;
  Journeys end in lovers meeting,
    Every wise man's son doth know.

WILLIAM SHAKESPEARE

What is love? 'tis not hereafter;
Present mirth hath present laughter;
What's to come is still unsure:
In delay there lies no plenty;
Then come kiss me, sweet-and-twenty!
Youth's a stuff will not endure.

134.   *Dirge*

COME away, come away, death,
   And in sad cypres let me be laid;
Fly away, fly away, breath;
   I am slain by a fair cruel maid.
My shroud of white, stuck all with yew,
      O prepare it!
My part of death, no one so true
      Did share it.

Not a flower, not a flower sweet,
   On my black coffin let there be strown;
Not a friend, not a friend greet
   My poor corse, where my bones shall be thrown:
A thousand thousand sighs to save,
      Lay me, O, where
Sad true lover never find my grave
      To weep there!

135.   *Under the Greenwood Tree*
Amiens sings:

UNDER the greenwood tree,
   Who loves to lie with me,
And turn his merry note
Unto the sweet bird's throat,

134. cypres] crape.

WILLIAM SHAKESPEARE

  Come hither, come hither, come hither:
   Here shall he see
   No enemy
  But winter and rough weather.

  Who doth ambition shun,
  And loves to live i' the sun,
  Seeking the food he eats,
  And pleased with what he gets,
  Come hither, come hither, come hither:
   Here shall he see
   No enemy
  But winter and rough weather.

Jaques replies :
  If it do come to pass
  That any man turn ass,
  Leaving his wealth and ease
  A stubborn will to please,
  Ducdamè, ducdamè, ducdamè :
   Here shall he see
   Gross fools as he,
  An if he will come to me.

136. *Blow, blow, thou Winter Wind*

  BLOW, blow, thou winter wind,
   Thou art not so unkind
    As man's ingratitude;
  Thy tooth is not so keen,
  Because thou art not seen,
    Although thy breath be rude.

Heigh ho! sing, heigh ho! unto the green holly:
Most friendship is feigning, most loving mere folly:
    Then heigh ho, the holly!
    This life is most jolly.

    Freeze, freeze, thou bitter sky,
    That dost not bite so nigh
      As benefits forgot:
    Though thou the waters warp,
    Thy sting is not so sharp
      As friend remember'd not.
Heigh ho! sing, heigh ho! unto the green holly:
Most friendship is feigning, most loving mere folly:
    Then heigh ho, the holly!
    This life is most jolly.

137. *It was a Lover and his Lass*

IT was a lover and his lass,
  With a hey, and a ho, and a hey nonino,
That o'er the green corn-field did pass,
  In the spring time, the only pretty ring time,
When birds do sing, hey ding a ding, ding;
Sweet lovers love the spring.

Between the acres of the rye,
  With a hey, and a ho, and a hey nonino,
These pretty country folks would lie,
  In the spring time, the only pretty ring time,
When birds do sing, hey ding a ding, ding;
Sweet lovers love the spring.

This carol they began that hour,
  With a hey, and a ho, and a hey nonino,

How that life was but a flower
   In the spring time, the only pretty ring time,
When birds do sing, hey ding a ding, ding;
Sweet lovers love the spring.

And, therefore, take the present time
   With a hey, and a ho, and a hey nonino,
For love is crownèd with the prime
   In the spring time, the only pretty ring time,
When birds do sing, hey ding a ding, ding;
Sweet lovers love the spring.

138. *Take, O take those Lips away*

TAKE, O take those lips away,
   That so sweetly were forsworn;
And those eyes, the break of day,
   Lights that do mislead the morn!
But my kisses bring again,
            Bring again;
Seals of love, but seal'd in vain,
            Seal'd in vain!

139. *Aubade*

HARK! hark! the lark at heaven's gate sings,
   And Phœbus 'gins arise,
His steeds to water at those springs
   On chaliced flowers that lies;
And winking Mary-buds begin
   To ope their golden eyes:
With everything that pretty bin,
   My lady sweet, arise!
      Arise, arise!

WILLIAM SHAKESPEARE

140. *Fidele*

FEAR no more the heat o' the sun,
    Nor the furious winter's rages;
Thou thy worldly task hast done,
    Home art gone, and ta'en thy wages:
Golden lads and girls all must,
As chimney-sweepers, come to dust.

Fear no more the frown o' the great,
    Thou art past the tyrant's stroke;
Care no more to clothe and eat;
    To thee the reed is as the oak:
The sceptre, learning, physic, must
All follow this, and come to dust.

Fear no more the lightning-flash,
    Nor the all-dreaded thunder-stone;
Fear not slander, censure rash;
    Thou hast finish'd joy and moan:
All lovers young, all lovers must
Consign to thee, and come to dust.

No exorciser harm thee!
Nor no witchcraft charm thee!
Ghost unlaid forbear thee!
Nothing ill come near thee!
Quiet consummation have;
And renownèd be thy grave!

WILLIAM SHAKESPEARE

141.   *Bridal Song*

ROSES, their sharp spines being gone,
    Not royal in their smells alone,
  But in their hue;
Maiden pinks, of odour faint,
Daisies smell-less, yet most quaint,
  And sweet thyme true;

Primrose, firstborn child of Ver;
Merry springtime's harbinger,
  With her bells dim;
Oxlips in their cradles growing,
Marigolds on death-beds blowing,
  Larks'-heels trim;

All dear Nature's children sweet
Lie 'fore bride and bridegroom's feet,
  Blessing their sense!
Not an angel of the air,
Bird melodious or bird fair,
  Be absent hence!

The crow, the slanderous cuckoo, nor
The boding raven, nor chough hoar,
  Nor chattering pye,
May on our bride-house perch or sing,
Or with them any discord bring,
  But from it fly!
            ? or *John Fletcher.*

WILLIAM SHAKESPEARE

142.   *Dirge of the Three Queens*

URNS and odours bring away!
　　Vapours, sighs, darken the day!
Our dole more deadly looks than dying;
　　Balms and gums and heavy cheers,
　　Sacred vials fill'd with tears,
And clamours through the wild air flying!

　　Come, all sad and solemn shows,
　　That are quick-eyed Pleasure's foes!
　　We convènt naught else but woes.
　　　　　　　　　　　　? or *John Fletcher.*

143.　　　　　*Orpheus*

ORPHEUS with his lute made trees
　　And the mountain tops that freeze
　　Bow themselves when he did sing:
　　To his music plants and flowers
　　Ever sprung; as sun and showers
　　　There had made a lasting spring.

　　Every thing that heard him play,
　　Even the billows of the sea,
　　　Hung their heads and then lay by.
　　In sweet music is such art,
　　　Killing care and grief of heart
　　Fall asleep, or hearing, die.
　　　　　　　　　　　　? or *John Fletcher.*

142. dole] lamentation.　　　　　convent] summon.

187

WILLIAM SHAKESPEARE

144. *The Phœnix and the Turtle*

LET the bird of loudest lay
    On the sole Arabian tree,
    Herald sad and trumpet be,
To whose sound chaste wings obey.

But thou shrieking harbinger,
    Foul precurrer of the fiend,
    Augur of the fever's end,
To this troop come thou not near.

From this session interdict
    Every fowl of tyrant wing
    Save the eagle, feather'd king:
Keep the obsequy so strict.

Let the priest in surplice white
    That defunctive music can,
    Be the death-divining swan,
Lest the requiem lack his right.

And thou, treble-dated crow,
    That thy sable gender mak'st
    With the breath thou giv'st and tak'st,
'Mongst our mourners shalt thou go.

Here the anthem doth commence :—
    Love and constancy is dead;
    Phœnix and the turtle fled
In a mutual flame from hence.

So they loved, as love in twain
    Had the essence but in one;
    Two distincts, division none;
Number there in love was slain.

can] knows.

WILLIAM SHAKESPEARE

Hearts remote, yet not asunder;
  Distance, and no space was seen
  'Twixt the turtle and his queen:
But in them it were a wonder.

So between them love did shine,
  That the turtle saw his right
  Flaming in the phœnix' sight;
Either was the other's mine.

Property was thus appall'd,
  That the self was not the same;
  Single nature's double name
Neither two nor one was call'd.

Reason, in itself confounded,
  Saw division grow together;
  To themselves yet either neither;
Simple were so well compounded,

That it cried, 'How true a twain
  Seemeth this concordant one!
  Love hath reason, reason none
If what parts can so remain.'

Whereupon it made this threne
  To the phœnix and the dove,
  Co-supremes and stars of love,
As chorus to their tragic scene.

THRENOS

BEAUTY, truth, and rarity,
  Grace in all simplicity,
Here enclosed in cinders lie.

Death is now the phœnix' nest;
And the turtle's loyal breast
To eternity doth rest,

Leaving no posterity:
'Twas not their infirmity,
It was married chastity.

Truth may seem, but cannot be;
Beauty brag, but 'tis not she;
Truth and beauty buried be.

To this urn let those repair
That are either true or fair;
For these dead birds sigh a prayer.

Sonnets

145.   i

SHALL I compare thee to a Summer's day?
Thou art more lovely and more temperate:
Rough winds do shake the darling buds of May,
And Summer's lease hath all too short a date:
Sometime too hot the eye of heaven shines,
And often is his gold complexion dimm'd;
And every fair from fair sometime declines,
By chance or nature's changing course untrimm'd:
But thy eternal Summer shall not fade
Nor lose possession of that fair thou owest;
Nor shall Death brag thou wanderest in his shade,
When in eternal lines to time thou growest:
  So long as men can breathe, or eyes can see,
  So long lives this, and this gives life to thee.

WILLIAM SHAKESPEARE

146.   ii

WHEN, in disgrace with Fortune and men's eyes,
   I all alone beweep my outcast state,
And trouble deaf heaven with my bootless cries,
And look upon myself, and curse my fate,
Wishing me like to one more rich in hope,
Featured like him, like him with friends possest,
Desiring this man's art and that man's scope,
With what I most enjoy contented least;
Yet in these thoughts myself almost despising—
Haply I think on thee: and then my state,
Like to the Lark at break of day arising
From sullen earth, sings hymns at Heaven's gate;
  For thy sweet love rememb'red such wealth brings
  That then I scorn to change my state with Kings.

147.   iii

WHEN to the Sessions of sweet silent thought
   I summon up remembrance of things past,
I sigh the lack of many a thing I sought,
And with old woes new wail my dear time's waste:
Then can I drown an eye, unused to flow,
For precious friends hid in death's dateless night,
And weep afresh love's long-since-cancell'd woe,
And moan th' expense of many a vanish'd sight:
Then can I grieve at grievances foregone,
And heavily from woe to woe tell o'er
The sad account of fore-bemoanèd moan,
Which I new pay as if not paid before.
  But if the while I think on thee, dear friend,
  All losses are restored and sorrows end.

WILLIAM SHAKESPEARE

148.   iv

THY bosom is endearèd with all hearts
  Which I, by lacking, have supposèd dead:
And there reigns Love, and all Love's loving parts,
And all those friends which I thought burièd.
How many a holy and obsequious tear
Hath dear religious love stol'n from mine eye,
As interest of the dead!—which now appear
But things removed that hidden in thee lie.
Thou art the grave where buried love doth live,
Hung with the trophies of my lovers gone,
Who all their parts of me to thee did give:
—That due of many now is thine alone:
  Their images I loved I view in thee,
  And thou, all they, hast all the all of me.

149.   v

WHAT is your substance, whereof are you made,
  That millions of strange shadows on you tend?
Since every one hath, every one, one shade,
And you, but one, can every shadow lend.
Describe Adonis, and the counterfeit
Is poorly imitated after you;
On Helen's cheek all art of beauty set,
And you in Grecian tires are painted new:
Speak of the spring and foison of the year,
The one doth shadow of your beauty show,
The other as your bounty doth appear;
And you in every blessèd shape we know.
  In all external grace you have some part,
  But you like none, none you, for constant heart.

149. foison] plenty.

WILLIAM SHAKESPEARE

150.   *vi.*

O HOW much more doth beauty beauteous seem
    By that sweet ornament which truth doth give!
The Rose looks fair, but fairer we it deem
For that sweet odour which doth in it live.
The Canker-blooms have full as deep a dye
As the perfumèd tincture of the Roses,
Hang on such thorns, and play as wantonly
When summer's breath their maskèd buds discloses:
But—for their virtue only is their show—
They live unwoo'd and unrespected fade,
Die to themselves. Sweet Roses do not so;
Of their sweet deaths are sweetest odours made.
    And so of you, beauteous and lovely youth,
    When that shall vade, my verse distils your truth.

151.   *vii*

BEING your slave, what should I do but tend
    Upon the hours and times of your desire?
I have no precious time at all to spend,
Nor services to do, till you require.
Nor dare I chide the world-without-end hour
Whilst I, my sovereign, watch the clock for you,
Nor think the bitterness of absence sour
When you have bid your servant once adieu;
Nor dare I question with my jealous thought
Where you may be, or your affairs suppose,
But, like a sad slave, stay and think of nought
Save, where you are how happy you make those!
    So true a fool is love, that in your Will,
    Though you do any thing, he thinks no ill.

WILLIAM SHAKESPEARE

152. *viii*

THAT time of year thou may'st in me behold
When yellow leaves, or none, or few, do hang
Upon those boughs which shake against the cold—
Bare ruin'd choirs where late the sweet birds sang.
In me thou see'st the twilight of such day
As after Sunset fadeth in the West,
Which by and by black night doth take away,
Death's second self, that seals up all in rest.
In me thou see'st the glowing of such fire
That on the ashes of his youth doth lie,
As the death-bed whereon it must expire,
Consumed with that which it was nourish'd by.
  This thou perceiv'st, which makes thy love more strong
  To love that well which thou must leave ere long.

153. *ix*

FAREWELL! thou art too dear for my possessing,
And like enough thou know'st thy estimate:
The charter of thy worth gives thee releasing;
My bonds in thee are all determinate.
For how do I hold thee but by thy granting?
And for that riches where is my deserving?
The cause of this fair gift in me is wanting,
And so my patent back again is swerving.
Thyself thou gav'st, thy own worth then not knowing,
Or me, to whom thou gav'st it, else mistaking;
So thy great gift, upon misprision growing,
Comes home again, on better judgment making.
  Thus have I had thee, as a dream doth flatter
  In sleep a King; but waking, no such matter.

WILLIAM SHAKESPEARE

154   *x*

THEN hate me when thou wilt; if ever, now;
   Now, while the world is bent my deeds to cross,
Join with the spite of fortune, make me bow,
And do not drop in for an after loss:
Ah! do not, when my heart hath 'scaped this sorrow,
Come in the rearward of a conquer'd woe;
Give not a windy night a rainy morrow,
To linger out a purposed overthrow.
If thou wilt leave me, do not leave me last,
When other petty griefs have done their spite,
But in the onset come: so shall I taste
At first the very worst of fortune's might;
   And other strains of woe, which now seem woe,
   Compared with loss of thee will not seem so!

155.   *xi*

THEY that have power to hurt and will do none,
   That do not do the thing they most do show,
Who, moving others, are themselves as stone,
Unmovèd, cold, and to temptation slow—
They rightly do inherit heaven's graces,
And husband nature's riches from expense;
They are the Lords and owners of their faces,
Others, but stewards of their excellence.
The summer's flower is to the summer sweet,
Though to itself it only live and die;
But if that flower with base infection meet,
The basest weed outbraves his dignity:
   For sweetest things turn sourest by their deeds;
   Lilies that fester smell far worse than weeds.

WILLIAM SHAKESPEARE

156. xii

How like a Winter hath my absence been
From thee, the pleasure of the fleeting year!
What freezings have I felt, what dark days seen,
What old December's bareness everywhere!
And yet this time removed was summer's time;
The teeming Autumn, big with rich increase,
Bearing the wanton burden of the prime
Like widow'd wombs after their Lord's decease:
Yet this abundant issue seem'd to me
But hope of orphans and unfather'd fruit;
For Summer and his pleasures wait on thee,
And, thou away, the very birds are mute:
  Or if they sing, 'tis with so dull a cheer
  That leaves look pale, dreading the Winter's near.

157. xiii

From you have I been absent in the spring,
When proud-pied April, dress'd in all his trim,
Hath put a spirit of youth in everything,
That heavy Saturn laugh'd and leap'd with him.
Yet nor the lays of birds, nor the sweet smell
Of different flowers in odour and in hue,
Could make me any summer's story tell,
Or from their proud lap pluck them where they grew;
Nor did I wonder at the Lily's white,
Nor praise the deep vermilion in the Rose;
They were but sweet, but figures of delight,
Drawn after you, you pattern of all those.
  Yet seem'd it Winter still, and, you away,
  As with your shadow I with these did play.

WILLIAM SHAKESPEARE

158.   xiv

MY love is strengthen'd, though more weak in seeming;
  I love not less, though less the show appear:
That love is merchandised whose rich esteeming
The owner's tongue doth publish everywhere.
Our love was new, and then but in the spring,
When I was wont to greet it with my lays;
As Philomel in summer's front doth sing
And stops her pipe in growth of riper days:
Not that the summer is less pleasant now
Than when her mournful hymns did hush the night,
But that wild music burthens every bough,
And sweets grown common lose their dear delight.
  Therefore, like her, I sometime hold my tongue,
  Because I would not dull you with my song.

159.   xv

TO me, fair friend, you never can be old;
  For as you were when first your eye I eyed,
Such seems your beauty still. Three Winters cold
Have from the forests shook three Summers' pride;
Three beauteous springs to yellow Autumn turn'd
In process of the seasons have I seen,
Three April perfumes in three hot Junes burn'd,
Since first I saw you fresh, which yet are green.
Ah! yet doth beauty, like a dial-hand,
Steal from his figure, and no pace perceived;
So your sweet hue, which methinks still doth stand,
Hath motion, and mine eye may be deceived:
  For fear of which, hear this, thou age unbred:
  Ere you were born was beauty's summer dead.

WILLIAM SHAKESPEARE

160.   *xvi*

WHEN in the chronicle of wasted time
   I see descriptions of the fairest wights,
And beauty making beautiful old rime
In praise of Ladies dead and lovely Knights;
Then, in the blazon of sweet beauty's best,
Of hand, of foot, of lip, of eye, of brow,
I see their antique pen would have exprest
Even such a beauty as you master now.
So all their praises are but prophecies
Of this our time, all you prefiguring;
And for they look'd but with divining eyes,
They had not skill enough your worth to sing:
  For we, which now behold these present days,
  Have eyes to wonder, but lack tongues to praise.

161.   *xvii*

O NEVER say that I was false of heart,
   Though absence seem'd my flame to qualify!
As easy might I from myself depart,
As from my soul, which in thy breast doth lie:
That is my home of love; if I have ranged,
Like him that travels I return again,
Just to the time, not with the time exchanged,
So that myself bring water for my stain.
Never believe, though in my nature reign'd
All frailties that besiege all kinds of blood,
That it could so prepost'rously be stain'd,
To leave for nothing all thy sum of good:
  For nothing this wide Universe I call,
  Save thou, my Rose; in it thou art my all.

WILLIAM SHAKESPEARE

162.   *xviii*

LET me not to the marriage of true minds
    Admit impediments. Love is not love
Which alters when it alteration finds,
Or bends with the remover to remove:
O, no! it is an ever-fixèd mark,
That looks on tempests and is never shaken;
It is the star to every wand'ring bark,
Whose worth's unknown, although his height be taken.
Love's not Time's fool, though rosy lips and cheeks
Within his bending sickle's compass come;
Love alters not with his brief hours and weeks,
But bears it out even to the edge of doom:—
    If this be error and upon me proved,
    I never writ, nor no man ever loved.

163.   *xix*

TH' expense of Spirit in a waste of shame
    Is lust in action; and till action, lust
Is perjured, murderous, bloody, full of blame,
Savage, extreme, rude, cruel, not to trust;
Enjoy'd no sooner but despisèd straight;
Past reason hunted; and, no sooner had,
Past reason hated, as a swallow'd bait
On purpose laid to make the taker mad:
Mad in pursuit, and in possession so;
Had, having, and in quest to have, extreme;
A bliss in proof, and proved, a very woe;
Before, a joy proposed; behind, a dream.
    All this the world well knows; yet none knows well
    To shun the heaven that leads men to this hell.

WILLIAM SHAKESPEARE

164.   *xx*

POOR soul, the centre of my sinful earth—
My sinful earth these rebel powers array—
Why dost thou pine within and suffer dearth,
Painting thy outward walls so costly gay?
Why so large cost, having so short a lease,
Dost thou upon thy fading mansion spend?
Shall worms, inheritors of this excess,
Eat up thy charge? Is this thy body's end?
Then, soul, live thou upon thy servant's loss,
And let that pine to aggravate thy store;
Buy terms divine in selling hours of dross;
Within be fed, without be rich no more:
  So shalt thou feed on Death, that feeds on men;
  And Death once dead, there's no more dying then.

RICHARD ROWLANDS
1565-1630?

165.   *Lullaby*

UPON my lap my sovereign sits
    And sucks upon my breast;
Meantime his love maintains my life
And gives my sense her rest.
    Sing lullaby, my little boy,
    Sing lullaby, mine only joy!

When thou hast taken thy repast,
Repose, my babe, on me;
So may thy mother and thy nurse
Thy cradle also be.
    Sing lullaby, my little boy,
    Sing lullaby, mine only joy!

RICHARD ROWLANDS

I grieve that duty doth not work
All that my wishing would;
Because I would not be to thee
But in the best I should.
    Sing lullaby, my little boy,
    Sing lullaby, mine only joy!

Yet as I am, and as I may,
I must and will be thine,
Though all too little for thyself
Vouchsafing to be mine.
    Sing lullaby, my little boy,
    Sing lullaby, mine only joy!

THOMAS NASHE
1567-1601

166.   Spring

SPRING, the sweet Spring, is the year's pleasant king;
   Then blooms each thing, then maids dance in a ring,
Cold doth not sting, the pretty birds do sing—
    Cuckoo, jug-jug, pu-we, to-witta-woo!

The palm and may make country houses gay,
Lambs frisk and play, the shepherds pipe all day,
And we hear aye birds tune this merry lay—
    Cuckoo, jug-jug, pu-we, to-witta-woo!

The fields breathe sweet, the daisies kiss our feet,
Young lovers meet, old wives a-sunning sit,
In every street these tunes our ears do greet—
    Cuckoo, jug-jug, pu-we, to-witta-woo!
    Spring, the sweet Spring!

THOMAS NASHE

167.   *In Time of Pestilence*
            1593

ADIEU, farewell earth's bliss!
This world uncertain is:
Fond are life's lustful joys,
Death proves them all but toys.
None from his darts can fly;
I am sick, I must die—
  Lord, have mercy on us!

Rich men, trust not in wealth,
Gold cannot buy you health;
Physic himself must fade;
All things to end are made;
The plague full swift goes by;
I am sick, I must die—
  Lord, have mercy on us!

Beauty is but a flower
Which wrinkles will devour;
Brightness falls from the air;
Queens have died young and fair;
Dust hath closed Helen's eye;
I am sick, I must die—
  Lord, have mercy on us!

Strength stoops unto the grave,
Worms feed on Hector brave;
Swords may not fight with fate;
Earth still holds ope her gate;
Come, come! the bells do cry;
I am sick, I must die—
  Lord, have mercy on us!

THOMAS NASHE

Wit with his wantonness
Tasteth death's bitterness;
Hell's executioner
Hath no ears for to hear
What vain art can reply;
I am sick, I must die—
   Lord, have mercy on us!

Haste therefore each degree
To welcome destiny;
Heaven is our heritage,
Earth but a player's stage.
Mount we unto the sky;
I am sick, I must die—
   Lord, have mercy on us!

THOMAS CAMPION
1567?–1619

168. *Cherry-Ripe*

THERE is a garden in her face
  Where roses and white lilies blow;
A heavenly paradise is that place,
  Wherein all pleasant fruits do flow:
    There cherries grow which none may buy
    Till 'Cherry-ripe' themselves do cry.

Those cherries fairly do enclose
  Of orient pearl a double row,
Which when her lovely laughter shows,
  They look like rose-buds fill'd with snow;
    Yet them nor peer nor prince can buy
    Till 'Cherry-ripe' themselves do cry.

Her eyes like angels watch them still;
Her brows like bended bows do stand,
Threat'ning with piercing frowns to kill
All that attempt with eye or hand
   Those sacred cherries to come nigh,
   Till 'Cherry-ripe' themselves do cry.

169.   *Laura*

ROSE-CHEEK'D *Laura*, come;
   Sing thou smoothly with thy beauty's
Silent music, either other
   Sweetly gracing.

Lovely forms do flow
From concent divinely framèd:
Heaven is music, and thy beauty's
   Birth is heavenly.

These dull notes we sing
Discords need for helps to grace them;
Only beauty purely loving
   Knows no discord;

But still moves delight,
Like clear springs renew'd by flowing,
Ever perfect, ever in them-
   selves eternal.

Devotion

170.   i

FOLLOW thy fair sun, unhappy shadow!
   Though thou be black as night,
   And she made all of light,
Yet follow thy fair sun, unhappy shadow!

Follow her, whose light thy light depriveth!
   Though here thou liv'st disgraced,
   And she in heaven is placed,
Yet follow her whose light the world reviveth!

Follow those pure beams, whose beauty burneth!
   That so have scorchèd thee
   As thou still black must be,
Till her kind beams thy black to brightness turneth.

Follow her, while yet her glory shineth!
   There comes a luckless night
   That will dim all her light;
And this the black unhappy shade divineth.

Follow still, since so thy fates ordainèd!
   The sun must have his shade,
   Till both at once do fade,—
The sun still proud, the shadow still disdainèd.

171.   *ii*

FOLLOW your saint, follow with accents sweet!
   Haste you, sad notes, fall at her flying feet!
There, wrapt in cloud of sorrow, pity move,
And tell the ravisher of my soul I perish for her love:
But if she scorns my never-ceasing pain,
Then burst with sighing in her sight, and ne'er return again!

All that I sung still to her praise did tend;
Still she was first, still she my songs did end;
Yet she my love and music both doth fly,
The music that her echo is and beauty's sympathy:
Then let my notes pursue her scornful flight!
It shall suffice that they were breathed and died for her delight.

THOMAS CAMPION

172.   *Vobiscum est Iope*

WHEN thou must home to shades of underground,
   And there arrived, a new admirèd guest,
The beauteous spirits do engirt thee round,
White Iope, blithe Helen, and the rest,
To hear the stories of thy finish'd love
From that smooth tongue whose music hell can move;

Then wilt thou speak of banqueting delights,
Of masques and revels which sweet youth did make,
Of tourneys and great challenges of knights,
And all these triumphs for thy beauty's sake:
When thou hast told these honours done to thee,
Then tell, O tell, how thou didst murder me!

173.   *A Hymn in Praise of Neptune*

OF Neptune's empire let us sing,
   At whose command the waves obey;
To whom the rivers tribute pay,
Down the high mountains sliding:
To whom the scaly nation yields
Homage for the crystal fields
   Wherein they dwell:
And every sea-dog pays a gem
Yearly out of his wat'ry cell
To deck great Neptune's diadem.

The Tritons dancing in a ring
Before his palace gates do make
The water with their echoes quake,
Like the great thunder sounding:

The sea-nymphs chant their accents shrill,
And the sirens, taught to kill
   With their sweet voice,
Make ev'ry echoing rock reply
Unto their gentle murmuring noise
The praise of Neptune's empery.

174.   *Winter Nights*

NOW winter nights enlarge
   The number of their hours,
And clouds their storms discharge
   Upon the airy towers.
Let now the chimneys blaze
   And cups o'erflow with wine;
Let well-tuned words amaze
   With harmony divine.
Now yellow waxen lights
   Shall wait on honey love,
While youthful revels, masques, and courtly sights
   Sleep's leaden spells remove.

This time doth well dispense
   With lovers' long discourse;
Much speech hath some defence,
   Though beauty no remorse.
All do not all things well;
   Some measures comely tread,
Some knotted riddles tell,
   Some poems smoothly read.
The summer hath his joys,
   And winter his delights;
Though love and all his pleasures are but toys,
   They shorten tedious nights.

175.   *Integer Vitae*

THE man of life upright,
　　Whose guiltless heart is free
From all dishonest deeds,
　　Or thought of vanity;

The man whose silent days
　　In harmless joys are spent,
Whom hopes cannot delude,
　　Nor sorrow discontent;

That man needs neither towers
　　Nor armour for defence,
Nor secret vaults to fly
　　From thunder's violence:

He only can behold
　　With unaffrighted eyes
The horrors of the deep
　　And terrors of the skies.

Thus, scorning all the cares
　　That fate or fortune brings,
He makes the heaven his book,
　　His wisdom heavenly things;

Good thoughts his only friends,
　　His wealth a well-spent age,
The earth his sober inn
　　And quiet pilgrimage.

THOMAS CAMPION

176. *O come quickly!*

NEVER weather-beaten sail more willing bent to shore,
    Never tirèd pilgrim's limbs affected slumber more,
Than my wearied sprite now longs to fly out of my
    troubled breast:
O come quickly, sweetest Lord, and take my soul to rest!

Ever blooming are the joys of heaven's high Paradise,
Cold age deafs not there our ears nor vapour dims our eyes:
Glory there the sun outshines; whose beams the Blessèd
    only see:
O come quickly, glorious Lord, and raise my sprite to Thee!

JOHN REYNOLDS
16th Cent.

177. *A Nosegay*

SAY, crimson Rose and dainty Daffodil,
    With Violet blue;
Since you have seen the beauty of my saint,
    And eke her view;
Did not her sight (fair sight!) you lonely fill,
    With sweet delight
Of goddess' grace and angels' sacred teint
    In fine, most bright?

Say, golden Primrose, sanguine Cowslip fair,
    With Pink most fine;
Since you beheld the visage of my dear,
    And eyes divine;

177. teint] tint, hue.

JOHN REYNOLDS

Did not her globy front, and glistering hair,
    With cheeks most sweet,
So gloriously like damask flowers appear,
    The gods to greet?

Say, snow-white Lily, speckled Gillyflower,
    With Daisy gay;
Since you have viewed the Queen of my desire,
    In her array;
Did not her ivory paps, fair Venus' bower,
    With heavenly glee,
A Juno's grace, conjure you to require
    Her face to see?

Say Rose, say Daffodil, and Violet blue,
    With Primrose fair,
Since ye have seen my nymph's sweet dainty face
    And gesture rare,
Did not (bright Cowslip, blooming Pink) her view
    (White Lily) shine—
(Ah, Gillyflower, ah Daisy!) with a grace
    Like stars divine?

SIR HENRY WOTTON
1568-1639

178. *Elizabeth of Bohemia*

YOU meaner beauties of the night,
    That poorly satisfy our eyes
More by your number than your light,
    You common people of the skies;
    What are you when the moon shall rise?

SIR HENRY WOTTON

You curious chanters of the wood,
  That warble forth Dame Nature's lays,
Thinking your passions understood
    By your weak accents; what's your praise
    When Philomel her voice shall raise?

You violets that first appear,
  By your pure purple mantles known
Like the proud virgins of the year,
    As if the spring were all your own;
    What are you when the rose is blown?

So, when my mistress shall be seen
  In form and beauty of her mind,
By virtue first, then choice, a Queen,
    Tell me, if she were not design'd
    Th' eclipse and glory of her kind.

179. *The Character of a Happy Life*

HOW happy is he born and taught
  That serveth not another's will;
Whose armour is his honest thought,
  And simple truth his utmost skill!

Whose passions not his masters are;
Whose soul is still prepared for death,
Untied unto the world by care
Of public fame or private breath;

Who envies none that chance doth raise,
Nor vice; who never understood
How deepest wounds are given by praise;
Nor rules of state, but rules of good;

SIR HENRY WOTTON

Who hath his life from rumours freed;
Whose conscience is his strong retreat;
Whose state can neither flatterers feed,
Nor ruin make oppressors great;

Who God doth late and early pray
More of His grace than gifts to lend;
And entertains the harmless day
With a religious book or friend;

—This man is freed from servile bands
Of hope to rise or fear to fall:
Lord of himself, though not of lands,
And having nothing, yet hath all.

180.   Upon the Death of Sir Albert Morton's Wife

HE first deceased; she for a little tried
To live without him, liked it not, and died.

SIR JOHN DAVIES
1569-1626

181.   Man

I KNOW my soul hath power to know all things,
Yet she is blind and ignorant in all:
I know I'm one of Nature's little kings,
Yet to the least and vilest things am thrall.

SIR JOHN DAVIES

I know my life's a pain and but a span;
I know my sense is mock'd in everything;
And, to conclude, I know myself a Man—
Which is a proud and yet a wretched thing.

SIR ROBERT AYTON
1570-1638

182. *To His Forsaken Mistress*

I DO confess thou'rt smooth and fair,
   And I might have gone near to love thee,
Had I not found the slightest prayer
   That lips could move, had power to move thee;
But I can let thee now alone
As worthy to be loved by none.

I do confess thou'rt sweet; yet find
   Thee such an unthrift of thy sweets,
Thy favours are but like the wind
   That kisseth everything it meets:
And since thou canst with more than one,
Thou'rt worthy to be kiss'd by none.

The morning rose that untouch'd stands
   Arm'd with her briers, how sweet she smells!
But pluck'd and strain'd through ruder hands,
   Her sweets no longer with her dwells:
But scent and beauty both are gone,
And leaves fall from her, one by one.

Such fate ere long will thee betide
   When thou hast handled been awhile,

With sere flowers to be thrown aside;
  And I shall sigh, while some will smile,
To see thy love to every one
Hath brought thee to be loved by none.

183.   *To an Inconstant One*

I LOVED thee once; I'll love no more—
  Thine be the grief as is the blame;
Thou art not what thou wast before,
  What reason I should be the same?
    He that can love unloved again,
    Hath better store of love than brain:
  God send me love my debts to pay,
  While unthrifts fool their love away!

Nothing could have my love o'erthrown
  If thou hadst still continued mine;
Yea, if thou hadst remain'd thy own,
  I might perchance have yet been thine.
    But thou thy freedom didst recall
    That it thou might elsewhere enthral:
  And then how could I but disdain
  A captive's captive to remain?

When new desires had conquer'd thee
  And changed the object of thy will,
It had been lethargy in me,
  Not constancy, to love thee still.
    Yea, it had been a sin to go
    And prostitute affection so:
  Since we are taught no prayers to say
  To such as must to others pray.

SIR ROBERT AYTON

Yet do thou glory in thy choice—
Thy choice of his good fortune boast;
I'll neither grieve nor yet rejoice
  To see him gain what I have lost:
    The height of my disdain shall be
    To laugh at him, to blush for thee;
To love thee still, but go no more
A-begging at a beggar's door.

BEN JONSON
1573-1637

184. *Hymn to Diana*

QUEEN and huntress, chaste and fair,
  Now the sun is laid to sleep,
Seated in thy silver chair,
  State in wonted manner keep:
    Hesperus entreats thy light,
    Goddess excellently bright.

Earth, let not thy envious shade
  Dare itself to interpose;
Cynthia's shining orb was made
  Heaven to clear when day did close:
    Bless us then with wishèd sight,
    Goddess excellently bright.

Lay thy bow of pearl apart,
  And thy crystal-shining quiver;
Give unto the flying hart
  Space to breathe, how short soever:
    Thou that mak'st a day of night—
    Goddess excellently bright.

185. *To Celia*

DRINK to me only with thine eyes,
   And I will pledge with mine;
Or leave a kiss but in the cup
   And I'll not look for wine.
The thirst that from the soul doth rise
   Doth ask a drink divine;
But might I of Jove's nectar sup,
   I would not change for thine.

I sent thee late a rosy wreath,
   Not so much honouring thee
As giving it a hope that there
   It could not wither'd be;
But thou thereon didst only breathe,
   And sent'st it back to me;
Since when it grows, and smells, I swear,
   Not of itself but thee!

186. *Simplex Munditiis*

STILL to be neat, still to be drest,
   As you were going to a feast;
Still to be powder'd, still perfumed:
Lady, it is to be presumed,
Though art's hid causes are not found,
All is not sweet, all is not sound.

Give me a look, give me a face
That makes simplicity a grace;
Robes loosely flowing, hair as free:
Such sweet neglect more taketh me
Than all th' adulteries of art;
They strike mine eyes, but not my heart.

BEN JONSON

187.   *The Shadow*

FOLLOW a shadow, it still flies you;
  Seem to fly it, it will pursue:
So court a mistress, she denies you;
  Let her alone, she will court you.
    Say, are not women truly, then,
    Styled but the shadows of us men?

At morn and even, shades are longest;
  At noon they are or short or none:
So men at weakest, they are strongest,
  But grant us perfect, they're not known.
    Say, are not women truly, then,
    Styled but the shadows of us men?

188.   *The Triumph*

SEE the Chariot at hand here of Love,
  Wherein my Lady rideth!
Each that draws is a swan or a dove,
  And well the car Love guideth.
As she goes, all hearts do duty
    Unto her beauty;
And enamour'd do wish, so they might
    But enjoy such a sight,
That they still were to run by her side,
Through swords, through seas, whither she would ride.

Do but look on her eyes, they do light
  All that Love's world compriseth!
Do but look on her hair, it is bright
  As Love's star when it riseth!

Do but mark, her forehead's smoother
    Than words that soothe her;
And from her arch'd brows such a grace
    Sheds itself through the face,
As alone there triumphs to the life
All the gain, all the good, of the elements' strife.

Have you seen but a bright lily grow
    Before rude hands have touch'd it?
Have you mark'd but the fall of the snow
    Before the soil hath smutch'd it?
Have you felt the wool of beaver,
    Or swan's down ever?
Or have smelt o' the bud o' the brier,
    Or the nard in the fire?
Or have tasted the bag of the bee?
O so white, O so soft, O so sweet is she!

189. *An Elegy*

THOUGH beauty be the mark of praise,
    And yours of whom I sing be such
      As not the world can praise too much,
Yet 'tis your Virtue now I raise.

A virtue, like allay so gone
    Throughout your form as, though that move
    And draw and conquer all men's love,
This subjects you to love of one.

Wherein you triumph yet—because
    'Tis of your flesh, and that you use
    The noblest freedom, not to choose
Against or faith or honour's laws.

189. allay] alloy.

But who should less expect from you?
  In whom alone Love lives again:
  By whom he is restored to men,
And kept and bred and brought up true.

His falling temples you have rear'd,
  The wither'd garlands ta'en away;
  His altars kept from that decay
That envy wish'd, and nature fear'd:

And on them burn so chaste a flame,
  With so much loyalty's expense,
  As Love to acquit such excellence
Is gone himself into your name.

And you are he—the deity
  To whom all lovers are design'd
  That would their better objects find;
Among which faithful troop am I—

Who as an off'ring at your shrine
  Have sung this hymn, and here entreat
  One spark of your diviner heat
To light upon a love of mine.

Which if it kindle not, but scant
  Appear, and that to shortest view;
  Yet give me leave to adore in you
What I in her am grieved to want!

190. *A Farewell to the World*

FALSE world, good night! since thou hast brought
  That hour upon my morn of age;
Henceforth I quit thee from my thought,
  My part is ended on thy stage.

BEN JONSON

Yes, threaten, do. Alas! I fear
    As little as I hope from thee:
I know thou canst not show nor bear
    More hatred than thou hast to me.

My tender, first, and simple years
    Thou didst abuse and then betray;
Since stir'd'st up jealousies and fears,
    When all the causes were away.

Then in a soil hast planted me
    Where breathe the basest of thy fools;
Where envious arts professèd be,
    And pride and ignorance the schools;

Where nothing is examined, weigh'd,
    But as 'tis rumour'd, so believed;
Where every freedom is betray'd,
    And every goodness tax'd or grieved.

But what we're born for, we must bear:
    Our frail condition it is such
That what to all may happen here,
    If 't chance to me, I must not grutch.

Else I my state should much mistake
    To harbour a divided thought
From all my kind—that, for my sake,
    There should a miracle be wrought.

No, I do know that I was born
    To age, misfortune, sickness, grief:
But I will bear these with that scorn
    As shall not need thy false relief.

Nor for my peace will I go far,
    As wanderers do, that still do roam;
But make my strengths, such as they are,
    Here in my bosom, and at home.

191.   *The Noble Balm*

HIGH-SPIRITED friend,
    I send nor balms nor cor'sives to your wound:
        Your fate hath found
A gentler and more agile hand to tend
The cure of that which is but corporal;
And doubtful days, which were named critical,
        Have made their fairest flight
        And now are out of sight.
Yet doth some wholesome physic for the mind
        Wrapp'd in this paper lie,
Which in the taking if you misapply,
        You are unkind.

        Your covetous hand,
Happy in that fair honour it hath gain'd,
        Must now be rein'd.
True valour doth her own renown command
In one full action; nor have you now more
To do, than be a husband of that store.
        Think but how dear you bought
        This fame which you have caught:
Such thoughts will make you more in love with truth.
        'Tis wisdom, and that high,
For men to use their fortune reverently,
        Even in youth.

BEN JONSON

Epitaphs

i

192.   *On Elizabeth L. H.*

WOULDST thou hear what Man can say
  In a little? Reader, stay.
Underneath this stone doth lie
As much Beauty as could die:
Which in life did harbour give
To more Virtue than doth live.
If at all she had a fault,
Leave it buried in this vault.
One name was *Elizabeth*,
The other, let it sleep with death:
Fitter, where it died, to tell
Than that it lived at all.   Farewell.

ii

193.   *On Salathiel Pavy*
  A child of Queen Elizabeth's Chapel

WEEP with me, all you that read
  This little story;
And know, for whom a tear you shed
  Death's self is sorry.
'Twas a child that so did thrive
  In grace and feature,
As Heaven and Nature seem'd to strive
  Which own'd the creature.
Years he number'd scarce thirteen
  When Fates turn'd cruel,
Yet three fill'd zodiacs had he been
  The stage's jewel;

And did act (what now we moan)
    Old men so duly,
As sooth the Parcae thought him one,
    He play'd so truly.
So, by error, to his fate
    They all consented;
But, viewing him since, alas, too late!
    They have repented;
And have sought, to give new birth,
    In baths to steep him;
But, being so much too good for earth,
    Heaven vows to keep him.

194. *A Part of an Ode*

to the Immortal Memory and Friendship of that noble pair, Sir Lucius Cary and Sir H. Morison

IT is not growing like a tree
    In bulk, doth make man better be;
Or standing long an oak, three hundred year,
To fall a log at last, dry, bald, and sere:
    A lily of a day
    Is fairer far in May,
Although it fall and die that night;
It was the plant and flower of light.
In small proportions we just beauties see;
And in short measures, life may perfect be.

    Call, noble *Lucius*, then for wine,
    And let thy looks with gladness shine:
Accept this garland, plant it on thy head,
And think—nay, know—thy *Morison*'s not dead.

BEN JONSON

He leap'd the present age,
Possest with holy rage
To see that bright eternal Day
Of which we Priests and Poets say
Such truths as we expect for happy men;
And there he lives with memory—and *Ben*

Jonson: who sung this of him, ere he went
Himself to rest,
Or tast a part of that full joy he meant
To have exprest
In this bright Asterism
Where it were friendship's schism—
Were not his *Lucius* long with us to tarry—
To separate these twy
Lights, the Dioscuri,
And keep the one half from his *Harry*.
But fate doth so alternate the design,
Whilst that in Heav'n, this light on earth must shine.

And shine as you exalted are!
Two names of friendship, but one star:
Of hearts the union: and those not by chance
Made, or indenture, or leased out to advance
The profits for a time.
No pleasures vain did chime
Of rimes or riots at your feasts,
Orgies of drink or feign'd protests;
But simple love of greatness and of good,
That knits brave minds and manners more than blood.

This made you first to know the *Why*
You liked, then after, to apply

BEN JONSON

That liking, and approach so one the t'other
Till either grew a portion of the other:
    Each stylèd by his end
    The copy of his friend.
  You lived to be the great surnames
  And titles by which all made claims
Unto the Virtue—nothing perfect done
But as a *CARY* or a *MORISON*.

And such the force the fair example had
    As they that saw
The good, and durst not practise it, were glad
    That such a law
  Was left yet to mankind,
  Where they might read and find
FRIENDSHIP indeed was written, not in words,
    And with the heart, not pen,
    Of two so early men,
Whose lines her rules were and records:
Who, ere the first down bloomèd on the chin,
Had sow'd these fruits, and got the harvest in.

JOHN DONNE
1573-1631

195. *Daybreak*

STAY, O sweet, and do not rise!
  The light that shines comes from thine eyes;
The day breaks not: it is my heart,
  Because that you and I must part.
    Stay! or else my joys will die
    And perish in their infancy.

JOHN DONNE

196.   *Song*

GO and catch a falling star,
    Get with child a mandrake root,
Tell me where all past years are,
    Or who cleft the Devil's foot;
Teach me to hear mermaids singing,
Or to keep off envy's stinging,
        And find
        What wind
Serves to advance an honest mind.

If thou be'st born to strange sights,
    Things invisible to see,
Ride ten thousand days and nights
    Till Age snow white hairs on thee;
Thou, when thou return'st, wilt tell me
All strange wonders that befell thee,
        And swear
        No where
Lives a woman true and fair.

If thou find'st one, let me know;
    Such a pilgrimage were sweet.
Yet do not; I would not go,
    Though at next door we might meet.
Though she were true when you met her,
And last till you write your letter,
        Yet she
        Will be
False, ere I come, to two or three.

JOHN DONNE

197.
That Time and Absence proves
Rather helps than hurts to loves

ABSENCE, hear thou my protestation
    Against thy strength,
    Distance and length:
Do what thou canst for alteration,
    For hearts of truest mettle
    Absence doth join and Time doth settle.

Who loves a mistress of such quality,
    His mind hath found
    Affection's ground
Beyond time, place, and all mortality.
    To hearts that cannot vary
    Absence is present, Time doth tarry.

My senses want their outward motion
    Which now within
    Reason doth win,
Redoubled by her secret notion:
    Like rich men that take pleasure
    In hiding more than handling treasure.

By Absence this good means I gain,
    That I can catch her
    Where none can watch her,
In some close corner of my brain:
    There I embrace and kiss her,
    And so enjoy her and none miss her.

198. *The Ecstasy*

WHERE, like a pillow on a bed,
    A pregnant bank swell'd up, to rest
The violet's reclining head,
    Sat we two, one another's best.

Our hands were firmly cèmented
    By a fast balm which thence did spring;
Our eye-beams twisted, and did thread
    Our eyes upon one double string.

So to engraft our hands, as yet
    Was all the means to make us one;
And pictures in our eyes to get
    Was all our propagation.

As 'twixt two equal armies Fate
    Suspends uncertain victory,
Our souls—which to advance their state
    Were gone out—hung 'twixt her and me.

And whilst our souls negotiate there,
    We like sepulchral statues lay;
All day the same our postures were,
    And we said nothing, all the day.

199. *The Dream*

DEAR love, for nothing less than thee
    Would I have broke this happy dream,
        It was a theme
For reason, much too strong for fantasy.
Therefore thou waked'st me wisely; yet
My dream thou brok'st not, but continued'st it.

Thou art so true that thoughts of thee suffice
To make dreams truths and fables histories;
Enter these arms, for since thou thought'st it best
Not to dream all my dream, let's act the rest.

As lightning, or a taper's light,
Thine eyes, and not thy noise, waked me;
    Yet I thought thee—
For thou lov'st truth—an angel, at first sight;
But when I saw thou saw'st my heart,
And knew'st my thoughts beyond an angel's art,
When thou knew'st what I dreamt, when thou knew'st when
Excess of joy would wake me, and cam'st then,
I must confess it could not choose but be
Profane to think thee anything but thee.

Coming and staying show'd thee thee,
But rising makes me doubt that now
    Thou art not thou.
That Love is weak where Fear's as strong as he;
'Tis not all spirit pure and brave
If mixture it of Fear, Shame, Honour have.
Perchance as torches, which must ready be,
Men light and put out, so thou deal'st with me.
Thou cam'st to kindle, go'st to come: then I
Will dream that hope again, but else would die.

200. *The Funeral*

WHOEVER comes to shroud me, do not harm
    Nor question much
That subtle wreath of hair about mine arm;
The mystery, the sign you must not touch,

  For 'tis my outward soul,
Viceroy to that which, unto heav'n being gone,
  Will leave this to control
And keep these limbs, her provinces, from dissolution.

For if the sinewy thread my brain lets fall
  Through every part
Can tie those parts, and make me one of all;
Those hairs, which upward grew, and strength and art
  Have from a better brain,
Can better do 't: except she meant that I
  By this should know my pain,
As prisoners then are manacled, when they're condemn'd to die.

Whate'er she meant by 't, bury it with me,
  For since I am
Love's martyr, it might breed idolatry
If into other hands these reliques came.
  As 'twas humility
T' afford to it all that a soul can do,
  So 'tis some bravery
That, since you would have none of me, I bury some of you.

201. *A Hymn to God the Father*

WILT Thou forgive that sin where I begun,
  Which was my sin, though it were done before?
Wilt Thou forgive that sin through which I run,
  And do run still, though still I do deplore?
    When Thou hast done, Thou hast not done;
      For I have more.

JOHN DONNE

Wilt Thou forgive that sin which I have won
  Others to sin, and made my sins their door?
Wilt Thou forgive that sin which I did shun
  A year or two, but wallow'd in a score?
When Thou hast done, Thou hast not done;
  For I have more.

I have a sin of fear, that when I've spun
  My last thread, I shall perish on the shore;
But swear by Thyself that at my death Thy Son
  Shall shine as He shines now and heretofore:
And having done that, Thou hast done;
  I fear no more.

202. *Death*

DEATH, be not proud, though some have callèd thee
  Mighty and dreadful, for thou art not so:
For those whom thou think'st thou dost overthrow
Die not, poor Death; nor yet canst thou kill me.
From Rest and Sleep, which but thy picture be,
Much pleasure, then from thee much more must flow;
And soonest our best men with thee do go—
Rest of their bones and souls' delivery!
Thou'rt slave to fate, chance, kings, and desperate men,
And dost with poison, war, and sickness dwell;
And poppy or charms can make us sleep as well
And better than thy stroke. Why swell'st thou then?
  One short sleep past, we wake eternally,
  And Death shall be no more: Death, thou shalt die!

RICHARD BARNEFIELD
1574-1627

203. *Philomel*

AS it fell upon a day
  In the merry month of May,
Sitting in a pleasant shade
Which a grove of myrtles made,
Beasts did leap and birds did sing,
Trees did grow and plants did spring;
Everything did banish moan
Save the Nightingale alone:
She, poor bird, as all forlorn
Lean'd her breast up-till a thorn,
And there sung the dolefull'st ditty,
That to hear it was great pity.
Fie, fie, fie! now would she cry;
Tereu, Tereu! by and by;
That to hear her so complain
Scarce I could from tears refrain;
For her griefs so lively shown
Made me think upon mine own.
Ah! thought I, thou mourn'st in vain,
None takes pity on thy pain:
Senseless trees they cannot hear thee,
Ruthless beasts they will not cheer thee:
King Pandion he is dead,
All thy friends are lapp'd in lead;
All thy fellow birds do sing
Careless of thy sorrowing:
Even so, poor bird, like thee,
None alive will pity me.

THOMAS DEKKER
1575-1641

204.   *Sweet Content*

ART thou poor, yet hast thou golden slumbers?
    O sweet content!
Art thou rich, yet is thy mind perplex'd?
    O punishment!
Dost thou laugh to see how fools are vex'd
To add to golden numbers golden numbers?
    O sweet content! O sweet, O sweet content!
Work apace, apace, apace, apace;
Honest labour bears a lovely face;
Then hey nonny nonny—hey nonny nonny!

Canst drink the waters of the crispèd spring?
    O sweet content!
Swim'st thou in wealth, yet sink'st in thine own tears?
    O punishment!
Then he that patiently want's burden bears,
No burden bears, but is a king, a king!
    O sweet content! O sweet, O sweet content!
Work apace, apace, apace, apace;
Honest labour bears a lovely face;
Then hey nonny nonny—hey nonny nonny!

THOMAS HEYWOOD
157?-1650

205.   *Matin Song*

PACK, clouds, away! and welcome, day!
    With night we banish sorrow.
Sweet air, blow soft; mount, lark, aloft
    To give my Love good-morrow!

Wings from the wind to please her mind,
  Notes from the lark I'll borrow:
Bird, prune thy wing! nightingale, sing!
  To give my Love good-morrow!
    To give my Love good-morrow
    Notes from them all I'll borrow.

Wake from thy nest, robin red-breast!
  Sing, birds, in every furrow!
And from each bill let music shrill
  Give my fair Love good-morrow!
Blackbird and thrush in every bush,
  Stare, linnet, and cocksparrow,
You pretty elves, among yourselves
  Sing my fair Love good-morrow!
    To give my Love good-morrow!
    Sing, birds, in every furrow!

206.   *The Message*

YE little birds that sit and sing
    Amidst the shady valleys,
And see how Phillis sweetly walks
    Within her garden-alleys;
Go, pretty birds, about her bower;
Sing, pretty birds, she may not lower;
Ah me! methinks I see her frown!
    Ye pretty wantons, warble.

Go tell her through your chirping bills,
    As you by me are bidden,
To her is only known my love,
    Which from the world is hidden.

205. stare] starling.

THOMAS HEYWOOD

Go, pretty birds, and tell her so,
See that your notes strain not too low,
For still methinks I see her frown;
    Ye pretty wantons, warble.

Go tune your voices' harmony
    And sing, I am her lover;
Strain loud and sweet, that every note
    With sweet content may move her:
And she that hath the sweetest voice,
Tell her I will not change my choice:
—Yet still methinks I see her frown!
    Ye pretty wantons, warble.

O fly! make haste! see, see, she falls
    Into a pretty slumber!
Sing round about her rosy bed
    That waking she may wonder:
Say to her, 'tis her lover true
That sendeth love to you, to you!
And when you hear her kind reply,
    Return with pleasant warblings.

JOHN FLETCHER
1579-1625

207.   *Sleep*

COME, Sleep, and with thy sweet deceiving
    Lock me in delight awhile;
    Let some pleasing dreams beguile
    All my fancies; that from thence
    I may feel an influence
All my powers of care bereaving!

Though but a shadow, but a sliding,
  Let me know some little joy!
We that suffer long annoy
Are contented with a thought
Through an idle fancy wrought:
O let my joys have some abiding!

208.   *Bridal Song*

CYNTHIA, to thy power and thee
      We obey.
Joy to this great company!
      And no day
Come to steal this night away
  Till the rites of love are ended,
And the lusty bridegroom say,
  Welcome, light, of all befriended!

Pace out, you watery powers below;
      Let your feet,
Like the galleys when they row,
      Even beat;
Let your unknown measures, set
  To the still winds, tell to all
That gods are come, immortal, great,
  To honour this great nuptial!

209.   *Aspatia's Song*

LAY a garland on my herse
      Of the dismal yew;
Maidens, willow branches bear;
      Say, I died true.

JOHN FLETCHER

My love was false, but I was firm
    From my hour of birth.
Upon my buried body lie
    Lightly, gentle earth!

210.   *Hymn to Pan*

SING his praises that doth keep
    Our flocks from harm,
Pan, the father of our sheep;
    And arm in arm
Tread we softly in a round,
Whilst the hollow neighbouring ground
Fills the music with her sound.

Pan, O great god Pan, to thee
    Thus do we sing!
Thou who keep'st us chaste and free
    As the young spring:
Ever be thy honour spoke
From that place the morn is broke
To that place day doth unyoke!

211.   *Away, Delights*

AWAY, delights! go seek some other dwelling,
    For I must die.
Farewell, false love! thy tongue is ever telling
    Lie after lie.
For ever let me rest now from thy smarts;
    Alas, for pity go
    And fire their hearts
That have been hard to thee! Mine was not so.

JOHN FLETCHER

Never again deluding love shall know me,
    For I will die;
And all those griefs that think to overgrow me
    Shall be as I:
For ever will I sleep, while poor maids cry—
    'Alas, for pity stay,
    And let us die
With thee! Men cannot mock us in the clay.'

212.   *Love's Emblems*

NOW the lusty spring is seen;
    Golden yellow, gaudy blue,
Daintily invite the view:
Everywhere on every green
Roses blushing as they blow,
    And enticing men to pull,
Lilies whiter than the snow,
    Woodbines of sweet honey full:
        All love's emblems, and all cry,
        'Ladies, if not pluck'd, we die.'

Yet the lusty spring hath stay'd;
    Blushing red and purest white
Daintily to love invite
Every woman, every maid:
Cherries kissing as they grow,
    And inviting men to taste,
Apples even ripe below,
    Winding gently to the waist:
        All love's emblems, and all cry,
        'Ladies, if not pluck'd, we die.'

JOHN FLETCHER

213.   *Hear, ye Ladies*

HEAR, ye ladies that despise
   What the mighty Love has done;
Fear examples and be wise:
   Fair Callisto was a nun;
   Leda, sailing on the stream
   To deceive the hopes of man,
   Love accounting but a dream,
   Doted on a silver swan;
      Danaë, in a brazen tower,
      Where no love was, loved a shower.

Hear, ye ladies that are coy,
   What the mighty Love can do;
Fear the fierceness of the boy:
   The chaste Moon he makes to woo;
   Vesta, kindling holy fires,
   Circled round about with spies,
   Never dreaming loose desires,
   Doting at the altar dies;
      Ilion, in a short hour, higher
      He can build, and once more fire.

214.   *God Lyaeus*

GOD Lyaeus, ever young,
   Ever honour'd, ever sung,
Stain'd with blood of lusty grapes,
In a thousand lusty shapes
   Dance upon the mazer's brim,
   In the crimson liquor swim;

214. mazer] a bowl of maple-wood.

JOHN FLETCHER

From thy plenteous hand divine
Let a river run with wine:
  God of youth, let this day here
  Enter neither care nor fear.

215.   *Beauty Clear and Fair*

BEAUTY clear and fair,
  Where the air
Rather like a perfume dwells;
  Where the violet and the rose
  Their blue veins and blush disclose,
And come to honour nothing else:

  Where to live near
  And planted there
Is to live, and still live new;
  Where to gain a favour is
  More than light, perpetual bliss—
Make me live by serving you!

Dear, again back recall
  To this light,
A stranger to himself and all!
  Both the wonder and the story
  Shall be yours, and eke the glory;
I am your servant, and your thrall.

216.   *Melancholy*

HENCE, all you vain delights,
  As short as are the nights
Wherein you spend your folly!
There's naught in this life sweet,

JOHN FLETCHER

If men were wise to see 't,
  But only melancholy—
  O sweetest melancholy!
Welcome, folded arms and fixèd eyes,
A sight that piercing mortifies,
A look that's fasten'd to the ground,
A tongue chain'd up without a sound!

Fountain-heads and pathless groves,
Places which pale passion loves!
Moonlight walks, when all the fowls
Are warmly housed, save bats and owls!
  A midnight bell, a parting groan—
  These are the sounds we feed upon:
Then stretch our bones in a still gloomy valley,
Nothing's so dainty sweet as lovely melancholy.

217. *Weep no more*

WEEP no more, nor sigh, nor groan,
  Sorrow calls no time that's gone:
Violets pluck'd, the sweetest rain
Makes not fresh nor grow again.
Trim thy locks, look cheerfully;
Fate's hid ends eyes cannot see.
Joys as wingèd dreams fly fast,
Why should sadness longer last?
Grief is but a wound to woe;
Gentlest fair, mourn, mourn no moe.

JOHN WEBSTER
?-1630?

218. *A Dirge*

CALL for the robin-redbreast and the wren,
   Since o'er shady groves they hover,
And with leaves and flowers do cover
The friendless bodies of unburied men.
Call unto his funeral dole
The ant, the field-mouse, and the mole,
To rear him hillocks that shall keep him warm,
And (when gay tombs are robb'd) sustain no harm;
But keep the wolf far thence, that's foe to men,
For with his nails he'll dig them up again.

219. *The Shrouding of the Duchess of Malfi*

HARK! Now everything is still,
   The screech-owl and the whistler shrill,
Call upon our dame aloud,
And bid her quickly don her shroud!

Much you had of land and rent;
Your length in clay's now competent:
A long war disturb'd your mind;
Here your perfect peace is sign'd.

Of what is't fools make such vain keeping?
Sin their conception, their birth weeping,
Their life a general mist of error,
Their death a hideous storm of terror.
Strew your hair with powders sweet,
Don clean linen, bathe your feet,

218. dole] lamentation.

And—the foul fiend more to check—
A crucifix let bless your neck:
'Tis now full tide 'tween night and day;
End your groan and come away.

220. *Vanitas Vanitatum*

ALL the flowers of the spring
  Meet to perfume our burying;
These have but their growing prime,
And man does flourish but his time:
Survey our progress from our birth—
We are set, we grow, we turn to earth.
Courts adieu, and all delights,
All bewitching appetites!
Sweetest breath and clearest eye
Like perfumes go out and die;
And consequently this is done
As shadows wait upon the sun.
Vain the ambition of kings
Who seek by trophies and dead things
To leave a living name behind,
And weave but nets to catch the wind.

WILLIAM ALEXANDER, EARL OF STIRLING
1580?-1640

221. *Aurora*

O HAPPY Tithon! if thou know'st thy hap,
  And valuest thy wealth, as I my want,
Then need'st thou not—which ah! I grieve to grant—
Repine at Jove, lull'd in his leman's lap:

EARL OF STIRLING

    That golden shower in which he did repose—
        One dewy drop it stains
        Which thy Aurora rains
        Upon the rural plains,
    When from thy bed she passionately goes.

Then, waken'd with the music of the merles,
    She not remembers Memnon when she mourns:
    That faithful flame which in her bosom burns
From crystal conduits throws those liquid pearls:
    Sad from thy sight so soon to be removed,
        She so her grief delates.
        —O favour'd by the fates
        Above the happiest states,
    Who art of one so worthy well-beloved!

PHINEAS FLETCHER
1580-1650

222.   *A Litany*

    DROP, drop, slow tears,
        And bathe those beauteous feet
    Which brought from Heaven
        The news and Prince of Peace:
    Cease not, wet eyes,
        His mercy to entreat;
    To cry for vengeance
        Sin doth never cease.
    In your deep floods
        Drown all my faults and fears;
    Nor let His eye
        See sin, but through my tears.

SIR JOHN BEAUMONT

1583-1627

223. *Of his Dear Son, Gervase*

DEAR Lord, receive my son, whose winning love
    To me was like a friendship, far above
The course of nature or his tender age;
Whose looks could all my bitter griefs assuage:
Let his pure soul, ordain'd seven years to be
In that frail body which was part of me,
Remain my pledge in Heaven, as sent to show
How to this port at every step I go.

WILLIAM DRUMMOND, OF HAWTHORNDEN

1585-1649

224. *Invocation*

PHŒBUS, arise!
    And paint the sable skies
With azure, white, and red;
Rouse Memnon's mother from her Tithon's bed,
That she thy career may with roses spread;
The nightingales thy coming each-where sing;
Make an eternal spring!
Give life to this dark world which lieth dead;
Spread forth thy golden hair
In larger locks than thou wast wont before,
And emperor-like decore
With diadem of pearl thy temples fair:
Chase hence the ugly night
Which serves but to make dear thy glorious light.

WILLIAM DRUMMOND

This is that happy morn,
That day, long wishèd day
Of all my life so dark
(If cruel stars have not my ruin sworn
And fates not hope betray),
Which, only white, deserves
A diamond for ever should it mark:
This is the morn should bring into this grove
My Love, to hear and recompense my love.
Fair King, who all preserves,
But show thy blushing beams,
And thou two sweeter eyes
Shalt see than those which by Penèus' streams
Did once thy heart surprise:
Nay, suns, which shine as clear
As thou when two thou did to Rome appear.
Now, Flora, deck thyself in fairest guise:
If that ye, winds, would hear
A voice surpassing far Amphion's lyre,
Your stormy chiding stay;
Let zephyr only breathe
And with her tresses play,
Kissing sometimes these purple ports of death.

The winds all silent are;
And Phœbus in his chair
Ensaffroning sea and air
Makes vanish every star:
Night like a drunkard reels
Beyond the hills to shun his flaming wheels:
The fields with flowers are deck'd in every hue,
The clouds bespangle with bright gold their blue:
Here is the pleasant place—
And everything, save Her, who all should grace.

WILLIAM DRUMMOND

225.   *Madrigal*

LIKE the Idalian queen,
　　Her hair about her eyne,
With neck and breast's ripe apples to be seen,
　　At first glance of the morn
　In Cyprus' gardens gathering those fair flow'rs
　　Which of her blood were born,
I saw, but fainting saw, my paramours.
　The Graces naked danced about the place,
　　The winds and trees amazed
　　With silence on her gazed,
The flowers did smile, like those upon her face;
And as their aspen stalks those fingers band,
　　That she might read my case,
A hyacinth I wish'd me in her hand.

226.   *Spring Bereaved 1*

THAT zephyr every year
　　So soon was heard to sigh in forests here,
It was for her: that wrapp'd in gowns of green
　　Meads were so early seen,
That in the saddest months oft sung the merles,
It was for her; for her trees dropp'd forth pearls.
　　That proud and stately courts
Did envy those our shades and calm resorts,
It was for her; and she is gone, O woe!
　　Woods cut again do grow,
Bud doth the rose and daisy, winter done;
But we, once dead, no more do see the sun.

225. paramours] = sing. paramour.　　band] bound.

WILLIAM DRUMMOND

227. *Spring Bereaved 2*

SWEET Spring, thou turn'st with all thy goodly train,
  Thy head with flames, thy mantle bright with flow'rs:
The zephyrs curl the green locks of the plain,
The clouds for joy in pearls weep down their show'rs.
Thou turn'st, sweet youth, but ah! my pleasant hours
And happy days with thee come not again;
The sad memorials only of my pain
Do with thee turn, which turn my sweets in sours.
Thou art the same which still thou wast before,
Delicious, wanton, amiable, fair;
But she, whose breath embalm'd thy wholesome air,
Is gone—nor gold nor gems her can restore.
  Neglected virtue, seasons go and come,
  While thine forgot lie closèd in a tomb.

228. *Spring Bereaved 3*

ALEXIS, here she stay'd; among these pines,
  Sweet hermitress, she did alone repair;
Here did she spread the treasure of her hair,
More rich than that brought from the Colchian mines.
She set her by these muskèd eglantines,
—The happy place the print seems yet to bear:
Her voice did sweeten here thy sugar'd lines,
To which winds, trees, beasts, birds, did lend their ear.
Me here she first perceived, and here a morn
Of bright carnations did o'erspread her face;
Here did she sigh, here first my hopes were born,
And I first got a pledge of promised grace:
  But ah! what served it to be happy so?
  Sith passèd pleasures double but new woe?

229. *Her Passing*

THE beauty and the life
  Of life's and beauty's fairest paragon
—O tears! O grief!—hung at a feeble thread
To which pale Atropos had set her knife;
  The soul with many a groan
  Had left each outward part,
And now did take his last leave of the heart:
Naught else did want, save death, ev'n to be dead;
When the afflicted band about her bed,
Seeing so fair him come in lips, cheeks, eyes,
Cried, '*Ah! and can Death enter Paradise?*'

230. *Inexorable*

MY thoughts hold mortal strife;
  I do detest my life,
  And with lamenting cries
  Peace to my soul to bring
Oft call that prince which here doth monarchise:
  —But he, grim-grinning King,
Who caitiffs scorns, and doth the blest surprise,
Late having deck'd with beauty's rose his tomb,
Disdains to crop a weed, and will not come.

231. *Change should breed Change*

NEW doth the sun appear,
  The mountains' snows decay,
Crown'd with frail flowers forth comes the baby year.
  My soul, time posts away;

WILLIAM DRUMMOND

    And thou yet in that frost
    Which flower and fruit hath lost,
As if all here immortal were, dost stay.
    For shame! thy powers awake,
Look to that Heaven which never night makes black,
And there at that immortal sun's bright rays,
Deck thee with flowers which fear not rage of days!

232.   *Saint John Baptist*

THE last and greatest Herald of Heaven's King,
  Girt with rough skins, hies to the deserts wild,
Among that savage brood the woods forth bring,
Which he than man more harmless found and mild.
His food was locusts, and what young doth spring
With honey that from virgin hives distill'd;
Parch'd body, hollow eyes, some uncouth thing
Made him appear, long since from earth exiled.
There burst he forth: 'All ye, whose hopes rely
On God, with me amidst these deserts mourn;
Repent, repent, and from old errors turn!'
—Who listen'd to his voice, obey'd his cry?
  Only the echoes, which he made relent,
  Rung from their marble caves 'Repent! Repent!

GILES FLETCHER
158?-1623

233.   *Wooing Song*

LOVE is the blossom where there blows
   Every thing that lives or grows:
Love doth make the Heav'ns to move,
And the Sun doth burn in love:

250

GILES FLETCHER

Love the strong and weak doth yoke,
And makes the ivy climb the oak,
Under whose shadows lions wild,
Soften'd by love, grow tame and mild:
Love no med'cine can appease,
He burns the fishes in the seas:
Not all the skill his wounds can stench,
Not all the sea his fire can quench.
Love did make the bloody spear
Once a leavy coat to wear,
While in his leaves there shrouded lay
Sweet birds, for love that sing and play
And of all love's joyful flame
I the bud and blossom am.
 Only bend thy knee to me,
 Thy wooing shall thy winning be!

See, see the flowers that below
Now as fresh as morning blow;
And of all the virgin rose
That as bright Aurora shows;
How they all unleavèd die,
Losing their virginity!
Like unto a summer shade,
But now born, and now they fade.
Every thing doth pass away;
There is danger in delay:
Come, come, gather then the rose,
Gather it, or it you lose!
All the sand of Tagus' shore
Into my bosom casts his ore:
All the valleys' swimming corn
To my house is yearly borne:

GILES FLETCHER

Every grape of every vine
Is gladly bruised to make me wine:
While ten thousand kings, as proud,
To carry up my train have bow'd,
And a world of ladies send me
In my chambers to attend me:
All the stars in Heav'n that shine,
And ten thousand more, are mine:
   Only bend thy knee to me,
   Thy wooing shall thy winning be!

FRANCIS BEAUMONT
1586-1616

234. *On the Tombs in Westminster Abbey*

MORTALITY, behold and fear!
   What a change of flesh is here!
Think how many royal bones
Sleep within this heap of stones:
Here they lie had realms and lands,
Who now want strength to stir their hands:
Where from their pulpits seal'd with dust
They preach, 'In greatness is no trust.'
Here's an acre sown indeed
With the richest, royall'st seed
That the earth did e'er suck in
Since the first man died for sin:
Here the bones of birth have cried—
'Though gods they were, as men they died.'
Here are sands, ignoble things,
Dropt from the ruin'd sides of kings;
Here's a world of pomp and state,
Buried in dust, once dead by fate.

JOHN FORD
1586-1639

235.   *Dawn*

FLY hence, shadows, that do keep
  Watchful sorrows charm'd in sleep!
Tho' the eyes be overtaken,
Yet the heart doth ever waken
Thoughts chain'd up in busy snares
Of continual woes and cares:
Love and griefs are so exprest
As they rather sigh than rest.
    Fly hence, shadows, that do keep
    Watchful sorrows charm'd in sleep!

GEORGE WITHER
1588-1667

236.   *I loved a Lass*

I LOVED a lass, a fair one,
  As fair as e'er was seen;
She was indeed a rare one,
  Another Sheba Queen:
But, fool as then I was,
  I thought she loved me too:
But now, alas! she's left me,
  Falero, lero, loo!

Her hair like gold did glister,
  Each eye was like a star,
She did surpass her sister,
  Which pass'd all others far;
She would me honey call,
  She'd—O she'd kiss me too!
But now, alas! she's left me,
  Falero, lero, loo!

GEORGE WITHER

Many a merry meeting
  My love and I have had;
She was my only sweeting,
  She made my heart full glad;
The tears stood in her eyes
  Like to the morning dew:
But now, alas! she's left me,
  Falero, lero, loo!

Her cheeks were like the cherry,
  Her skin was white as snow;
When she was blithe and merry
  She angel-like did show;
Her waist exceeding small,
  The fives did fit her shoe:
But now, alas! she's left me,
  Falero, lero, loo!

In summer time or winter
  She had her heart's desire;
I still did scorn to stint her
  From sugar, sack, or fire;
The world went round about,
  No cares we ever knew:
But now, alas! she's left me,
  Falero, lero, loo!

To maidens' vows and swearing
  Henceforth no credit give;
You may give them the hearing,
  But never them believe;
They are as false as fair,
  Unconstant, frail, untrue:
For mine, alas! hath left me,
  Falero, lero, loo!

GEORGE WITHER

237.   *The Lover's Resolution*

SHALL I, wasting in despair,
Die because a woman's fair?
Or make pale my cheeks with care
'Cause another's rosy are?
Be she fairer than the day,
Or the flow'ry meads in May,
  If she think not well of me,
  What care I how fair she be?

Shall my silly heart be pined
'Cause I see a woman kind?
Or a well disposèd nature
Joinèd with a lovely feature?
Be she meeker, kinder, than
Turtle-dove or pelican,
  If she be not so to me,
  What care I how kind she be?

Shall a woman's virtues move
Me to perish for her love?
Or her well-deservings known
Make me quite forget my own?
Be she with that goodness blest
Which may merit name of Best,
  If she be not such to me,
  What care I how good she be?

'Cause her fortune seems too high,
Shall I play the fool and die?
She that bears a noble mind,
If not outward helps she find,

Thinks* what with them he would do
That without them dares her woo;
　And unless that mind I see,
　What care I how great she be?

Great, or good, or kind, or fair,
I will ne'er the more despair;
If she love me, this believe,
I will die ere she shall grieve;
If she slight me when I woo,
I can scorn and let her go;
　For if she be not for me,
　What care I for whom she be?

238.　　　　*The Choice*

ME so oft my fancy drew
　　Here and there, that I ne'er knew
Where to place desire before
So that range it might no more;
But as he that passeth by
Where, in all her jollity,
Flora's riches in a row
Do in seemly order grow,
And a thousand flowers stand
Bending as to kiss his hand;
Out of which delightful store
One he may take and no more;
Long he pausing doubteth whether
Of those fair ones he should gather.

First the Primrose courts his eyes,
Then the Cowslip he espies;

GEORGE WITHER

Next the Pansy seems to woo him,
Then Carnations bow unto him;
Which whilst that enamour'd swain
From the stalk intends to strain,
(As half-fearing to be seen)
Prettily her leaves between
Peeps the Violet, pale to see
That her virtues slighted be;
Which so much his liking wins
That to seize her he begins.

Yet before he stoop'd so low
He his wanton eye did throw
On a stem that grew more high,
And the Rose did there espy.
Who, beside her previous scent,
To procure his eyes content
Did display her goodly breast,
Where he found at full exprest
All the good that Nature showers
On a thousand other flowers;
Wherewith he affected takes it,
His belovèd flower he makes it,
And without desire of more
Walks through all he saw before.

So I wand'ring but erewhile
Through the garden of this Isle,
Saw rich beauties, I confess,
And in number numberless.
Yea, so differing lovely too,
That I had a world to do
Ere I could set up my rest,
Where to choose and choose the best.

GEORGE WITHER

Thus I fondly fear'd, till Fate
(Which I must confess in that
Did a greater favour to me
Than the world can malice do me)
Show'd to me that matchless flower,
Subject for this song of our;
Whose perfection having eyed,
Reason instantly espied
That Desire, which ranged abroad,
There would find a period:
And no marvel if it might,
For it there hath all delight,
And in her hath nature placed
What each several fair one graced.

Let who list, for me, advance
The admirèd flowers of France,
Let who will praise and behold
The reservèd Marigold;
Let the sweet-breath'd Violet now
Unto whom she pleaseth bow;
And the fairest Lily spread
Where she will her golden head;
I have such a flower to wear
That for those I do not care.

Let the young and happy swains
Playing on the Britain plains
Court unblamed their shepherdesses,
And with their gold curlèd tresses
Toy uncensured, until I
Grudge at their prosperity.

GEORGE WITHER

Let all times, both present, past,
And the age that shall be last,
Vaunt the beauties they bring forth.
I have found in one such worth,
That content I neither care
What the best before me were;
Nor desire to live and see
Who shall fair hereafter be;
For I know the hand of Nature
Will not make a fairer creature.

239. *A Widow's Hymn*

HOW near me came the hand of Death,
    When at my side he struck my dear,
And took away the precious breath
    Which quicken'd my belovèd peer!
      How helpless am I thereby made!
      By day how grieved, by night how sad!
And now my life's delight is gone,
—Alas! how am I left alone!

The voice which I did more esteem
    Than music in her sweetest key,
Those eyes which unto me did seem
    More comfortable than the day;
      Those now by me, as they have been,
      Shall never more be heard or seen;
But what I once enjoy'd in them
Shall seem hereafter as a dream.

239. peer] companion.

GEORGE WITHER

Lord! keep me faithful to the trust
  Which my dear spouse reposed in me:
To him now dead preserve me just
  In all that should performèd be!
For though our being man and wife
  Extendeth only to this life,
Yet neither life nor death should end
The being of a faithful friend.

WILLIAM BROWNE, OF TAVISTOCK
1588-1643

240. *A Welcome*

WELCOME, welcome! do I sing,
  Far more welcome than the spring;
He that parteth from you never
Shall enjoy a spring for ever.

He that to the voice is near
  Breaking from your iv'ry pale,
Need not walk abroad to hear
  The delightful nightingale.
    Welcome, welcome, then . . .

He that looks still on your eyes,
  Though the winter have begun
To benumb our arteries,
  Shall not want the summer's sun.
    Welcome, welcome, then . . .

He that still may see your cheeks,
  Where all rareness still reposes,
Is a fool if e'er he seeks
  Other lilies, other roses.
    Welcome, welcome, then . . .

He to whom your soft lip yields,
  And perceives your breath in kissing,
All the odours of the fields
  Never, never shall be missing.
        Welcome, welcome, then . . .

He that question would anew
  What fair Eden was of old,
Let him rightly study you,
  And a brief of that behold.
        Welcome, welcome, then . . .

241. *The Sirens' Song*

STEER, hither steer your wingèd pines,
  All beaten mariners!
Here lie Love's undiscover'd mines,
  A prey to passengers—
Perfumes far sweeter than the best
Which make the Phœnix' urn and nest.
    Fear not your ships,
Nor any to oppose you save our lips;
    But come on shore,
Where no joy dies till Love hath gotten more.

For swelling waves our panting breasts,
  Where never storms arise,
Exchange, and be awhile our guests:
  For stars gaze on our eyes.
The compass Love shall hourly sing,
And as he goes about the ring,
    We will not miss
To tell each point he nameth with a kiss.
    —Then come on shore,
Where no joy dies till Love hath gotten more.

242.   *The Rose*

A ROSE, as fair as ever saw the North,
  Grew in a little garden all alone;
A sweeter flower did Nature ne'er put forth,
Nor fairer garden yet was never known:
The maidens danced about it morn and noon,
And learnèd bards of it their ditties made;
The nimble fairies by the pale-faced moon
Water'd the root and kiss'd her pretty shade.
But well-a-day!—the gardener careless grew;
The maids and fairies both were kept away,
And in a drought the caterpillars threw
Themselves upon the bud and every spray.
  God shield the stock! If heaven send no supplies,
  The fairest blossom of the garden dies.

243.   *Song*

FOR her gait, if she be walking;
  Be she sitting, I desire her
For her state's sake; and admire her
For her wit if she be talking;
    Gait and state and wit approve her;
    For which all and each I love her.

Be she sullen, I commend her
For a modest. Be she merry,
For a kind one her prefer I.
Briefly, everything doth lend her
    So much grace, and so approve her,
    That for everything I love her.

244. *Memory*

SO shuts the marigold her leaves
    At the departure of the sun;
So from the honeysuckle sheaves
    The bee goes when the day is done;
So sits the turtle when she is but one,
And so all woe, as I since she is gone.

To some few birds kind Nature hath
    Made all the summer as one day:
Which once enjoy'd, cold winter's wrath
    As night they sleeping pass away.
Those happy creatures are, that know not yet
The pain to be deprived or to forget.

I oft have heard men say there be
    Some that with confidence profess
The helpful Art of Memory:
    But could they teach Forgetfulness,
I'd learn; and try what further art could do
To make me love her and forget her too.

Epitaphs

245.   *In Obitum M.S. X° Maij, 1614*

MAY! Be thou never graced with birds that sing,
    Nor Flora's pride!
In thee all flowers and roses spring,
    Mine only died.

WILLIAM BROWNE

246. *On the Countess Dowager of Pembroke*

UNDERNEATH this sable herse
Lies the subject of all verse:
Sidney's sister, Pembroke's mother:
Death, ere thou hast slain another
Fair and learn'd and good as she,
Time shall throw a dart at thee.

ROBERT HERRICK
1591-1674

247. *Corinna's going a-Maying*

GET up, get up for shame! The blooming morn
Upon her wings presents the god unshorn.
See how Aurora throws her fair
Fresh-quilted colours through the air:
Get up, sweet slug-a-bed, and see
The dew bespangling herb and tree!
Each flower has wept and bow'd toward the east
Above an hour since, yet you not drest;
Nay! not so much as out of bed?
When all the birds have matins said
And sung their thankful hymns, 'tis sin,
Nay, profanation, to keep in,
Whereas a thousand virgins on this day
Spring sooner than the lark, to fetch in May.

Rise and put on your foliage, and be seen
To come forth, like the spring-time, fresh and green,
And sweet as Flora. Take no care
For jewels for your gown or hair:
Fear not; the leaves will strew
Gems in abundance upon you:

ROBERT HERRICK

Besides, the childhood of the day has kept,
Against you come, some orient pearls unwept.
    Come, and receive them while the light
    Hangs on the dew-locks of the night:
    And Titan on the eastern hill
    Retires himself, or else stands still
Till you come forth! Wash, dress, be brief in praying:
Few beads are best when once we go a-Maying.

Come, my Corinna, come; and coming, mark
How each field turns a street, each street a park,
    Made green and trimm'd with trees! see how
    Devotion gives each house a bough
    Or branch! each porch, each door, ere this,
    An ark, a tabernacle is,
Made up of white-thorn neatly interwove,
As if here were those cooler shades of love.
    Can such delights be in the street
    And open fields, and we not see't?
    Come, we'll abroad: and let's obey
    The proclamation made for May,
And sin no more, as we have done, by staying;
But, my Corinna, come, let's go a-Maying.

There's not a budding boy or girl this day
But is got up and gone to bring in May.
    A deal of youth ere this is come
    Back, and with white-thorn laden home.
    Some have despatch'd their cakes and cream,
    Before that we have left to dream:
And some have wept and woo'd, and plighted troth,
And chose their priest, ere we can cast off sloth:

beads] prayers.

ROBERT HERRICK

Many a green-gown has been given,
Many a kiss, both odd and even:
Many a glance, too, has been sent
From out the eye, love's firmament:
Many a jest told of the keys betraying
This night, and locks pick'd: yet we're not a-Maying!

Come, let us go, while we are in our prime,
And take the harmless folly of the time!
We shall grow old apace, and die
Before we know our liberty.
Our life is short, and our days run
As fast away as does the sun.
And, as a vapour or a drop of rain,
Once lost, can ne'er be found again,
So when or you or I are made
A fable, song, or fleeting shade,
All love, all liking, all delight
Lies drown'd with us in endless night.
Then, while time serves, and we are but decaying,
Come, my Corinna, come, let's go a-Maying.

248. *To the Virgins, to make much of Time*

GATHER ye rosebuds while ye may,
  Old Time is still a-flying:
And this same flower that smiles to-day
  To-morrow will be dying.

The glorious lamp of heaven, the sun,
  The higher he's a-getting,
The sooner will his race be run,
  And nearer he's to setting.

247. green-gown] tumble on the grass.

That age is best which is the first,
    When youth and blood are warmer;
But being spent, the worse, and worst
    Times still succeed the former.

Then be not coy, but use your time,
    And while ye may, go marry:
For having lost but once your prime,
    You may for ever tarry.

249. *To the Western Wind*

SWEET western wind, whose luck it is,
    Made rival with the air,
To give Perenna's lip a kiss,
    And fan her wanton hair:

Bring me but one, I'll promise thee,
    Instead of common showers,
Thy wings shall be embalm'd by me,
    And all beset with flowers.

250. *To Electra*

I DARE not ask a kiss,
    I dare not beg a smile,
Lest having that, or this,
    I might grow proud the while.

No, no, the utmost share
    Of my desire shall be
Only to kiss that air
    That lately kissèd thee.

251. *To Violets*

WELCOME, maids of honour!
  You do bring
  In the spring,
And wait upon her.

She has virgins many,
  Fresh and fair;
  Yet you are
More sweet than any.

You're the maiden posies,
  And so graced
  To be placed
'Fore damask roses.

Yet, though thus respected,
  By-and-by
  Ye do lie,
Poor girls, neglected.

252. *To Daffodils*

FAIR daffodils, we weep to see
  You haste away so soon;
As yet the early-rising sun
  Has not attain'd his noon.
    Stay, stay
  Until the hasting day
    Has run
  But to the evensong;
And, having pray'd together, we
  Will go with you along.

We have short time to stay, as you,
  We have as short a spring;
As quick a growth to meet decay,
  As you, or anything.
    We die
  As your hours do, and dry
    Away
Like to the summer's rain;
Or as the pearls of morning's dew,
  Ne'er to be found again.

253.   *To Blossoms*

FAIR pledges of a fruitful tree,
  Why do ye fall so fast?
  Your date is not so past
But you may stay yet here awhile
  To blush and gently smile,
    And go at last.

What! were ye born to be
  An hour or half's delight,
  And so to bid good night?
'Twas pity Nature brought you forth
  Merely to show your worth
    And lose you quite.

But you are lovely leaves, where we
  May read how soon things have
  Their end, though ne'er so brave:
And after they have shown their pride
  Like you awhile, they glide
    Into the grave.

ROBERT HERRICK

254. *The Primrose*

ASK me why I send you here
This sweet Infanta of the year?
Ask me why I send to you
This primrose, thus bepearl'd with dew?
I will whisper to your ears:—
The sweets of love are mix'd with tears.

Ask me why this flower does show
So yellow-green, and sickly too?
Ask me why the stalk is weak
And bending (yet it doth not break)?
I will answer:—These discover
What fainting hopes are in a lover.

255. *The Funeral Rites of the Rose*

THE Rose was sick and smiling died
And, being to be sanctified,
About the bed there sighing stood
The sweet and flowery sisterhood:
Some hung the head, while some did bring,
To wash her, water from the spring;
Some laid her forth, while others wept,
But all a solemn fast there kept:
The holy sisters, some among,
The sacred dirge and trental sung.
But ah! what sweets smelt everywhere,
As Heaven had spent all perfumes there.
At last, when prayers for the dead
And rites were all accomplishèd,
They, weeping, spread a lawny loom,
And closed her up as in a tomb.

255. trental] services for the dead, of thirty masses.

256. *Cherry-Ripe*

CHERRY-RIPE, ripe, ripe, I cry,
  Full and fair ones; come and buy.
If so be you ask me where
They do grow, I answer: There
Where my Julia's lips do smile;
There's the land, or cherry-isle,
Whose plantations fully show
All the year where cherries grow.

257. *A Meditation for his Mistress*

YOU are a tulip seen to-day,
  But, dearest, of so short a stay
That where you grew scarce man can say.

You are a lovely July-flower,
Yet one rude wind or ruffling shower
Will force you hence, and in an hour.

You are a sparkling rose i' th' bud,
Yet lost ere that chaste flesh and blood
Can show where you or grew or stood.

You are a full-spread, fair-set vine,
And can with tendrils love entwine,
Yet dried ere you distil your wine.

You are like balm enclosèd well
In amber or some crystal shell,
Yet lost ere you transfuse your smell.

ROBERT HERRICK

You are a dainty violet,
Yet wither'd ere you can be set
Within the virgin's coronet.

You are the queen all flowers among;
But die you must, fair maid, ere long,
As he, the maker of this song.

258. *Delight in Disorder*

A SWEET disorder in the dress
Kindles in clothes a wantonness:
A lawn about the shoulders thrown
Into a fine distraction:
An erring lace, which here and there
Enthrals the crimson stomacher:
A cuff neglectful, and thereby
Ribbands to flow confusedly:
A winning wave, deserving note,
In the tempestuous petticoat:
A careless shoe-string, in whose tie
I see a wild civility:
Do more bewitch me than when art
Is too precise in every part.

259. *Upon Julia's Clothes*

WHENAS in silks my Julia goes,
Then, then, methinks, how sweetly flows
The liquefaction of her clothes!

Next, when I cast mine eyes and see
That brave vibration each way free,
—O how that glittering taketh me!

260.   *The Bracelet: To Julia*

WHY I tie about thy wrist,
    Julia, this silken twist;
For what other reason is 't
But to show thee how, in part,
Thou my pretty captive art?
But thy bond-slave is my heart:
'Tis but silk that bindeth thee,
Knap the thread and thou art free;
But 'tis otherwise with me:
—I am bound and fast bound, so
That from thee I cannot go;
If I could, I would not so.

261.   *To Daisies, not to shut so soon*

SHUT not so soon; the dull-eyed night
    Has not as yet begun
To make a seizure on the light,
    Or to seal up the sun.

No marigolds yet closèd are,
    No shadows great appear;
Nor doth the early shepherd's star
    Shine like a spangle here.

Stay but till my Julia close
    Her life-begetting eye,
And let the whole world then dispose
    Itself to live or die.

262. *The Night-piece: To Julia*

HER eyes the glow-worm lend thee,
The shooting stars attend thee;
And the elves also,
Whose little eyes glow
Like the sparks of fire, befriend thee.

No Will-o'-the-wisp mislight thee,
Nor snake or slow-worm bite thee;
But on, on thy way
Not making a stay,
Since ghost there's none to affright thee.

Let not the dark thee cumber:
What though the moon does slumber?
The stars of the night
Will lend thee their light
Like tapers clear without number.

Then, Julia, let me woo thee,
Thus, thus to come unto me;
And when I shall meet
Thy silv'ry feet,
My soul I'll pour into thee.

263. *To Music, to becalm his Fever*

CHARM me asleep, and melt me so
With thy delicious numbers,
That, being ravish'd, hence I go
Away in easy slumbers.
Ease my sick head,
And make my bed,

ROBERT HERRICK

Thou power that canst sever
   From me this ill,
   And quickly still,
   Though thou not kill
     My fever.

Thou sweetly canst convert the same
   From a consuming fire
Into a gentle licking flame,
   And make it thus expire.
     Then make me weep
     My pains asleep;
   And give me such reposes
     That I, poor I,
     May think thereby
     I live and die
       'Mongst roses.

Fall on me like the silent dew,
   Or like those maiden showers
Which, by the peep of day, do strew
   A baptim o'er the flowers.
     Melt, melt my pains
     With thy soft strains;
   That, having ease me given,
     With full delight
     I leave this light,
     And take my flight
       For Heaven.

264.   *To Dianeme*

SWEET, be not proud of those two ey
    Which starlike sparkle in their skies;
Nor be you proud that you can see
All hearts your captives, yours yet free;
Be you not proud of that rich hair
Which wantons with the love-sick air;
Whenas that ruby which you wear,
Sunk from the tip of your soft ear,
Will last to be a precious stone
When all your world of beauty's gone.

265.   *To Œnone*

WHAT conscience, say, is it in thee
    When I a heart had one,
To take away that heart from me,
    And to retain thy own?

For shame or pity now incline
    To play a loving part;
Either to send me kindly thine,
    Or give me back my heart.

Covet not both; but if thou dost
    Resolve to part with neither,
Why, yet to show that thou art just,
    Take me and mine together!

ROBERT HERRICK

266. *To Anthea, who may command him Anything*

BID me to live, and I will live
    Thy Protestant to be;
Or bid me love, and I will give
    A loving heart to thee.

A heart as soft, a heart as kind,
    A heart as sound and free
As in the whole world thou canst find,
    That heart I'll give to thee.

Bid that heart stay, and it will stay
    To honour thy decree:
Or bid it languish quite away,
    And 't shall do so for thee.

Bid me to weep, and I will weep
    While I have eyes to see:
And, having none, yet will I keep
    A heart to weep for thee.

Bid me despair, and I'll despair
    Under that cypress-tree:
Or bid me die, and I will dare
    E'en death to die for thee.

Thou art my life, my love my heart,
    The very eyes of me:
And hast command of every part
    To live and die for thee.

267. *To the Willow-tree*

THOU art to all lost love the best,
  The only true plant found,
Wherewith young men and maids distre
  And left of love, are crown'd.

When once the lover's rose is dead,
  Or laid aside forlorn:
Then willow-garlands 'bout the head
  Bedew'd with tears are worn.

When with neglect, the lovers' bane,
  Poor maids rewarded be
For their love lost, their only gain
  Is but a wreath from thee.

And underneath thy cooling shade,
  When weary of the light,
The love-spent youth and love-sick maic
  Come to weep out the night.

268. *The Mad Maid's Song*

GOOD-MORROW to the day so fair,
  Good-morning, sir, to you;
Good-morrow to mine own torn hair
  Bedabbled with the dew.

Good-morning to this primrose too,
  Good-morrow to each maid
That will with flowers the tomb bestrew
  Wherein my love is laid.

Ah! woe is me, woe, woe is me!
   Alack and well-a-day!
For pity, sir, find out that bee
   Which bore my love away.

I'll seek him in your bonnet brave,
   I'll seek him in your eyes;
Nay, now I think they've made his grave
   I' th' bed of strawberries.

I'll seek him there; I know ere this
   The cold, cold earth doth shake him;
But I will go, or send a kiss
   By you, sir, to awake him.

Pray hurt him not; though he be dead,
   He knows well who do love him,
And who with green turfs rear his head,
   And who do rudely move him.

He's soft and tender (pray take heed);
   With bands of cowslips bind him,
And bring him home—but 'tis decreed
   That I shall never find him!

269. *Comfort to a Youth that had lost his Love*

WHAT needs complaints,
   When she a place
   Has with the race
     Of saints?

In endless mirth
   She thinks not on
   What's said or done
     In Earth.

ROBERT HERRICK

She sees no tears,
Or any tone
Of thy deep groan
She hears:

Nor does she mind
Or think on't now
That ever thou
Wast kind;

But changed above,
She likes not there,
As she did here,
Thy love.

Forbear therefore,
And lull asleep
Thy woes, and weep
No more.

270. *To Meadows*

YE have been fresh and green,
  Ye have been fill'd with flowers,
And ye the walks have been
  Where maids have spent their hours.

You have beheld how they
  With wicker arks did come
To kiss and bear away
  The richer cowslips home.

You've heard them sweetly sing,
  And seen them in a round:
Each virgin like a spring,
  With honeysuckles crown'd.

But now we see none here
  Whose silv'ry feet did tread
And with dishevell'd hair
  Adorn'd this smoother mead.

Like unthrifts, having spent
  Your stock and needy grown,
You're left here to lament
  Your poor estates, alone.

271.   *A Child's Grace*

HERE a little child I stand
  Heaving up my either hand;
Cold as paddocks though they be,
Here I lift them up to Thee,
For a benison to fall
On our meat and on us all. Amen.

272.   *Epitaph*
   upon a Child that died

HERE she lies, a pretty bud,
  Lately made of flesh and blood:
Who as soon fell fast asleep
As her little eyes did peep.
Give her strewings, but not stir
The earth that lightly covers her.

273.   *Another*

HERE a pretty baby lies
  Sung asleep with lullabies:
Pray be silent and not stir
Th' easy earth that covers her.

271. paddocks] frogs.

274.   *His Winding-sheet*

 COME thou, who art the wine and wit
  Of all I've writ:
The grace, the glory, and the best
  Piece of the rest.
Thou art of what I did intend
  The all and end;
And what was made, was made to meet
  Thee, thee, my sheet.
Come then and be to my chaste side
  Both bed and bride:
We two, as reliques left, will have
  One rest, one grave:
And hugging close, we will not fear
  Lust entering here:
Where all desires are dead and cold
  As is the mould;
And all affections are forgot,
  Or trouble not.
Here, here, the slaves and prisoners be
  From shackles free:
And weeping widows long oppress'd
  Do here find rest.
The wrongèd client ends his laws
  Here, and his cause.
Here those long suits of Chancery lie
  Quiet, or die:
And all Star-Chamber bills do cease
  Or hold their peace.
Here needs no Court for our Request
  Where all are best,
All wise, all equal, and all just
  Alike i' th' dust.

Nor need we here to fear the frown
    Of court or crown:
Where fortune bears no sway o'er things,
    There all are kings.
In this securer place we'll keep
    As lull'd asleep;
Or for a little time we'll lie
    As robes laid by;
To be another day re-worn,
    Turn'd, but not torn:
Or like old testaments engross'd,
    Lock'd up, not lost.
And for a while lie here conceal'd,
    To be reveal'd
Next at the great Platonick year,
    And then meet here.

275. *Litany to the Holy Spirit*

IN the hour of my distress,
  When temptations me oppress,
And when I my sins confess,
    Sweet Spirit, comfort me!

When I lie within my bed,
Sick in heart and sick in head,
And with doubts discomforted,
    Sweet Spirit, comfort me!

When the house doth sigh and weep,
And the world is drown'd in sleep,
Yet mine eyes the watch do keep,
    Sweet Spirit, comfort me!

274. Platonick year] the perfect or cyclic year, when the sun, moon, and five planets end their revolutions together and start anew. See *Timæus*, p. 39.

ROBERT HERRICK

When the passing bell doth toll,
And the Furies in a shoal
Come to fright a parting soul,
    Sweet Spirit, comfort me!

When the tapers now burn blue,
And the comforters are few,
And that number more than true,
    Sweet Spirit, comfort me!

When the priest his last hath pray'd
And I nod to what is said,
'Cause my speech is now decay'd,
    Sweet Spirit, comfort me!

When, God knows, I'm toss'd about
Either with despair or doubt;
Yet before the glass be out,
    Sweet Spirit, comfort me!

When the tempter me pursu'th
With the sins of all my youth,
And half damns me with untruth,
    Sweet Spirit, comfort me!

When the flames and hellish cries
Fright mine ears and fright mine eyes,
And all terrors me surprise,
    Sweet Spirit, comfort me!

When the Judgment is reveal'd,
And that open'd which was seal'd,
When to Thee I have appeal'd,
    Sweet Spirit, comfort me!

FRANCIS QUARLES
1592-1644

276. *A Divine Rapture*

E'EN like two little bank-dividing brooks,
   That wash the pebbles with their wanton streams,
And having ranged and search'd a thousand nooks,
   Meet both at length in silver-breasted Thames,
     Where in a greater current they conjoin:
So I my Best-belovèd's am; so He is mine.

E'en so we met; and after long pursuit,
   E'en so we joined; we both became entire;
No need for either to renew a suit,
   For I was flax, and He was flames of fire:
     Our firm-united souls did more than twine;
So I my Best-belovèd's am; so He is mine.

If all those glittering Monarchs, that command
   The servile quarters of this earthly ball,
Should tender in exchange their shares of land,
   I would not change my fortunes for them all:
     Their wealth is but a counter to my coin:
The world's but theirs; but my Belovèd's mine.

277. *Epigram*

Respice Finem

MY soul, sit thou a patient looker-on;
   Judge not the play before the play is done:
Her plot hath many changes; every day
Speaks a new scene; the last act crowns the play.

HENRY KING, BISHOP OF CHICHESTER
1592-1669

278. *A Contemplation upon Flowers*

BRAVE flowers—that I could gallant it like you,
    And be as little vain!
You come abroad, and make a harmless show,
    And to your beds of earth again.
You are not proud: you know your birth:
For your embroider'd garments are from earth.

You do obey your months and times, but I
    Would have it ever Spring:
My fate would know no Winter, never die,
    Nor think of such a thing.
O that I could my bed of earth but view
And smile, and look as cheerfully as you!

O teach me to see Death and not to fear,
    But rather to take truce!
How often have I seen you at a bier,
    And there look fresh and spruce!
You fragrant flowers! then teach me, that my breath
Like yours may sweeten and perfume my death.

279. *A Renunciation*

WE, that did nothing study but the way
    To love each other, with which thoughts the day
Rose with delight to us and with them set,
Must learn the hateful art, how to forget.
We, that did nothing wish that Heaven could give
Beyond ourselves, nor did desire to live

Beyond that wish, all these now cancel must,
As if not writ in faith, but words and dust.
Yet witness those clear vows which lovers make,
Witness the chaste desires that never brake
Into unruly heats; witness that breast
Which in thy bosom anchor'd his whole rest—
'Tis no default in us : I dare acquite
Thy maiden faith, thy purpose fair and white
As thy pure self. Cross planets did envỳ
Us to each other, and Heaven did untie
Faster than vows could bind. Oh, that the stars,
When lovers meet, should stand opposed in wars!

Since then some higher Destinies command,
Let us not strive, nor labour to withstand
What is past help. The longest date of grief
Can never yield a hope of our relief:
Fold back our arms; take home our fruitless loves,
That must new fortunes try, like turtle-doves
Dislodgèd from their haunts. We must in tears
Unwind a love knit up in many years.
In this last kiss I here surrender thee
Back to thyself.—So, thou again art free:
Thou in another, sad as that, resend
The truest heart that lover e'er did lend.
Now turn from each : so fare our sever'd hearts
As the divorced soul from her body parts.

280. *Exequy on his Wife*

ACCEPT, thou shrine of my dead saint,
Instead of dirges this complaint;
And for sweet flowers to crown thy herse
Receive a strew of weeping verse

From thy grieved friend, whom thou might'st see
Quite melted into tears for thee.
  Dear loss! since thy untimely fate,
My task hath been to meditate
On thee, on thee! Thou art the book,
The library whereon I look,
Tho' almost blind. For thee, loved clay,
I languish out, not live, the day. . . .
Thou hast benighted me; thy set
This eve of blackness did beget,
Who wast my day (tho' overcast
Before thou hadst thy noontide past):
And I remember must in tears
Thou scarce hadst seen so many years
As day tells hours. By thy clear sun
My love and fortune first did run;
But thou wilt never more appear
Folded within my hemisphere,
Since both thy light and motion,
Like a fled star, is fall'n and gone,
And 'twixt me and my soul's dear wish
The earth now interposèd is. . . .
  I could allow thee for a time
To darken me and my sad clime;
Were it a month, a year, or ten,
I would thy exile live till then,
And all that space my mirth adjourn—
So thou wouldst promise to return,
And putting off thy ashy shroud
At length disperse this sorrow's cloud.
  But woe is me! the longest date
Too narrow is to calculate
These empty hopes: never shall I

HENRY KING

Be so much blest as to descry
A glimpse of thee, till that day come
Which shall the earth to cinders doom,
And a fierce fever must calcine
The body of this world—like thine,
My little world! That fit of fire
Once off, our bodies shall aspire
To our souls' bliss: then we shall rise
And view ourselves with clearer eyes
In that calm region where no night
Can hide us from each other's sight.

    Meantime thou hast her, earth: much good
May my harm do thee! Since it stood
With Heaven's will I might not call
Her longer mine, I give thee all
My short-lived right and interest
In her whom living I loved best.
Be kind to her, and prithee look
Thou write into thy Doomsday book
Each parcel of this rarity
Which in thy casket shrined doth lie,
As thou wilt answer Him that lent—
Not gave—thee my dear monument.
So close the ground, and 'bout her shade
Black curtains draw: my bride is laid.

    Sleep on, my Love, in thy cold bed
Never to be disquieted!
My last good-night! Thou wilt not wake
Till I thy fate shall overtake:
Till age, or grief, or sickness must
Marry my body to that dust
It so much loves; and fill the room
My heart keeps empty in thy tomb.

HENRY KING

Stay for me there: I will not fail
To meet thee in that hollow vale.
And think not much of my delay:
I am already on the way,
And follow thee with all the speed
Desire can make, or sorrows breed.
Each minute is a short degree
And every hour a step towards thee. . . .
   'Tis true—with shame and grief I yield—
Thou, like the van, first took'st the field;
And gotten hast the victory
In thus adventuring to die
Before me, whose more years might crave
A just precedence in the grave.
But hark! my pulse, like a soft drum,
Beats my approach, tells thee I come;
And slow howe'er my marches be
I shall at last sit down by thee.
   The thought of this bids me go on
And wait my dissolution
With hope and comfort. Dear—forgive
The crime—I am content to live
Divided, with but half a heart,
Till we shall meet and never part.

GEORGE HERBERT
1593-1632

281.   *Virtue*

SWEET day, so cool, so calm, so bright!
   The bridal of the earth and sky—
The dew shall weep thy fall to-night;
     For thou must die.

GEORGE HERBERT

Sweet rose, whose hue angry and brave
Bids the rash gazer wipe his eye,
Thy root is ever in its grave,
    And thou must die.

Sweet spring, full of sweet days and roses,
A box where sweets compacted lie,
My music shows ye have your closes,
    And all must die.

Only a sweet and virtuous soul,
Like season'd timber, never gives;
But though the whole world turn to coal,
    Then chiefly lives.

282.   *Easter*

I GOT me flowers to straw Thy way,
  I got me boughs off many a tree;
But Thou wast up by break of day,
  And brought'st Thy sweets along with Thee.

Yet though my flowers be lost, they say
  A heart can never come too late;
Teach it to sing Thy praise this day,
  And then this day my life shall date.

283.   *Discipline*

THROW away Thy rod,
  Throw away Thy wrath;
    O my God,
  Take the gentle path!

GEORGE HERBERT

For my heart's desire
Unto Thine is bent:
  I aspire
To a full consent.

Not a word or look
I affect to own,
  But by book,
And Thy Book alone.

Though I fail, I weep;
Though I halt in pace,
  Yet I creep
To the throne of grace.

Then let wrath remove;
Love will do the deed;
  For with love
Stony hearts will bleed.

Love is swift of foot;
Love's a man of war,
  And can shoot,
And can hit from far.

Who can 'scape his bow?
That which wrought on Thee,
  Brought Thee low,
Needs must work on me.

Throw away Thy rod;
Though man frailties hath,
  Thou art God:
Throw away Thy wrath!

284. *A Dialogue*

Man. SWEETEST Saviour, if my soul
    Were but worth the having,
Quickly should I then control
    Any thought of waving.
But when all my care and pains
Cannot give the name of gains
To Thy wretch so full of stains,
What delight or hope remains?

Saviour. What, child, is the balance thine,
    Thine the poise and measure?
If I say, 'Thou shalt be Mine,'
    Finger not My treasure.
What the gains in having thee
Do amount to, only He
Who for man was sold can see;
That transferr'd th' accounts to Me.

Man. But as I can see no merit
    Leading to this favour,
So the way to fit me for it
    Is beyond my savour.
As the reason, then, is Thine,
So the way is none of mine;
I disclaim the whole design;
Sin disclaims and I resign.

Saviour. That is all: if that I could
    Get without repining;
And My clay, My creature, would
    Follow My resigning;

savour] savoir, knowing.

GEORGE HERBERT

    That as I did freely part
    With My glory and desert,
    Left all joys to feel all smart——

Man. Ah, no more! Thou break'st my heart!

285.   The Pulley

    WHEN God at first made Man,
      Having a glass of blessings standing by—
Let us (said He) pour on him all we can;
Let the world's riches, which dispersèd lie,
    Contract into a span.

    So strength first made a way,
Then beauty flow'd, then wisdom, honour, pleasure:
When almost all was out, God made a stay,
Perceiving that, alone of all His treasure,
    Rest in the bottom lay.

    For if I should (said He)
Bestow this jewel also on My creature,
He would adore My gifts instead of Me,
And rest in Nature, not the God of Nature:
    So both should losers be.

    Yet let him keep the rest,
But keep them with repining restlessness;
Let him be rich and weary, that at least,
If goodness lead him not, yet weariness
    May toss him to My breast.

GEORGE HERBERT

286. *Love*

LOVE bade me welcome; yet my soul drew back,
    Guilty of dust and sin.
But quick-eyed Love, observing me grow slack
    From my first entrance in,
Drew nearer to me, sweetly questioning
    If I lack'd anything.

'A guest,' I answer'd, 'worthy to be here:'
    Love said, 'You shall be he.'
'I, the unkind, ungrateful? Ah, my dear,
    I cannot look on Thee.'
Love took my hand and smiling did reply,
    'Who made the eyes but I?'

'Truth, Lord; but I have marr'd them: let my shame
    Go where it doth deserve.'
'And know you not,' says Love, 'Who bore the blame?'
    'My dear, then I will serve.'
'You must sit down,' says Love, 'and taste my meat.'
    So I did sit and eat.

JAMES SHIRLEY
1596-1666

287. *A Hymn*

O FLY, my Soul! What hangs upon
    Thy drooping wings,
    And weighs them down
With love of gaudy mortal things?

The Sun is now i' the east: each shade
    As he doth rise
    Is shorter made,
That earth may lessen to our eyes.

JAMES SHIRLEY

O be not careless then and play
    Until the Star of Peace
Hide all his beams in dark recess!
Poor pilgrims needs must lose their way
When all the shadows do increase.

288.   *Death the Leveller*

THE glories of our blood and state
    Are shadows, not substantial things;
There is no armour against Fate;
Death lays his icy hand on kings:
    Sceptre and Crown
    Must tumble down,
And in the dust be equal made
With the poor crookèd scythe and spade

Some men with swords may reap the fie
    And plant fresh laurels where they ki
But their strong nerves at last must yiel
They tame but one another still:
    Early or late
    They stoop to fate,
And must give up their murmuring breath
When they, pale captives, creep to death.

The garlands wither on your brow;
    Then boast no more your mighty deeds!
Upon Death's purple altar now
    See where the victor-victim bleeds.
    Your heads must come
    To the cold tomb:
Only the actions of the just
Smell sweet and blossom in their dust.

THOMAS CAREW

1595?-1639?

289.   Song

ASK me no more where Jove bestows,
   When June is past, the fading rose;
For in your beauty's orient deep
These flowers, as in their causes, sleep.

Ask me no more whither do stray
The golden atoms of the day;
For in pure love heaven did prepare
Those powders to enrich your hair.

Ask me no more whither doth haste
The nightingale when May is past;
For in your sweet dividing throat
She winters and keeps warm her note.

Ask me no more where those stars 'light
That downwards fall in dead of night;
For in your eyes they sit, and there
Fixèd become as in their sphere.

Ask me no more if east or west
The Phœnix builds her spicy nest;
For unto you at last she flies,
And in your fragrant bosom dies.

290.   *Persuasions to Joy: a Song*

IF the quick spirits in your eye
   Now languish and anon must die;
If every sweet and every grace
Must fly from that forsaken face;

Then, Celia, let us reap our joys
Ere Time such goodly fruit destroys.

Or if that golden fleece must grow
For ever free from agèd snow;
If those bright suns must know no shade,
Nor your fresh beauties ever fade;
   Then fear not, Celia, to bestow
   What, still being gather'd, still must grow.

Thus either Time his sickle brings
In vain, or else in vain his wings.

291. *To His Inconstant Mistress*

WHEN thou, poor Excommunicate
   From all the joys of Love, shalt see
The full reward and glorious fate
   Which my strong faith shall purchase me,
   Then curse thine own inconstancy!

A fairer hand than thine shall cure
   That heart which thy false oaths did wound;
And to my soul a soul more pure
   Than thine shall by Love's hand be bound,
   And both with equal glory crown'd.

Then shalt thou weep, entreat, complain
   To Love, as I did once to thee;
When all thy tears shall be as vain
   As mine were then: for thou shalt be
   Damn'd for thy false apostasy.

THOMAS CAREW

292. *The Unfading Beauty*

HE that loves a rosy cheek,
    Or a coral lip admires,
Or from star-like eyes doth seek
    Fuel to maintain his fires:
As old Time makes these decay,
So his flames must waste away.

But a smooth and steadfast mind,
    Gentle thoughts and calm desires,
Hearts with equal love combined,
    Kindle never-dying fires.
Where these are not, I despise
Lovely cheeks or lips or eyes.

293. *Ingrateful Beauty threatened*

KNOW, Celia, since thou art so proud,
    'Twas I that gave thee thy renown.
Thou hadst in the forgotten crowd
    Of common beauties lived unknown,
Had not my verse extoll'd thy name,
And with it imp'd the wings of Fame.

That killing power is none of thine;
    I gave it to thy voice and eyes;
Thy sweets, thy graces, all are mine;
    Thou art my star, shin'st in my skies;
Then dart not from thy borrow'd sphere
Lightning on him that fix'd thee there.

293. imp'd] grafted with new feathers.

Tempt me with such affrights no more,
    Lest what I made I uncreate;
Let fools thy mystic form adore,
    I know thee in thy mortal state.
Wise poets, that wrapt Truth in tales,
Knew her themselves through all her veils.

294. Epitaph
On the Lady Mary Villiers

THE Lady Mary Villiers lies
    Under this stone; with weeping eyes
The parents that first gave her birth,
And their sad friends, laid her in earth.
If any of them, Reader, were
Known unto thee, shed a tear;
Or if thyself possess a gem
As dear to thee, as this to them,
Though a stranger to this place,
Bewail in theirs thine own hard case:
    For thou perhaps at thy return
    May'st find thy Darling in an urn.

295. Another

THIS little vault, this narrow room,
    Of Love and Beauty is the tomb;
The dawning beam, that 'gan to clear
Our clouded sky, lies darken'd here,
For ever set to us: by Death
Sent to enflame the World Beneath.
    'Twas but a bud, yet did contain
More sweetness than shall spring again;

THOMAS CAREW

A budding Star, that might have grown
Into a Sun when it had blown.
This hopeful Beauty did create
New life in Love's declining state;
But now his empire ends, and we
From fire and wounding darts are free:
His brand, his bow, let no man fear:
The flames, the arrows, all lie here.

JASPER MAYNE
1604-1672

296.   *Time*

TIME is the feather'd thing,
    And, whilst I praise
The sparklings of thy looks and call them rays,
    Takes wing,
    Leaving behind him as he flies
An unperceivèd dimness in thine eyes.
    His minutes, whilst they're told,
        Do make us old;
    And every sand of his fleet glass,
    Increasing age as it doth pass,
    Insensibly sows wrinkles there
    Where flowers and roses do appear.
    Whilst we do speak, our fire
        Doth into ice expire,
        Flames turn to frost;
    And ere we can
    Know how our crow turns swan,
        Or how a silver snow
    Springs there where jet did grow,
Our fading spring is in dull winter lost.

JASPER MAYNE

    Since then the Night hath hurl'd
      Darkness, Love's shade,
  Over its enemy the Day, and made
        The world
  Just such a blind and shapeless thing,
As 'twas before light did from darkness
    Let us employ its treasure
    And make shade pleasure:
Let's number out the hours by blisses,
And count the minutes by our kisses;
    Let the heavens new motions feel
    And by our embraces wheel;
    And whilst we try the way
    By which Love doth convey
      Soul unto soul,
      And mingling so
    Makes them such raptures know
    As makes them entrancèd lie
      In mutual ecstasy,
Let the harmonious spheres in music ro

WILLIAM HABINGTON
1605-1654
297. *To Roses in the Bosom of Castara*

YE blushing virgins happy are
  In the chaste nunnery of her breasts—
For he'd profane so chaste a fair,
  Whoe'er should call them Cupid's nests.

Transplanted thus how bright ye grow!
  How rich a perfume do ye yield!
In some close garden cowslips so
  Are sweeter than i' th' open field.

In those white cloisters live secure
  From the rude blasts of wanton breath!—
Each hour more innocent and pure,
  Till you shall wither into death.

Then that which living gave you room,
  Your glorious sepulchre shall be. .
There wants no marble for a tomb
  Whose breast hath marble been to me.

298. *Nox Nocti Indicat Scientiam*

WHEN I survey the bright
    Celestial sphere;
So rich with jewels hung, that Night
  Doth like an Ethiop bride appear:

My soul her wings doth spread
    And heavenward flies,
Th' Almighty's mysteries to read
  In the large volumes of the skies.

For the bright firmament
    Shoots forth no flame
So silent, but is eloquent
  In speaking the Creator's name.

No unregarded star
    Contracts its light
Into so small a character,
  Removed far from our human sight,

But if we steadfast look
    We shall discern
In it, as in some holy book,
  How man may heavenly knowledge learn.

WILLIAM HABINGTON

It tells the conqueror
    That far-stretch'd power,
Which his proud dangers traffic for,
    Is but the triumph of an hour:

That from the farthest North,
    Some nation may,
Yet undiscover'd, issue forth,
    And o'er his new-got conquest sw

Some nation yet shut in
    With hills of ice
May be let out to scourge his sin,
    Till they shall equal him in vice.

And then they likewise shall
    Their ruin have;
For as yourselves your empires fall,
    And every kingdom hath a grave.

Thus those celestial fires,
    Though seeming mute,
The fallacy of our desires
    And all the pride of life confute:—

For they have watch'd since first
    The World had birth:
And found sin in itself accurst,
    And nothing permanent on Earth.

THOMAS RANDOLPH
1605–1635

299. *A Devout Lover*

I HAVE a mistress, for perfections rare
  In every eye, but in my thoughts most fair.
Like tapers on the altar shine her eyes;
Her breath is the perfume of sacrifice;
And wheresoe'er my fancy would begin,
Still her perfection lets religion in.
We sit and talk, and kiss away the hours
As chastely as the morning dews kiss flowers:
I touch her, like my beads, with devout care,
And come unto my courtship as my prayer.

300. *An Ode to Master Anthony Stafford*
to hasten Him into the Country

COME, spur away,
  I have no patience for a longer stay,
    But must go down
And leave the chargeable noise of this great town:
    I will the country see,
    Where old simplicity,
      Though hid in gray,
      Doth look more gay
Than foppery in plush and scarlet clad.
    Farewell, you city wits, that are
      Almost at civil war—
'Tis time that I grow wise, when all the world grows mad.

THOMAS RANDOLPH

      More of my days
I will not spend to gain an idiot's praise;
     Or to make sport
For some slight Puisne of the Inns of Court.
   Then, worthy Stafford, say,
    How shall we spend the day?
     With what delights
     Shorten the nights?
When from this tumult we are got secure,
  Where mirth with all her freedom goes,
    Yet shall no finger lose;
Where every word is thought, and every thought is pure?

     There from the tree
We'll cherries pluck, and pick the strawberry;
     And every day
Go see the wholesome country girls make hay,
   Whose brown hath lovelier grace
   Than any painted face
    That I do know
    Hyde Park can show:
Where I had rather gain a kiss than meet
  (Though some of them in greater state
    Might court my love with plate)
The beauties of the Cheap, and wives of Lombard Street.

    But think upon
Some other pleasures: these to me are none.
    Why do I prate
Of women, that are things against my fate!
   I never mean to wed
    That torture to my bed:
     My Muse is she
     My love shall be.

Let clowns get wealth and heirs: when I am gone
   And that great bugbear, grisly Death,
    Shall take this idle breath,
If I a poem leave, that poem is my son.
     Of this no more!
  We'll rather taste the bright Pomona's store.
    No fruit shall 'scape
Our palates, from the damson to the grape.
   Then, full, we'll seek a shade,
   And hear what music's made;
    How Philomel
    Her tale doth tell,
And how the other birds do fill the quire;
  The thrush and blackbird lend their throats,
   Warbling melodious notes;
We will all sports enjoy which others but desire.

    Ours is the sky,
Where at what fowl we please our hawk shall fly:
    Nor will we spare
To hunt the crafty fox or timorous hare;
   But let our hounds run loose
   In any ground they'll choose;
    The buck shall fall,
    The stag, and all.
Our pleasures must from their own warrants be,
   For to my Muse, if not to me,
    I'm sure all game is free:
Heaven, earth, are all but parts of her great royalty.

    And when we mean
To taste of Bacchus' blessings now and then,
    And drink by stealth
A cup or two to noble Barkley's health,

THOMAS RANDOLPH

I'll take my pipe and try
The Phrygian melody;
Which he that hears,
Lets through his ears
A madness to distemper all the brain:
Then I another pipe will take
And Doric music make,
To civilize with graver notes our wits again.

SIR WILLIAM DAVENANT
1606-1668

301. *Aubade*

THE lark now leaves his wat'ry nest,
And climbing shakes his dewy wings.
He takes this window for the East,
And to implore your light he sings—
Awake, awake! the morn will never rise
Till she can dress her beauty at your eyes.

The merchant bows unto the seaman's star,
The ploughman from the sun his season takes;
But still the lover wonders what they are
Who look for day before his mistress wakes.
Awake, awake! break thro' your veils of lawn!
Then draw your curtains, and begin the dawn!

302. *To a Mistress Dying*

Lover. YOUR beauty, ripe and calm and fresh
As eastern summers are,
Must now, forsaking time and flesh,
Add light to some small star.

Philosopher. Whilst she yet lives, were stars decay'd,
  Their light by hers relief might find;
  But Death will lead her to a shade
  Where Love is cold and Beauty blind.

Lover. Lovers, whose priests all poets are,
  Think every mistress, when she dies,
  Is changed at least into a star:
  And who dares doubt the poets wise?

Philosopher. But ask not bodies doom'd to die
  To what abode they go;
  Since Knowledge is but Sorrow's spy,
  It is not safe to know.

303. *Praise and Prayer*

PRAISE is devotion fit for mighty minds,
  The diff'ring world's agreeing sacrifice;
Where Heaven divided faiths united finds:
  But Prayer in various discord upward flies.

For Prayer the ocean is where diversely
  Men steer their course, each to a sev'ral coast;
Where all our interests so discordant be
  That half beg winds by which the rest are lost.

By Penitence when we ourselves forsake,
  'Tis but in wise design on piteous Heaven;
In Praise we nobly give what God may take,
  And are, without a beggar's blush, forgiven.

EDMUND WALLER

1606-1687

304. *On a Girdle*

THAT which her slender waist confined
Shall now my joyful temples bind;
No monarch but would give his crown
His arms might do what this has done.

It was my Heaven's extremest sphere,
The pale which held that lovely deer:
My joy, my grief, my hope, my love,
Did all within this circle move.

A narrow compass! and yet there
Dwelt all that's good, and all that's fair!
Give me but what this ribband bound,
Take all the rest the sun goes round!

305. *Go, lovely Rose*

GO, lovely Rose—
 Tell her that wastes her time and me
 That now she knows,
When I resemble her to thee,
How sweet and fair she seems to be.

 Tell her that's young,
And shuns to have her graces spied,
 That hadst thou sprung
In deserts where no men abide,
Thou must have uncommended died.

 Small is the worth
Of beauty from the light retired:
 Bid her come forth,
Suffer herself to be desired,
And not blush so to be admired.

EDMUND WALLER

    Then die—that she
The common fate of all things rare
    May read in thee;
How small a part of time they share
That are so wondrous sweet and fair!

306. *Old Age*

THE seas are quiet when the winds give o'er;
  So calm are we when passions are no more.
For then we know how vain it was to boast
Of fleeting things, so certain to be lost.
Clouds of affection from our younger eyes
Conceal that emptiness which age descries.

The soul's dark cottage, batter'd and decay'd,
Lets in new light through chinks that Time hath made:
Stronger by weakness, wiser men become
As they draw near to their eternal home.
Leaving the old, both worlds at once they view
That stand upon the threshold of the new.

JOHN MILTON
1608-1674

307. *Hymn on the Morning of Christ's Nativity*

IT was the Winter wilde,
  While the Heav'n-born-childe,
    All meanly wrapt in the rude manger lies;
Nature in aw to him
Had doff't her gawdy trim,
    With her great Master so to sympathize:
It was no season then for her
To wanton with the Sun her lusty Paramour.

JOHN MILTON

Only with speeches fair
She woo's the gentle Air
   To hide her guilty front with innocent Snow,
And on her naked shame,
Pollute with sinfull blame,
   The Saintly Vail of Maiden white to throw,
Confounded, that her Makers eyes
Should look so neer upon her foul deformities.

But he her fears to cease,
Sent down the meek-eyd Peace,
   She crown'd with Olive green, came softly sliding
Down through the turning sphear
His ready Harbinger,
   With Turtle wing the amorous clouds dividing,
And waving wide her mirtle wand,
She strikes a universall Peace through Sea and Land.

No War, or Battails sound
Was heard the World around,
   The idle spear and shield were high up hung;
The hookèd Chariot stood
Unstain'd with hostile blood,
   The Trumpet spake not to the armèd throng,
And Kings sate still with awfull eye,
As if they surely knew their sovran Lord was by.

But peacefull was the night
Wherin the Prince of light
   His raign of peace upon the earth began:
The Windes with wonder whist,
Smoothly the waters kist,
   Whispering new joyes to the milde Ocean,
Who now hath quite forgot to rave,
While Birds of Calm sit brooding on the charmèd wave.

312

JOHN MILTON

The Stars with deep amaze
Stand fixt in stedfast gaze,
  Bending one way their pretious influence,
And will not take their flight,
For all the morning light,
  Or Lucifer that often warn'd them thence ;
But in their glimmering Orbs did glow,
Untill their Lord himself bespake, and bid them go.

And though the shady gloom
Had given day her room,
  The Sun himself with-held his wonted speed,
And hid his head for shame,
As his inferiour flame,
  The new enlightn'd world no more should need ;
He saw a greater Sun appear
Then his bright Throne, or burning Axletree could bear.

The Shepherds on the Lawn,
Or ere the point of dawn,
  Sate simply chatting in a rustick row ;
Full little thought they than,
That the mighty Pan
  Was kindly com to live with them below ;
Perhaps their loves, or els their sheep,
Was all that did their silly thoughts so busie keep.

When such musick sweet
Their hearts and ears did greet,
  As never was by mortall finger strook,
Divinely-warbled voice
Answering the stringèd noise,
  As all their souls in blisfull rapture took
The Air such pleasure loth to lose,
With thousand echo's still prolongs each heav'nly close.

JOHN MILTON

Nature that heard such sound
Beneath the hollow round
  Of Cynthia's seat, the Airy region thrilling,
Now was almost won
To think her part was don,
  And that her raign had here its last fulfilling;
She knew such harmony alone
Could hold all Heav'n and Earth in happier union.

At last surrounds their sight
A Globe of circular light,
  That with long beams the shame-fac't night array'd,
The helmèd Cherubim
And sworded Seraphim,
  Are seen in glittering ranks with wings displaid,
Harping in loud and solemn quire,
With unexpressive notes to Heav'ns new-born Heir.

Such musick (as 'tis said)
Before was never made,
  But when of old the sons of morning sung,
While the Creator Great
His constellations set,
  And the well-ballanc't world on hinges hung,
And cast the dark foundations deep,
And bid the weltring waves their oozy channel keep.

Ring out ye Crystall sphears,
Once bless our human ears,
  (If ye have power to touch our senses so)
And let your silver chime
Move in melodious time;
  And let the Base of Heav'ns deep Organ blow
And with your ninefold harmony
Make up full consort to th'Angelike symphony.

JOHN MILTON

For if such holy Song
Enwrap our fancy long,
   Time will run back, and fetch the age of gold,
And speckl'd vanity
Will sicken soon and die,
   And leprous sin will melt from earthly mould,
And Hell it self will pass away,
And leave her dolorous mansions to the peering day.

Yea Truth, and Justice then
Will down return to men,
   Th'enameld Arras of the Rain-bow wearing,
And Mercy set between,
Thron'd in Celestiall sheen,
   With radiant feet the tissued clouds down stearing,
And Heav'n as at som festivall,
Will open wide the Gates of her high Palace Hall.

But wisest Fate sayes no,
This must not yet be so,
   The Babe lies yet in smiling Infancy,
That on the bitter cross
Must redeem our loss;
   So both himself and us to glorifie:
Yet first to those ychain'd in sleep,
The wakefull trump of doom must thunder through the deep,

With such a horrid clang
As on mount Sinai rang
   While the red fire, and smouldring clouds out brake:
The agèd Earth agast
With terrour of that blast,
   Shall from the surface to the center shake;
When at the worlds last session,
The dreadfull Judge in middle Air shall spread his throne.

JOHN MILTON

And then at last our bliss
Full and perfect is,
  But now begins; for from this happy day
Th'old Dragon under ground
In straiter limits bound,
  Not half so far casts his usurpèd sway,
And wrath to see his Kingdom fail,
Swindges the scaly Horrour of his foulded tail.

The Oracles are dumm,
No voice or hideous humm
  Runs through the archèd roof in words deceiving.
Apollo from his shrine
Can no more divine,
  With hollow shreik the steep of Delphos leaving.
No nightly trance, or breathèd spell,
Inspire's the pale-ey'd Priest from the prophetic cell.

The lonely mountains o're,
And the resounding shore,
  A voice of weeping heard, and loud lament;
From haunted spring, and dale
Edg'd with poplar pale,
  The parting Genius is with sighing sent,
With flowre-inwov'n tresses torn
The Nimphs in twilight shade of tangled thickets mourn.

In consecrated Earth,
And on the holy Hearth,
  The Lars, and Lemures moan with midnight plaint,
In Urns, and Altars round,
A drear, and dying sound
  Affrights the Flamins at their service quaint;
And the chill Marble seems to sweat,
While each peculiar power forgoes his wonted seat.

JOHN MILTON

Peor, and Baalim,
Forsake their Temples dim,
  With that twise-batter'd god of Palestine,
And moonèd Ashtaroth,
Heav'ns Queen and Mother both,
  Now sits not girt with Tapers holy shine,
The Libyc Hammon shrinks his horn,
In vain the Tyrian Maids their wounded Thamuz mourn.

And sullen Moloch fled,
Hath left in shadows dred,
  His burning Idol all of blackest hue,
In vain with Cymbals ring,
They call the grisly king,
  In dismall dance about the furnace blue;
The brutish gods of Nile as fast,
Isis and Orus, and the Dog Anubis hast.

Nor is Osiris seen
In Memphian Grove, or Green,
  Trampling the unshowr'd Grasse with lowings loud:
Nor can he be at rest
Within his sacred chest,
  Naught but profoundest Hell can be his shroud,
In vain with Timbrel'd Anthems dark
The sable-stolèd Sorcerers bear his worshipt Ark.

He feels from Juda's Land
The dredded Infants hand,
  The rayes of Bethlehem blind his dusky eyn;
Nor all the gods beside,
Longer dare abide,
  Not Typhon huge ending in snaky twine:
Our Babe to shew his Godhead true,
Can in his swadling bands controul the damnèd crew.

JOHN MILTON

So when the Sun in bed,
Curtain'd with cloudy red,
  Pillows his chin upon an Orient wave,
The flocking shadows pale,
Troop to th'infernall jail,
  Each fetter'd Ghost slips to his severall grave,
And the yellow-skirted Fayes,
Fly after the Night-steeds, leaving their Moon-lov'd maze.

But see the Virgin blest,
Hath laid her Babe to rest.
  Time is our tedious Song should here have ending,
Heav'ns youngest teemèd Star,
Hath fixt her polisht Car,
  Her sleeping Lord with Handmaid Lamp attending:
And all about the Courtly Stable,
Bright-harnest Angels sit in order serviceable.

308.   *On Time*

FLY envious Time, till thou run out thy race,
    Call on the lazy leaden-stepping hours,
Whose speed is but the heavy Plummets pace;
And glut thy self with what thy womb devours,
Which is no more then what is false and vain,
    And meerly mortal dross;
    So little is our loss,
    So little is thy gain.
For when as each thing bad thou hast entomb'd,
And last of all, thy greedy self consum'd,
Then long Eternity shall greet our bliss
With an individual kiss;
And Joy shall overtake us as a flood,
When every thing that is sincerely good

318

JOHN MILTON

And perfectly divine,
With Truth, and Peace, and Love shall ever shine
About the supreme Throne
Of him, t'whose happy-making sight alone,
When once our heav'nly-guided soul shall clime,
Then all this Earthy grosnes quit,
Attir'd with Stars, we shall for ever sit,
  Triumphing over Death, and Chance, and thee O Time.

309. *At a Solemn Musick*

BLEST pair of Sirens, pledges of Heav'ns joy,
  Sphear-born harmonious Sisters, Voice, and Vers,
Wed your divine sounds, and mixt power employ
Dead things with inbreath'd sense able to pierce,
And to our high-rais'd phantasie present,
That undisturbèd Song of pure content,
Ay sung before the saphire-colour'd throne
To him that sits theron
With Saintly shout, and solemn Jubily,
Where the bright Seraphim in burning row
Their loud up-lifted Angel trumpets blow,
And the Cherubick host in thousand quires
Touch their immortal Harps of golden wires,
With those just Spirits that wear victorious Palms,
Hymns devout and holy Psalms
Singing everlastingly;
That we on Earth with undiscording voice
May rightly answer that melodious noise;
As once we did, till disproportion'd sin
Jarr'd against natures chime, and with harsh din
Broke the fair musick that all creatures made
To their great Lord, whose love their motion sway'd

In perfect Diapason, whilst they stood
In first obedience, and their state of good.
O may we soon again renew that Song,
And keep in tune with Heav'n, till God ere long
To his celestial consort us unite,
To live with him, and sing in endles morn of light.

310. *L'Allegro*

HENCE loathèd Melancholy
   Of Cerberus and blackest midnight born,
In Stygian Cave forlorn
   'Mongst horrid shapes, and shreiks, and sights unholy.
Find out som uncouth cell,
   Where brooding darknes spreads his jealous wings,
And the night-Raven sings;
   There, under Ebon shades, and low-brow'd Rocks,
As ragged as thy Locks,
   In dark Cimmerian desert ever dwell.
But com thou Goddes fair and free,
In Heav'n ycleap'd Euphrosyne,
And by men, heart-easing Mirth,
Whom lovely Venus, at a birth
With two sister Graces more
To Ivy-crownèd Bacchus bore;
Or whether (as som Sager sing)
The frolick Wind that breathes the Spring,
Zephir with Aurora playing,
As he met her once a Maying,
There on Beds of Violets blew,
And fresh-blown Roses washt in dew,
Fill'd her with thee a daughter fair,
So bucksom, blith, and debonair.

JOHN MILTON

Haste thee nymph, and bring with thee
Jest and youthful Jollity,
Quips and Cranks, and wanton Wiles,
Nods, and Becks, and Wreathèd Smiles,
Such as hang on Hebe's cheek,
And love to live in dimple sleek;
Sport that wrincled Care derides,
And Laughter holding both his sides.
Com, and trip it as ye go
On the light fantastick toe,
And in thy right hand lead with thee,
The Mountain Nymph, sweet Liberty;
And if I give thee honour due,
Mirth, admit me of thy crue
To live with her, and live with thee,
In unprovèd pleasures free;
To hear the Lark begin his flight,
And singing startle the dull night,
From his watch-towre in the skies,
Till the dappled dawn doth rise;
Then to com in spight of sorrow,
And at my window bid good morrow,
Through the Sweet-Briar, or the Vine,
Or the twisted Eglantine.
While the Cock with lively din,
Scatters the rear of darknes thin,
And to the stack, or the Barn dore,
Stoutly struts his Dames before,
Oft list'ning how the Hounds and horn
Chearly rouse the slumbring morn,
From the side of som Hoar Hill,
Through the high wood echoing shrill.
Som time walking not unseen

JOHN MILTON

By Hedge-row Elms, on Hillocks green,
Right against the Eastern gate,
Wher the great Sun begins his state,
Rob'd in flames, and Amber light,
The clouds in thousand Liveries dight.
While the Plowman neer at hand,
Whistles ore the Furrow'd Land,
And the Milkmaid singeth blithe,
And the Mower whets his sithe,
And every Shepherd tells his tale
Under the Hawthorn in the dale.
Streit mine eye hath caught new pleasu
Whilst the Lantskip round it measures,
Russet Lawns, and Fallows Gray,
Where the nibling flocks do stray,
Mountains on whose barren brest
The labouring clouds do often rest:
Meadows trim with Daisies pide,
Shallow Brooks, and Rivers wide.
Towers, and Battlements it sees
Boosom'd high in tufted Trees,
Wher perhaps som beauty lies,
The Cynosure of neighbouring eyes.
Hard by, a Cottage chimney smokes,
From betwixt two agèd Okes,
Where Corydon and Thyrsis met,
Are at their savory dinner set
Of Hearbs, and other Country Messes,
Which the neat-handed Phillis dresses;
And then in haste her Bowre she leaves,
With Thestylis to bind the Sheaves;
Or if the earlier season lead
To the tann'd Haycock in the Mead,

JOHN MILTON

Som times with secure delight
The up-land Hamlets will invite,
When the merry Bells ring round,
And the jocond rebecks sound
To many a youth, and many a maid,
Dancing in the Chequer'd shade;
And young and old com forth to play
On a Sunshine Holyday,
Till the live-long day-light fail,
Then to the Spicy Nut-brown Ale.
With stories told of many a feat,
How Faery Mab the junkets eat,
She was pincht, and pull'd she sed,
And he by Friars Lanthorn led
Tells how the drudging Goblin swet,
To ern his Cream-bowle duly set,
When in one night, ere glimps of morn,
His shadowy Flale hath thresh'd the Corn
That ten day-labourers could not end,
Then lies him down the Lubbar Fend,
And stretch'd out all the Chimney's length,
Basks at the fire his hairy strength;
And Crop-full out of dores he flings,
Ere the first Cock his Mattin rings.
Thus don the Tales, to bed they creep,
By whispering Windes soon lull'd asleep.
 Towred Cities please us then,
And the busie humm of men,
Where throngs of Knights and Barons bold,
In weeds of Peace high triumphs hold,
With store of Ladies, whose bright eies
Rain influence, and judge the prise
Of Wit, or Arms, while both contend

JOHN MILTON

To win her Grace, whom all commend.
There let Hymen oft appear
In Saffron robe, with Taper clear,
And pomp, and feast, and revelry,
With mask, and antique Pageantry,
Such sights as youthfull Poets dream
On Summer eeves by haunted stream.
Then to the well-trod stage anon,
If Jonsons learnèd Sock be on,
Or sweetest Shakespear fancies childe,
Warble his native Wood-notes wilde,
And ever against eating Cares,
Lap me in soft Lydian Aires,
Married to immortal verse
Such as the meeting soul may pierce
In notes, with many a winding bout
Of linckèd sweetnes long drawn out,
With wanton heed, and giddy cunning,
The melting voice through mazes runni
Untwisting all the chains that ty
The hidden soul of harmony.
That Orpheus self may heave his head
From golden slumber on a bed
Of heapt Elysian flowres, and hear
Such streins as would have won the ear
Of Pluto, to have quite set free
His half regain'd Eurydice.
These delights, if thou canst give,
Mirth with thee, I mean to live.

JOHN MILTON

311.   *Il Penseroso*

HENCE vain deluding joyes,
 The brood of folly without father bred,
How little you bested,
 Or fill the fixèd mind with all your toyes;
Dwell in som idle brain,
 And fancies fond with gaudy shapes possess,
As thick and numberless
 As the gay motes that people the Sun Beams,
Or likest hovering dreams
 The fickle Pensioners of Morpheus train.
But hail thou Goddes, sage and holy,
Hail divinest Melancholy,
Whose Saintly visage is too bright
To hit the Sense of human sight;
And therfore to our weaker view,
Ore laid with black staid Wisdoms hue.
Black, but such as in esteem,
Prince Memnons sister might beseem,
Or that Starr'd Ethiope Queen that strove
To set her beauties praise above
The Sea Nymphs, and their powers offended.
Yet thou art higher far descended,
Thee bright-hair'd Vesta long of yore,
To solitary Saturn bore;
His daughter she (in Saturns raign,
Such mixture was not held a stain)
Oft in glimmering Bowres, and glades
He met her, and in secret shades
Of woody Ida's inmost grove,
Whilst yet there was no fear of Jove.
Com pensive Nun, devout and pure,

JOHN MILTON

Sober, stedfast, and demure,
All in a robe of darkest grain,
Flowing with majestick train,
And sable stole of Cipres Lawn,
Over thy decent shoulders drawn.
Com, but keep thy wonted state,
With eev'n step, and musing gate,
And looks commercing with the skies,
Thy rapt soul sitting in thine eyes:
There held in holy passion still,
Forget thy self to Marble, till
With a sad Leaden downward cast,
Thou fix them on the earth as fast.
And joyn with thee calm Peace, and Quiet,
Spare Fast, that oft with gods doth diet,
And hears the Muses in a ring,
Ay round about Joves Altar sing.
And adde to these retirèd Leasure,
That in trim Gardens takes his pleasure;
But first, and chiefest, with thee bring,
Him that yon soars on golden wing,
Guiding the fiery-wheelèd throne,
The Cherub Contemplation,
And the mute Silence hist along,
'Less Philomel will daign a Song,
In her sweetest, saddest plight,
Smoothing the rugged brow of night,
While Cynthia checks her Dragon yoke,
Gently o're th'accustom'd Oke;
Sweet Bird that shunn'st the noise of folly,
Most musicall, most melancholy!
Thee Chauntress oft the Woods among,
I woo to hear thy eeven-Song;

JOHN MILTON

And missing thee, I walk unseen
On the dry smooth-shaven Green,
To behold the wandring Moon,
Riding neer her highest noon,
Like one that had bin led astray
Through the Heav'ns wide pathles way;
And oft, as if her head she bow'd,
Stooping through a fleecy cloud.
Oft on a Plat of rising ground,
I hear the far-off Curfeu sound,
Over som wide-water'd shoar,
Swinging slow with sullen roar;
Or if the Ayr will not permit,
Som still removèd place will fit,
Where glowing Embers through the room
Teach light to counterfeit a gloom,
Far from all resort of mirth,
Save the Cricket on the hearth,
Or the Belmans drousie charm,
To bless the dores from nightly harm:
Or let my Lamp at midnight hour,
Be seen in som high lonely Towr,
Where I may oft out-watch the Bear,
With thrice great Hermes, or unsphear
The spirit of Plato to unfold
What Worlds, or what vast Regions hold
The immortal mind that hath forsook
Her mansion in this fleshly nook:
And of those Dæmons that are found
In fire, air, flood, or under ground,
Whose power hath a true consent
With Planet, or with Element.
Som time let Gorgeous Tragedy

JOHN MILTON

In Scepter'd Pall com sweeping by,
Presenting Thebs, or Pelops line,
Or the tale of Troy divine.
Or what (though rare) of later age,
Ennoblèd hath the Buskind stage.
 But, O sad Virgin, that thy power
Might raise Musæus from his bower
Or bid the soul of Orpheus sing
Such notes as warbled to the string,
Drew Iron tears down Pluto's cheek,
And made Hell grant what Love did seek.
Or call up him that left half told
The story of Cambuscan bold,
Of Camball, and of Algarsife,
And who had Canace to wife,
That own'd the vertuous Ring and Glass,
And of the wondrous Hors of Brass,
On which the Tartar King did ride;
And if ought els, great Bards beside,
In sage and solemn tunes have sung,
Of Turneys and of Trophies hung;
Of Forests, and inchantments drear,
Where more is meant then meets the ear.
Thus night oft see me in thy pale career,
Till civil-suited Morn appeer,
Not trickt and frounc't as she was wont,
With the Attick Boy to hunt,
But Chercheft in a comly Cloud,
While rocking Winds are Piping loud,
Or usher'd with a shower still,
When the gust hath blown his fill,
Ending on the russling Leaves,
With minute drops from off the Eaves.

JOHN MILTON

And when the Sun begins to fling
His flaring beams, me Goddes bring
To archèd walks of twilight groves,
And shadows brown that Sylvan loves,
Of Pine, or monumental Oake,
Where the rude Ax with heavèd stroke,
Was never heard the Nymphs to daunt,
Or fright them from their hallow'd haunt.
There in close covert by som Brook,
Where no profaner eye may look,
Hide me from Day's garish eie,
While the Bee with Honied thie,
That at her flowry work doth sing,
And the Waters murmuring
With such consort as they keep,
Entice the dewy-feather'd Sleep;
And let som strange mysterious dream,
Wave at his Wings in Airy stream,
Of lively portrature display'd,
Softly on my eye-lids laid.
And as I wake, sweet musick breath
Above, about, or underneath,
Sent by som spirit to mortals good,
Or th'unseen Genius of the Wood.
But let my due feet never fail,
To walk the studious Cloysters pale,
And love the high embowèd Roof,
With antick Pillars massy proof,
And storied Windows richly dight,
Casting a dimm religious light.
There let the pealing Organ blow,
To the full voic'd Quire below,
In Service high, and Anthems cleer,

As may with sweetnes, through mine ear,
Dissolve me into extasies,
And bring all Heav'n before mine eyes.
And may at last my weary age
Find out the peacefull hermitage,
The Hairy Gown and Mossy Cell,
Where I may sit and rightly spell
Of every Star that Heav'n doth shew,
And every Herb that sips the dew;
Till old experience do attain
To somthing like Prophetic strain.
These pleasures Melancholy give,
And I with thee will choose to live.

312. *From 'Arcades'*

O'RE the smooth enameld green
   Where no print of step hath been,
    Follow me as I sing,
    And touch the warbled string.
Under the shady roof
Of branching Elm Star-proof,
    Follow me,
I will bring you where she sits
Clad in splendor as befits
    Her deity.
Such a rural Queen
All Arcadia hath not seen.

From 'Comus'

313.
i

THE Star that bids the Shepherd fold,
  Now the top of Heav'n doth hold,

JOHN MILTON

And the gilded Car of Day,
His glowing Axle doth allay
In the steep Atlantick stream,
And the slope Sun his upward beam
Shoots against the dusky Pole,
Pacing toward the other gole
Of his Chamber in the East.
Mean while welcom Joy, and Feast,
Midnight shout, and revelry,
Tipsie dance, and Jollity.
Braid your Locks with rosie Twine
Dropping odours, dropping Wine.
Rigor now is gon to bed,
And Advice with scrupulous head,
Strict Age, and sowre Severity,
With their grave Saws in slumber ly.
We that are of purer fire
Imitate the Starry Quire,
Who in their nightly watchfull Sphears,
Lead in swift round the Months and Years.
The Sounds, and Seas with all their finny drove
Now to the Moon in wavering Morrice move,
And on the Tawny Sands and Shelves,
Trip the pert Fairies and the dapper Elves;
By dimpled Brook, and Fountain brim,
The Wood-Nymphs deckt with Daisies trim,
Their merry wakes and pastimes keep:
What hath night to do with sleep?
Night hath better sweets to prove,
Venus now wakes, and wak'ns Love. . . .
Com, knit hands, and beat the ground,
In a light fantastick round.

JOHN MILTON

314. ii
Echo

SWEET Echo, sweetest Nymph that liv'st unseen
    Within thy airy shell
  By slow Meander's margent green,
And in the violet imbroider'd vale
    Where the love-lorn Nightingale
Nightly to thee her sad Song mourneth well.
Canst thou not tell me of a gentle Pair
    That likest thy Narcissus are?
    O if thou have
    Hid them in som flowry Cave,
    Tell me but where
Sweet Queen of Parly, Daughter of the Sphear!
So maist thou be translated to the skies,
And give resounding grace to all Heav'ns Harmonies!

315. iii
Sabrina

The Spirit sings:

SABRINA fair
  Listen where thou art sitting
    Under the glassie, cool, translucent wave,
      In twisted braids of Lillies knitting
    The loose train of thy amber-dropping hair,
      Listen for dear honour's sake,
      Goddess of the silver lake,
          Listen and save!

  Listen and appear to us,
  In name of great Oceanus,
  By the earth-shaking Neptune's mace,
  And Tethys grave majestick pace,

JOHN MILTON

By hoary Nereus wrincled look,
And the Carpathian wisards hook,
By scaly Tritons winding shell,
And old sooth-saying Glaucus spell,
By Leucothea's lovely hands,
And her son that rules the strands,
By Thetis tinsel-slipper'd feet,
And the Songs of Sirens sweet,
By dead Parthenope's dear tomb,
And fair Ligea's golden comb,
Wherwith she sits on diamond rocks
Sleeking her soft alluring locks,
By all the Nymphs that nightly dance
Upon thy streams with wily glance,
Rise, rise, and heave thy rosie head
From thy coral-pav'n bed,
And bridle in thy headlong wave,
Till thou our summons answered have.
                    Listen and save!

Sabrina replies :
    By the rushy-fringèd bank,
Where grows the Willow and the Osier dank,
    My sliding Chariot stayes,
Thick set with Agat, and the azurn sheen
Of Turkis blew, and Emrauld green
    That in the channell strayes,
Whilst from off the waters fleet
Thus I set my printless feet
O're the Cowslips Velvet head,
    That bends not as I tread,
Gentle swain at thy request
    I am here.

316.   iv

The Spirit epiloguizes:

TO the Ocean now I fly,
And those happy climes that ly
Where day never shuts his eye,
Up in the broad fields of the sky:
There I suck the liquid ayr
All amidst the Gardens fair
Of Hesperus, and his daughters three
That sing about the golden tree:
Along the crispèd shades and bowres
Revels the spruce and jocond Spring,
The Graces, and the rosie-boosom'd Howres,
Thither all their bounties bring,
That there eternal Summer dwels,
And West winds, with musky wing
About the cedar'n alleys fling
Nard, and Cassia's balmy smels.
Iris there with humid bow,
Waters the odorous banks that blow
Flowers of more mingled hew
Than her purfl'd scarf can shew,
And drenches with Elysian dew
(List mortals, if your ears be true)
Beds of Hyacinth, and roses
Where young Adonis oft reposes,
Waxing well of his deep wound
In slumber soft, and on the ground
Sadly sits th' Assyrian Queen;
But far above in spangled sheen
Celestial Cupid her fam'd son advanc't,
Holds his dear Psyche sweet intranc't

JOHN MILTON

After her wandring labours long,
Till free consent the gods among
Make her his eternal Bride,
And from her fair unspotted side
Two blissful twins are to be born,
Youth and Joy; so Jove hath sworn.
  But now my task is smoothly don,
I can fly, or I can run
Quickly to the green earths end,
Where the bow'd welkin slow doth bend,
And from thence can soar as soon
To the corners of the Moon.
  Mortals that would follow me,
Love vertue, she alone is free.
She can teach ye how to clime
Higher then the Spheary chime;
Or if Vertue feeble were,
Heav'n it self would stoop to her.

317. *Lycidas*

A Lament for a friend drowned in his passage from Chester on the Irish Seas, 1637

YET once more, O ye Laurels, and once more
Ye Myrtles brown, with Ivy never-sear,
I com to pluck your Berries harsh and crude,
And with forc'd fingers rude,
Shatter your leaves before the mellowing year.
Bitter constraint, and sad occasion dear,
Compels me to disturb your season due:
For Lycidas is dead, dead ere his prime
Young Lycidas, and hath not left his peer:
Who would not sing for Lycidas? he knew

JOHN MILTON

Himself to sing, and build the lofty rhyme.
He must not flote upon his watry bear
Unwept, and welter to the parching wind,
Without the meed of som melodious tear.
  Begin, then, Sisters of the sacred well,
That from beneath the seat of Jove doth spring,
Begin, and somwhat loudly sweep the string.
Hence with denial vain, and coy excuse,
So may som gentle Muse
With lucky words favour my destin'd Urn,
And as he passes turn,
And bid fair peace be to my sable shrowd.
For we were nurst upon the self-same hill,
Fed the same flock, by fountain, shade, and rill.
  Together both, ere the high Lawns appear'd
Under the opening eye-lids of the morn,
We drove a field, and both together heard
What time the Gray-fly winds her sultry horn,
Batt'ning our flocks with the fresh dews of night,
Oft till the Star that rose, at Ev'ning, bright
Toward Heav'ns descent had slop'd his westering wheel.
Mean while the Rural ditties were not mute,
Temper'd to th'Oaten Flute;
Rough Satyrs danc'd, and Fauns with clov'n heel,
From the glad sound would not be absent long,
And old Damætas lov'd to hear our song
  But O the heavy change, now thou art gon,
Now thou art gon, and never must return!
Thee Shepherd, thee the Woods, and desert Caves,
With wilde Thyme and the gadding Vine o'regrown,
And all their echoes mourn.
The Willows, and the Hazle Copses green,
Shall now no more be seen,

Fanning their joyous Leaves to thy soft layes.
As killing as the Canker to the Rose,
Or Taint-worm to the weanling Herds that graze,
Or Frost to Flowers, that their gay wardrop wear,
When first the White thorn blows;
Such, Lycidas, thy loss to Shepherds ear.
 Where were ye Nymphs when the remorseless deep
Clos'd o're the head of your lov'd Lycidas?
For neither were ye playing on the steep,
Where your old Bards, the famous Druids ly,
Nor on the shaggy top of Mona high,
Nor yet where Deva spreads her wisard stream:
Ay me, I fondly dream!
Had ye bin there—for what could that have don?
What could the Muse her self that Orpheus bore,
The Muse her self, for her inchanting son
Whom Universal nature did lament,
When by the rout that made the hideous roar,
His goary visage down the stream was sent,
Down the swift Hebrus to the Lesbian shore.
 Alas! what boots it with uncessant care
To tend the homely slighted Shepherds trade,
And strictly meditate the thankles Muse,
Were it not better don as others use,
To sport with Amaryllis in the shade,
Or with the tangles of Neæra's hair?
Fame is the spur that the clear spirit doth raise
(That last infirmity of Noble mind)
To scorn delights, and live laborious dayes;
But the fair Guerdon when we hope to find,
And think to burst out into sudden blaze,
Comes the blind Fury with th'abhorrèd shears,
And slits the thin spun life. But not the praise,

JOHN MILTON

Phœbus repli'd, and touch'd my trembling ears;
Fame is no plant that grows on mortal soil,
Nor in the glistering foil
Set off to th'world, nor in broad rumour lies,
But lives and spreds aloft by those pure eyes,
And perfet witnes of all judging Jove;
As he pronounces lastly on each deed,
Of so much fame in Heav'n expect thy meed.
  O fountain Arethuse, and thou honour'd flo҅
Smooth-sliding Mincius, crown'd with vocall re
That strain I heard was of a higher mood:
But now my Oate proceeds,
And listens to the Herald of the Sea
That came in Neptune's plea,
He ask'd the Waves, and ask'd the Fellon w҅
What hard mishap hath doom'd this gentle sw
And question'd every gust of rugged wings
That blows from off each beakèd Promontory,
They knew not of his story,
And sage Hippotades their answer brings,
That not a blast was from his dungeon stray'd,
The Ayr was calm, and on the level brine,
Sleek Panope with all her sisters play'd.
It was that fatall and perfidious Bark
Built in th'eclipse, and rigg'd with curses dark,
That sunk so low that sacred head of thine.
  Next Camus, reverend Sire, went footing slow,
His Mantle hairy, and his Bonnet sedge,
Inwrought with figures dim, and on the edge
Like to that sanguine flower inscrib'd with woe.
Ah; Who hath reft (quoth he) my dearest pledge?
Last came, and last did go,
The Pilot of the Galilean lake,

JOHN MILTON

Two massy Keyes he bore of metals twain,
(The Golden opes, the Iron shuts amain)
He shook his Miter'd locks, and stern bespake,
How well could I have spar'd for thee, young swain,
Anow of such as for their bellies sake,
Creep and intrude, and climb into the fold?
Of other care they little reck'ning make,
Then how to scramble at the shearers feast,
And shove away the worthy bidden guest.
Blind mouthes! that scarce themselves know how to hold
A Sheep-hook, or have learn'd ought els the least
That to the faithfull Herdmans art belongs!
What recks it them? What need they? They are sped;
And when they list, their lean and flashy songs
Grate on their scrannel Pipes of wretched straw,
The hungry Sheep look up, and are not fed,
But swoln with wind, and the rank mist they draw,
Rot inwardly, and foul contagion spread:
Besides what the grim Woolf with privy paw
Daily devours apace, and nothing sed,
But that two-handed engine at the door,
Stands ready to smite once, and smite no more.
  Return Alpheus, the dread voice is past,
That shrunk thy streams; Return Sicilian Muse,
And call the Vales, and bid them hither cast
Their Bels, and Flourets of a thousand hues.
Ye valleys low where the milde whispers use,
Of shades and wanton winds, and gushing brooks,
On whose fresh lap the swart Star sparely looks,
Throw hither all your quaint enameld eyes,
That on the green terf suck the honied showres,
And purple all the ground with vernal flowres.
Bring the rathe Primrose that forsaken dies.

JOHN MILTON

The tufted Crow-toe, and pale Gessamine,
The white Pink, and the Pansie freakt with jeat,
The glowing Violet.
The Musk-rose, and the well attir'd Woodbine.
With Cowslips wan that hang the pensive hed,
And every flower that sad embroidery wears:
Bid Amaranthus all his beauty shed,
And Daffadillies fill their cups with tears,
To strew the Laureat Herse where Lycid lies.
For so to interpose a little ease,
Let our frail thoughts dally with false surmise.
Ay me! Whilst thee the shores, and sounding Seas
Wash far away, where ere thy bones are hurld,
Whether beyond the stormy Hebrides,
Where thou perhaps under the whelming tide
Visit'st the bottom of the monstrous world;
Or whether thou to our moist vows deny'd,
Sleep'st by the fable of Bellerus old,
Where the great vision of the guarded Mount
Looks toward Namancos and Bayona's hold;
Look homeward Angel now, and melt with ruth.
And, O ye Dolphins, waft the haples youth.

Weep no more, woful Shepherds weep no more,
For Lycidas your sorrow is not dead,
Sunk though he be beneath the watry floar,
So sinks the day-star in the Ocean bed,
And yet anon repairs his drooping head,
And tricks his beams, and with new spangled Ore,
Flames in the forehead of the morning sky:
So Lycidas sunk low, but mounted high,
Through the dear might of him that walk'd the waves
Where other groves, and other streams along,
With Nectar pure his oozy Lock's he laves,
And hears the unexpressive nuptiall Song,

In the blest Kingdoms meek of joy and love.
There entertain him all the Saints above,
In solemn troops, and sweet Societies
That sing, and singing in their glory move,
And wipe the tears for ever from his eyes.
Now Lycidas the Shepherds weep no more;
Hence forth thou art the Genius of the shore,
In thy large recompense, and shalt be good
To all that wander in that perilous flood.

 Thus sang the uncouth Swain to th'Okes and rills,
While the still morn went out with Sandals gray,
He touch'd the tender stops of various Quills,
With eager thought warbling his Dorick lay:
And now the Sun had stretch'd out all the hills,
And now was dropt into the Western bay;
At last he rose, and twitch'd his Mantle blew:
To morrow to fresh Woods, and Pastures new.

317.* *To the Lady Margaret Ley*

DAUGHTER to that good Earl, once President
 Of Englands Counsel, and her Treasury,
Who liv'd in both, unstain'd with gold or fee,
 And left them both, more in himself content,
Till the sad breaking of that Parlament
 Broke him, as that dishonest victory
 At Chæronèa, fatal to liberty
Kil'd with report that Old man eloquent,
Though later born, then to have known the dayes
 Wherin your Father flourisht, yet by you
 Madam, me thinks I see him living yet;
So well your words his noble vertues praise,
 That all both judge you to relate them true,
 And to possess them, Honour'd Margaret.

JOHN MILTON

318. *On His Blindness*

WHEN I consider how my light is spent,
  E're half my days, in this dark world and wide,
  And that one Talent which is death to hide,
  Lodg'd with me useless, though my Soul more bent
To serve therewith my Maker, and present
  My true account, least he returning chide,
  Doth God exact day-labour, light deny'd,
  I fondly ask; But patience to prevent
That murmur, soon replies, God doth not need
  Either man's work or his own gifts, who best
  Bear his milde yoak, they serve him best, his State
Is Kingly. Thousands at his bidding speed
  And post o're Land and Ocean without rest:
  They also serve who only stand and waite.

319. *To Mr. Lawrence*

LAWRENCE of vertuous Father vertuous Son,
  Now that the Fields are dank, and ways are mire,
  Where shall we sometimes meet, and by the fire
  Help wast a sullen day; what may be won
From the hard Season gaining: time will run
  On smoother, till Favonius re-inspire
  The frozen earth; and cloth in fresh attire
  The Lillie and Rose, that neither sow'd nor spun.
What neat repast shall feast us, light and choice,
  Of Attick tast, with Wine, whence we may rise
  To hear the Lute well toucht, or artfull voice
Warble immortal Notes and Tuskan Ayre?
  He who of those delights can judge, and spare
  To interpose them oft, is not unwise.

JOHN MILTON

320. *To Cyriack Skinner*

CYRIACK, whose Grandsire on the Royal Bench
   Of Brittish Themis, with no mean applause
   Pronounc't and in his volumes taught our Lawes,
   Which others at their Barr so often wrench:
To day deep thoughts resolve with me to drench
   In mirth, that after no repenting drawes;
   Let Euclid rest and Archimedes pause,
   And what the Swede intend, and what the French.
To measure life, learn thou betimes, and know
   Toward solid good what leads the nearest way;
   For other things mild Heav'n a time ordains,
And disapproves that care, though wise in show,
   That with superfluous burden loads the day,
   And when God sends a cheerful hour, refrains.

321. *On His Deceased Wife*

METHOUGHT I saw my late espousèd Saint
   Brought to me like Alcestis from the grave,
   Whom Joves great Son to her glad Husband gave,
   Rescu'd from death by force though pale and faint.
Mine as whom washt from spot of child-bed taint,
   Purification in the old Law did save,
   And such, as yet once more I trust to have
   Full sight of her in Heaven without restraint,
Came vested all in white, pure as her mind:
   Her face was vail'd, yet to my fancied sight,
   Love, sweetness, goodness, in her person shin'd
So clear, as in no face with more delight.
   But O as to embrace me she enclin'd
   I wak'd, she fled, and day brought back my night.

JOHN MILTON

322. *Light*

HAIL holy light, ofspring of Heav'n first-born,
   Or of th' Eternal Coeternal beam
May I express thee unblam'd? since God is light,
And never but in unapproachèd light
Dwelt from Eternitie, dwelt then in thee,
Bright effluence of bright essence increate.
Or hear'st thou rather pure Ethereal stream,
Whose Fountain who shall tell? before the Sun,
Before the Heavens thou wert, and at the voice
Of God, as with a Mantle didst invest
The rising world of waters dark and deep,
Won from the void and formless infinite.
Thee I re-visit now with bolder wing,
Escap't the Stygian Pool, though long detain'd
In that obscure sojourn, while in my flight
Through utter and through middle darkness borne
With other notes then to th' Orphean Lyre
I sung of Chaos and Eternal Night,
Taught by the heav'nly Muse to venture down
The dark descent, and up to reascend,
Though hard and rare: thee I revisit safe,
And feel thy sovran vital Lamp; but thou
Revisit'st not these eyes, that rowle in vain
To find thy piercing ray, and find no dawn;
So thick a drop serene hath quencht thir Orbs,
Or dim suffusion veild. Yet not the more
Cease I to wander where the Muses haunt
Cleer Spring, or shadie Grove, or Sunnie Hill,

JOHN MILTON

Smit with the love of sacred song; but chief
Thee *Sion* and the flowrie Brooks beneath
That wash thy hallowd feet, and warbling flow,
Nightly I visit: nor somtimes forget
Those other two equal'd with me in Fate,
So were I equal'd with them in renown,
Blind Thamyris and blind Mæonides,
And Tiresias and Phineus Prophets old.
Then feed on thoughts, that voluntarie move
Harmonious numbers; as the wakeful Bird
Sings darkling, and in shadiest Covert hid
Tunes her nocturnal Note. Thus with the Year
Seasons return, but not to me returns
Day, or the sweet approach of Ev'n or Morn,
Or sight of vernal bloom, or Summers Rose,
Or flocks, or herds, or human face divine;
But cloud in stead, and ever-during dark
Surrounds me, from the chearful waies of men
Cut off, and for the Book of knowledg fair
Presented with a Universal blanc
Of Natures works to mee expung'd and ras'd,
And wisdome at one entrance quite shut out.
So much the rather thou Celestial light
Shine inward, and the mind through all her powers
Irradiate, there plant eyes, all mist from thence
Purge and disperse, that I may see and tell
Of things invisible to mortal sight.

JOHN MILTON

From 'Samson Agonistes'

323.   *i*

OH how comely it is and how reviving
   To the Spirits of just men long opprest!
When God into the hands of thir deliverer
Puts invincible might
To quell the mighty of the Earth, th' oppressour,
The brute and boist'rous force of violent men
Hardy and industrious to support
Tyrannic power, but raging to pursue
The righteous and all such as honour Truth;
He all thir Ammunition
And feats of War defeats
With plain Heroic magnitude of mind
And celestial vigour arm'd,
Thir Armories and Magazins contemns,
Renders them useless, while
With wingèd expedition
Swift as the lightning glance he executes
His errand on the wicked, who surpris'd
Lose thir defence distracted and amaz'd.

324.   *ii*

ALL is best, though we oft doubt,
   What th' unsearchable dispose
Of highest wisdom brings about,
And ever best found in the close.
Oft he seems to hide his face,
But unexpectedly returns
And to his faithful Champion hath in place
Bore witness gloriously; whence Gaza mourns

JOHN MILTON

And all that band them to resist
His uncontroulable intent.
His servants he with new acquist
Of true experience from this great event
With peace and consolation hath dismist,
And calm of mind all passion spent.

SIR JOHN SUCKLING
1609–1642
325. *A Doubt of Martyrdom*

O FOR some honest lover's ghost,
  Some kind unbodied post
    Sent from the shades below!
    I strangely long to know
Whether the noble chaplets wear
Those that their mistress' scorn did bear
    Or those that were used kindly.

For whatsoe'er they tell us here
  To make those sufferings dear,
    'Twill there, I fear, be found
    That to the being crown'd
T' have loved alone will not suffice,
Unless we also have been wise
    And have our loves enjoy'd.

What posture can we think him in
  That, here unloved, again
    Departs, and 's thither gone
    Where each sits by his own?
Or how can that Elysium be
Where I my mistress still must see
    Circled in other's arms?

For there the judges all are just,
  And Sophonisba must
    Be his whom she held dear,
    Not his who loved her here.
The sweet Philoclea, since she died,
Lies by her Pirocles his side,
    Not by Amphialus.

Some bays, perchance, or myrtle bough
  For difference crowns the brow
    Of those kind souls that were
    The noble martyrs here :
And if that be the only odds
(As who can tell?), ye kinder gods,
    Give me the woman here!

326. *The Constant Lover*

OUT upon it, I have loved
    Three whole days together!
And am like to love three more,
    If it prove fair weather.

Time shall moult away his wings
    Ere he shall discover
In the whole wide world again
    Such a constant lover.

But the spite on 't is, no praise
    Is due at all to me:
Love with me had made no stays,
    Had it any been but she.

Had it any been but she,
    And that very face,
There had been at least ere this
    A dozen dozen in her place.

SIR JOHN SUCKLING

327. *Why so Pale and Wan?*

WHY so pale and wan, fond lover?
    Prithee, why so pale?
Will, when looking well can't move her,
    Looking ill prevail?
    Prithee, why so pale?

Why so dull and mute, young sinner?
    Prithee, why so mute?
Will, when speaking well can't win her,
    Saying nothing do 't?
    Prithee, why so mute?

Quit, quit for shame! This will not move;
    This cannot take her.
If of herself she will not love,
    Nothing can make her:
    The devil take her!

328. *When, Dearest, I but think of Thee*

WHEN, dearest, I but think of thee,
    Methinks all things that lovely be
Are present, and my soul delighted:
For beauties that from worth arise
Are like the grace of deities,
    Still present with us, tho' unsighted.

Thus while I sit and sigh the day
With all his borrow'd lights away,
    Till night's black wings do overtake me,
Thinking on thee, thy beauties then,
As sudden lights do sleepy men,
    So they by their bright rays awake me.

SIR JOHN SUCKLING

Thus absence dies, and dying proves
No absence can subsist with loves
   That do partake of fair perfection:
Since in the darkest night they may
By love's quick motion find a way
   To see each other by reflection.

The waving sea can with each flood
Bathe some high promont that hath stood
   Far from the main up in the river:
O think not then but love can do
As much! for that's an ocean too,
   Which flows not every day, but ever!

SIR RICHARD FANSHAWE
1608-1666

329.   *A Rose*

BLOWN in the morning, thou shalt fade ere noon.
   What boots a life which in such haste forsakes thee?
Thou'rt wondrous frolic, being to die so soon,
And passing proud a little colour makes thee.
If thee thy brittle beauty so deceives,
Know then the thing that swells thee is thy bane;
For the same beauty doth, in bloody leaves,
The sentence of thy early death contain.
Some clown's coarse lungs will poison thy sweet flower,
If by the careless plough thou shalt be torn;
And many Herods lie in wait each hour
To murder thee as soon as thou art born—
   Nay, force thy bud to blow—their tyrant breath
   Anticipating life, to hasten death!

WILLIAM CARTWRIGHT
1611-1643

330. *To Chloe*
Who for his sake wished herself younger

THERE are two births; the one when light
  First strikes the new awaken'd sense;
The other when two souls unite,
  And we must count our life from thence:
When you loved me and I loved you
Then both of us were born anew.

Love then to us new souls did give
  And in those souls did plant new powers;
Since when another life we live,
  The breath we breathe is his, not ours:
Love makes those young whom age doth chill,
And whom he finds young keeps young still.

331. *Falsehood*

STILL do the stars impart their light
  To those that travel in the night;
Still time runs on, nor doth the hand
Or shadow on the dial stand;
The streams still glide and constant are:
  Only thy mind
  Untrue I find,
  Which carelessly
  Neglects to be
Like stream or shadow, hand or star.

Fool that I am! I do recall
My words, and swear thou'rt like them all,

Thou seem'st like stars to nourish fire,
But O how cold is thy desire!
And like the hand upon the brass
    Thou point'st at me
    In mockery;
    If I come nigh
    Shade-like thou'lt fly,
And as the stream with murmur pass.

332. *On the Queen's Return from the Low Countries*

HALLOW the threshold, crown the posts anew!
    The day shall have its due.
Twist all our victories into one bright wreath,
    On which let honour breathe;
Then throw it round the temples of our Queen!
'Tis she that must preserve those glories green.

When greater tempests than on sea before
    Received her on the shore;
When she was shot at 'for the King's own good'
    By legions hired to blood;
How bravely did she do, how bravely bear!
And show'd, though they durst rage, she durst not fear.

Courage was cast about her like a dress
    Of solemn comeliness:
A gather'd mind and an untroubled face
    Did give her dangers grace:
Thus, arm'd with innocence, secure they move
Whose highest 'treason' is but highest love.

WILLIAM CARTWRIGHT

333. *On a Virtuous Young Gentlewoman that died suddenly*

SHE who to Heaven more Heaven doth annex,
　Whose lowest thought was above all our sex,
Accounted nothing death but t' be repriev'd,
And died as free from sickness as she lived.
Others are dragg'd away, or must be driven,
She only saw her time and stept to Heaven;
Where seraphims view all her glories o'er,
As one return'd that had been there before.
For while she did this lower world adorn,
Her body seem'd rather assumed than born;
So rarified, advanced, so pure and whole,
That body might have been another's soul;
And equally a miracle it were
That she could die, or that she could live here.

JAMES GRAHAM, MARQUIS OF MONTROSE
1612-1650

334. *I'll never love Thee more*

MY dear and only Love, I pray
　That little world of thee
Be govern'd by no other sway
　Than purest monarchy;
For if confusion have a part
　(Which virtuous souls abhor),
And hold a synod in thine heart,
　I'll never love thee more.

Like Alexander I will reign,
　And I will reign alone;
My thoughts did evermore disdain
　A rival on my throne.

MARQUIS OF MONTROSE

He either fears his fate too much,
    Or his deserts are small,
That dares not put it to the touch,
    To gain or lose it all.

And in the empire of thine heart,
    Where I should solely be,
If others do pretend a part
    Or dare to vie with me,
Or if *Committees* thou erect,
    And go on such a score,
I'll laugh and sing at thy neglect,
    And never love thee more.

But if thou wilt prove faithful then,
    And constant of thy word,
I'll make thee glorious by my pen
    And famous by my sword;
I'll serve thee in such noble ways
    Was never heard before;
I'll crown and deck thee all with bay
    And love thee more and more.

THOMAS JORDAN
1612?-1685

335. *Coronemus nos Rosis antequam marcescant*

LET us drink and be merry, dance, joke, and rejoice,
    With claret and sherry, theorbo and voice!
The changeable world to our joy is unjust,
    All treasure's uncertain,
    Then down with your dust!
In frolics dispose your pounds, shillings, and pence,
For we shall be nothing a hundred years hence.

THOMAS JORDAN

We'll sport and be free with Moll, Betty, and Dolly,
Have oysters and lobsters to cure melancholy:
Fish-dinners will make a man spring like a flea,
    Dame Venus, love's lady,
    Was born of the sea;
With her and with Bacchus we'll tickle the sense,
For we shall be past it a hundred years hence.

Your most beautiful bride who with garlands is crown'd
And kills with each glance as she treads on the ground,
Whose lightness and brightness doth shine in such splendour
    That none but the stars
    Are thought fit to attend her,
Though now she be pleasant and sweet to the sense,
Will be damnable mouldy a hundred years hence.

Then why should we turmoil in cares and in fears,
Turn all our tranquill'ty to sighs and to tears?
Let's eat, drink, and play till the worms do corrupt us,
    'Tis certain, *Post mortem*
    Nulla voluptas.
For health, wealth and beauty, wit, learning and sense,
Must all come to nothing a hundred years hence.

RICHARD CRASHAW
1613?-1649

336. *Wishes to His Supposed Mistress*

WHOE'ER she be—
    That not impossible She
That shall command my heart and me:

Where'er she lie,
Lock'd up from mortal eye
In shady leaves of destiny:

RICHARD CRASHAW

Till that ripe birth
Of studied Fate stand forth,
And teach her fair steps to our earth:

Till that divine
Idea take a shrine
Of crystal flesh, through which to shi

Meet you her, my Wishes,
Bespeak her to my blisses,
And be ye call'd my absent kisses.

I wish her Beauty,
That owes not all its duty
To gaudy tire, or glist'ring shoe-tie:

Something more than
Taffata or tissue can,
Or rampant feather, or rich fan.

A Face, that's best
By its own beauty drest,
And can alone commend the rest.

A Face, made up
Out of no other shop
Than what Nature's white hand sets ope.

A Cheek, where youth
And blood, with pen of truth,
Write what the reader sweetly ru'th.

A Cheek, where grows
More than a morning rose,
Which to no box his being owes.

RICHARD CRASHAW

Lips, where all day
A lover's kiss may play,
Yet carry nothing thence away.

Looks, that oppress
Their richest tires, but dress
And clothe their simplest nakedness.

Eyes, that displace
The neighbour diamond, and outface
That sunshine by their own sweet grace.

Tresses, that wear
Jewels but to declare
How much themselves more precious are:

Whose native ray
Can tame the wanton day
Of gems that in their bright shades play.

Each ruby there,
Or pearl that dare appear,
Be its own blush, be its own tear.

A well-tamed Heart,
For whose more noble smart
Love may be long choosing a dart.

Eyes, that bestow
Full quivers on love's bow,
Yet pay less arrows than they owe.

Smiles, that can warm
The blood, yet teach a charm,
That chastity shall take no harm.

RICHARD CRASHAW

Blushes, that bin
The burnish of no sin,
Nor flames of aught too hot within.

Joys, that confess
Virtue their mistress,
And have no other head to dress.

Fears, fond and slight
As the coy bride's, when night
First does the longing lover right.

Days, that need borrow
No part of their good-morrow
From a fore-spent night of sorrow.

Days, that in spite
Of darkness, by the light
Of a clear mind, are day all night.

Nights, sweet as they,
Made short by lovers' play,
Yet long by th' absence of the day.

Life, that dares send
A challenge to his end,
And when it comes, say, 'Welcome, friend!'

Sydneian showers
Of sweet discourse, whose powers
Can crown old Winter's head with flowers.

Soft silken hours,
Open suns, shady bowers;
'Bove all, nothing within that lowers.

RICHARD CRASHAW

Whate'er delight
Can make Day's forehead bright,
Or give down to the wings of Night.

I wish her store
Of worth may leave her poor
Of wishes; and I wish—no more.

Now, if Time knows
That Her, whose radiant brows
Weave them a garland of my vows;

Her, whose just bays
My future hopes can raise,
A trophy to her present praise;

Her, that dares be
What these lines wish to see;
I seek no further, it is She.

'Tis She, and here,
Lo! I unclothe and clear
My Wishes' cloudy character.

May she enjoy it
Whose merit dare apply it,
But modesty dares still deny it!

Such worth as this is
Shall fix my flying Wishes,
And determine them to kisses.

Let her full glory,
My fancies, fly before ye;
Be ye my fictions—but her story.

RICHARD CRASHAW

337.   *The Weeper*

HAIL, sister springs,
    Parents of silver-footed rills!
Ever bubbling things,
Thawing crystal, snowy hills!
    Still spending, never spent; I mean
    Thy fair eyes, sweet Magdalene.

Heavens thy fair eyes be;
Heavens of ever-falling stars;
'Tis seed-time still with thee,
And stars thou sow'st whose harvest dares
    Promise the earth to countershine
    Whatever makes Heaven's forehead fine.

Every morn from hence
A brisk cherub something sips
Whose soft influence
Adds sweetness to his sweetest lips;
    Then to his music: and his song
    Tastes of this breakfast all day long.

When some new bright guest
Takes up among the stars a room,
And Heaven will make a feast,
Angels with their bottles come,
    And draw from these full eyes of thine
    Their Master's water, their own wine.

The dew no more will weep
The primrose's pale cheek to deck;
The dew no more will sleep
Nuzzled in the lily's neck:
    Much rather would it tremble here,
    And leave them both to be thy tear.

RICHARD CRASHAW

When sorrow would be seen
In her brightest majesty,
—For she is a Queen—
Then is she drest by none but thee:
   Then and only then she wears
   Her richest pearls—I mean thy tears.

Not in the evening's eyes,
When they red with weeping are
For the Sun that dies,
Sits Sorrow with a face so fair.
   Nowhere but here did ever meet
   Sweetness so sad, sadness so sweet.

Does the night arise?
Still thy tears do fall and fall.
Does night lose her eyes?
Still the fountain weeps for all.
   Let day and night do what they will,
   Thou hast thy task, thou weepest still.

Not *So long she lived*
Will thy tomb report of thee;
But *So long she grieved*:
Thus must we date thy memory.
   Others by days, by months, by years,
   Measure their ages, thou by tears.

Say, ye bright brothers,
The fugitive sons of those fair eyes
Your fruitful mothers,
What make you here? What hopes can 'tice
   You to be born? What cause can borrow
   You from those nests of noble sorrow?

RICHARD CRASHAW

    Whither away so fast
For sure the sordid earth
    Your sweetness cannot taste,
Nor does the dust deserve your birth.
       Sweet, whither haste you then? O say,
    Why you trip so fast away?

We go not to seek
The darlings of Aurora's bed,
*   The rose's modest cheek,*
Nor the violet's humble head.
*   No such thing: we go to meet*
*   A worthier object—our Lord's feet.*

338. *A Hymn to the Name and Honour of the Admirable Saint Teresa*

LOVE, thou art absolute, sole Lord
    Of life and death. To prove the word,
We'll now appeal to none of all
Those thy old soldiers, great and tall,
Ripe men of martyrdom, that could reach down
With strong arms their triumphant crown:
Such as could with lusty breath
Speak loud, unto the face of death,
Their great Lord's glorious name; to none
Of those whose spacious bosoms spread a throne
For love at large to fill. Spare blood and sweat:
We'll see Him take a private seat,
And make His mansion in the mild
And milky soul of a soft child.

RICHARD CRASHAW

Scarce has she learnt to lisp a name
Of martyr, yet she thinks it shame
Life should so long play with that breath
Which spent can buy so brave a death.
She never undertook to know
What death with love should have to do.
Nor has she e'er yet understood
Why, to show love, she should shed blood;
Yet, though she cannot tell you why,
She can love, and she can die.
Scarce has she blood enough to make
A guilty sword-blush for her sake;
Yet has a heart dares hope to prove
How much less strong is death than love. . . .

Since 'tis not to be had at home,
She'll travel for a martyrdom.
No home for her, confesses she,
But where she may a martyr be.
She'll to the Moors, and trade with them
For this unvalued diadem;
She offers them her dearest breath,
With Christ's name in 't, in change for death:
She'll bargain with them, and will give
Them God, and teach them how to live
In Him; or, if they this deny,
For Him she'll teach them how to die.
So shall she leave amongst them sown
Her Lord's blood, or at least her own.

Farewell then, all the world, adieu!
Teresa is no more for you.
Farewell all pleasures, sports, and joys,
Never till now esteemèd toys!

RICHARD CRASHAW

Farewell whatever dear may be—
Mother's arms, or father's knee!
Farewell house, and farewell home!
She 's for the Moors and Martyrdom.

Sweet, not so fast; lo! thy fair spouse,
Whom thou seek'st with so swift vows,
Calls thee back, and bids thee come
T' embrace a milder martyrdom. . . .
O how oft shalt thou complain
Of a sweet and subtle pain!
Of intolerable joys!
Of a death, in which who dies
Loves his death, and dies again,
And would for ever so be slain;
And lives and dies, and knows not why
To live, but that he still may die!
How kindly will thy gentle heart
Kiss the sweetly-killing dart!
And close in his embraces keep
Those delicious wounds, that weep
Balsam, to heal themselves with thus,
When these thy deaths, so numerous,
Shall all at once die into one,
And melt thy soul's sweet mansion;
Like a soft lump of incense, hasted
By too hot a fire, and wasted
Into perfuming clouds, so fast
Shalt thou exhale to heaven at last
In a resolving sigh, and then,—
O what? Ask not the tongues of men.

Angels cannot tell; suffice,
Thyself shalt feel thine own full joys,

RICHARD CRASHAW

And hold them fast for ever there.
So soon as thou shalt first appear,
The moon of maiden stars, thy white
Mistress, attended by such bright
Souls as thy shining self, shall come,
And in her first ranks make thee room;
Where, 'mongst her snowy family,
Immortal welcomes wait for thee.
O what delight, when she shall stand
And teach thy lips heaven, with her hand,
On which thou now may'st to thy wishes
Heap up thy consecrated kisses!
What joy shall seize thy soul, when she,
Bending her blessèd eyes on thee,
Those second smiles of heaven, shall dart
Her mild rays through thy melting heart!

Angels, thy old friends, there shall greet thee,
Glad at their own home now to meet thee.
All thy good works which went before,
And waited for thee at the door,
Shall own thee there; and all in one
Weave a constellation
Of crowns, with which the King, thy spouse,
Shall build up thy triumphant brows.
All thy old woes shall now smile on thee,
And thy pains sit bright upon thee:
All thy sorrows here shall shine,
And thy sufferings be divine.
Tears shall take comfort, and turn gems,
And wrongs repent to diadems.
Even thy deaths shall live, and new
Dress the soul which late they slew.

RICHARD CRASHAW

Thy wounds shall blush to such bright scars
As keep account of the Lamb's wars.

Those rare works, where thou shalt leave writ
Love's noble history, with wit
Taught thee by none but Him, while here
They feed our souls, shall clothe thine there.
Each heavenly word by whose hid flame
Our hard hearts shall strike fire, the same
Shall flourish on thy brows, and be
Both fire to us and flame to thee;
Whose light shall live bright in thy face
By glory, in our hearts by grace.
Thou shalt look round about, and see
Thousands of crown'd souls throng to be
Themselves thy crown, sons of thy vows,
The virgin-births with which thy spouse
Made fruitful thy fair soul; go now,
And with them all about thee bow
To Him; put on, He'll say, put on,
My rosy Love, that thy rich zone,
Sparkling with the sacred flames
Of thousand souls, whose happy names
Heaven keeps upon thy score : thy bright
Life brought them first to kiss the light
That kindled them to stars; and so
Thou with the Lamb, thy Lord, shalt go.
And, wheresoe'er He sets His white
Steps, walk with Him those ways of light,
Which who in death would live to see,
Must learn in life to die like thee.

RICHARD CRASHAW

339. *Upon the Book and Picture of the Seraphical Saint Teresa*

O THOU undaunted daughter of desires!
   By all thy dower of lights and fires;
By all the eagle in thee, all the dove;
By all thy lives and deaths of love;
By thy large draughts of intellectual day,
And by thy thirsts of love more large than they;
By all thy brim-fill'd bowls of fierce desire,
By thy last morning's draught of liquid fire;
By the full kingdom of that final kiss
That seized thy parting soul, and seal'd thee His;
By all the Heav'n thou hast in Him
(Fair sister of the seraphim!);
By all of Him we have in thee;
Leave nothing of myself in me.
Let me so read thy life, that I
Unto all life of mine may die!

340. *Verses from the Shepherds' Hymn*

WE saw Thee in Thy balmy nest,
   Young dawn of our eternal day;
We saw Thine eyes break from the East,
   And chase the trembling shades away:
We saw Thee, and we blest the sight,
We saw Thee by Thine own sweet light.

Poor world, said I, what wilt thou do
   To entertain this starry stranger?
Is this the best thou canst bestow—
   A cold and not too cleanly manger?

RICHARD CRASHAW

Contend, the powers of heaven and earth,
To fit a bed for this huge birth.

Proud world, said I, cease your contest.
   And let the mighty babe alone ;
The phœnix builds the phœnix' nest,
   Love's architecture is His own.
The babe, whose birth embraves this n
Made His own bed ere He was born.

I saw the curl'd drops, soft and slow,
   Come hovering o'er the place's head,
Off'ring their whitest sheets of snow,
   To furnish the fair infant's bed.
Forbear, said I, be not too bold ;
Your fleece is white, but 'tis too cold.

I saw th' obsequious seraphim
   Their rosy fleece of fire bestow,
For well they now can spare their wir.
   Since Heaven itself lies here below.
Well done, said I ; but are you sure
Your down, so warm, will pass for pure?

No, no, your King's not yet to seek
   Where to repose His royal head ;
See, see how soon His new-bloom'd cheek
   'Twixt mother's breasts is gone to bed!
Sweet choice, said we ; no way but so,
Not to lie cold, yet sleep in snow!

She sings Thy tears asleep, and dips
   Her kisses in Thy weeping eye ;
She spreads the red leaves of Thy lips,
   That in their buds yet blushing lie.

She 'gainst those mother diamonds tries
The points of her young eagle's eyes.

Welcome—tho' not to those gay flies,
   Gilded i' th' beams of earthly kings,
Slippery souls in smiling eyes—
   But to poor shepherds, homespun things,
Whose wealth 's their flocks, whose wit 's
Well read in their simplicity.

Yet, when young April's husband show'rs
   Shall bless the fruitful Maia's bed,
We'll bring the first-born of her flowers,
   To kiss Thy feet and crown Thy head.
To Thee, dread Lamb! whose love must
The shepherds while they feed their sheep.

To Thee, meek Majesty, soft King
   Of simple graces and sweet loves!
Each of us his lamb will bring,
   Each his pair of silver doves!
At last, in fire of Thy fair eyes,
Ourselves become our own best sacrifice!

341. *Christ Crucified*

THY restless feet now cannot go
   For us and our eternal good,
As they were ever wont. What though
   They swim, alas! in their own flood?

Thy hands to give Thou canst not lift,
   Yet will Thy hand still giving be;
It gives, but O, itself's the gift!
   It gives tho' bound, tho' bound 'tis free!

RICHARD CRASHAW

342. *An Epitaph upon Husband and Wife*
Who died and were buried together.

TO these whom death again did wed
 This grave's the second marriage-bed.
For though the hand of Fate could force
'Twixt soul and body a divorce,
It could not sever man and wife,
Because they both lived but one life.
Peace, good reader, do not weep;
Peace, the lovers are asleep.
They, sweet turtles, folded lie
In the last knot that love could tie.
Let them sleep, let them sleep on,
Till the stormy night be gone,
And the eternal morrow dawn;
Then the curtains will be drawn,
And they wake into a light
Whose day shall never die in night.

RICHARD LOVELACE
1618-1658
343. *To Lucasta, going to the Wars*

TELL me not, Sweet, I am unkind,
 That from the nunnery
Of thy chaste breast and quiet mind
 To war and arms I fly.

True, a new mistress now I chase,
 The first foe in the field;
And with a stronger faith embrace
 A sword, a horse, a shield.

Yet this inconstancy is such
As thou too shalt adore;
I could not love thee, Dear, so much,
Loved I not Honour more.

344. *To Lucasta, going beyond the Seas*

IF to be absent were to be
    Away from thee;
  Or that when I am gone
  You or I were alone;
Then, my Lucasta, might I crave
Pity from blustering wind or swallowing wave.

But I'll not sigh one blast or gale
    To swell my sail,
  Or pay a tear to 'suage
  The foaming blue god's rage;
For whether he will let me pass
Or no, I'm still as happy as I was.

Though seas and land betwixt us both,
    Our faith and troth,
  Like separated souls,
  All time and space controls:
Above the highest sphere we meet
Unseen, unknown; and greet as Angels greet.

So then we do anticipate
    Our after-fate,
  And are alive i' the skies,
  If thus our lips and eyes
Can speak like spirits unconfined
In Heaven, their earthy bodies left behind.

RICHARD LOVELACE

345. *Gratiana Dancing*

SHE beat the happy pavèment—
By such a star made firmament,
Which now no more the roof envies!
But swells up high, with Atlas even,
Bearing the brighter nobler heaven,
And, in her, all the deities.

Each step trod out a Lover's thought,
And the ambitious hopes he brought
Chain'd to her brave feet with such arts,
Such sweet command and gentle awe,
As, when she ceased, we sighing saw
The floor lay paved with broken hearts.

346. *To Amarantha, that she would dishevel her Hair*

AMARANTHA sweet and fair,
Ah, braid no more that shining hair!
As my curious hand or eye
Hovering round thee, let it fly!

Let it fly as unconfined
As its calm ravisher the wind,
Who hath left his darling, th' East,
To wanton o'er that spicy nest.

Every tress must be confest,
But neatly tangled at the best;
Like a clew of golden thread
Most excellently ravellèd.

Do not then wind up that light
  In ribbands, and o'ercloud in night,
Like the Sun in 's early ray;
  But shake your head, and scatter day!

347.   *The Grasshopper*

O THOU that swing'st upon the waving hair
    Of some well-fillèd oaten beard,
Drunk every night with a delicious tear
    Dropt thee from heaven, where thou wert rear'd!

The joys of earth and air are thine entire,
    That with thy feet and wings dost hop and fly;
And when thy poppy works, thou dost retire
    To thy carved acorn-bed to lie.

Up with the day, the Sun thou welcom'st then,
    Sport'st in the gilt plaits of his beams,
And all these merry days mak'st merry men,
    Thyself, and melancholy streams.

348.   *To Althea, from Prison*

WHEN Love with unconfinèd wings
    Hovers within my gates,
And my divine Althea brings
    To whisper at the grates;
When I lie tangled in her hair
    And fetter'd to her eye,
The birds that wanton in the air
    Know no such liberty.

When flowing cups run swiftly round
    With no allaying Thames,

RICHARD LOVELACE

Our careless heads with roses bound,
    Our hearts with loyal flames;
When thirsty grief in wine we steep,
    When healths and draughts go free
Fishes that tipple in the deep
    Know no such liberty.

When, like committed linnets, I
    With shriller throat shall sing
The sweetness, mercy, majesty,
    And glories of my King;
When I shall voice aloud how good
    He is, how great should be,
Enlargèd winds, that curl the flood,
    Know no such liberty.

Stone walls do not a prison make,
    Nor iron bars a cage;
Minds innocent and quiet take
    That for an hermitage;
If I have freedom in my love
    And in my soul am free,
Angels alone, that soar above,
    Enjoy such liberty.

ABRAHAM COWLEY
Anacreontics

1618-1667

349. *1. Drinking*

THE thirsty earth soaks up the rain,
    And drinks and gapes for drink again;
The plants suck in the earth, and are
With constant drinking fresh and fair;

ABRAHAM COWLEY

The sea itself (which one would think
Should have but little need of drink)
Drinks twice ten thousand rivers up,
So fill'd that they o'erflow the cup.
The busy Sun (and one would guess
By 's drunken fiery face no less)
Drinks up the sea, and when he 's done,
The Moon and Stars drink up the Sun :
They drink and dance by their own light,
They drink and revel all the night :
Nothing in Nature 's sober found,
But an eternal health goes round.
Fill up the bowl, then, fill it high,
Fill all the glasses there—for why
Should every creature drink but I ?
Why, man of morals, tell me why ?

350. *2. The Epicure*

UNDERNEATH this myrtle shade,
   On flowery beds supinely laid,
With odorous oils my head o'erflowing,
And around it roses growing,
What should I do but drink away
The heat and troubles of the day ?
In this more than kingly state
Love himself on me shall wait.
Fill to me, Love ! nay, fill it up !
And mingled cast into the cup
Wit and mirth and noble fires,
Vigorous health and gay desires.
The wheel of life no less will stay
In a smooth than rugged way :

Since it equally doth flee,
Let the motion pleasant be.
Why do we precious ointments shower?—
Nobler wines why do we pour?—
Beauteous flowers why do we spread
Upon the monuments of the dead?
Nothing they but dust can show,
Or bones that hasten to be so.
Crown me with roses while I live,
Now your wines and ointments give:
After death I nothing crave,
Let me alive my pleasures have:
All are Stoics in the grave.

351. *3. The Swallow*

FOOLISH prater, what dost thou
   So early at my window do?
Cruel bird, thou'st ta'en away
A dream out of my arms to-day;
A dream that ne'er must equall'd be
By all that waking eyes may see.
Thou this damage to repair
Nothing half so sweet and fair,
Nothing half so good, canst bring,
Tho' men say thou bring'st the Spring.

352. *On the Death of Mr. William Hervey*

IT was a dismal and a fearful night:
   Scarce could the Morn drive on th' unwilling Light,
When Sleep, Death's image, left my troubled breast
    By something liker Death possest.

ABRAHAM COWLEY

My eyes with tears did uncommanded flow,
    And on my soul hung the dull weight
    Of some intolerable fate.
What bell was that? Ah me! too much I know!

My sweet companion and my gentle peer,
Why hast thou left me thus unkindly here,
Thy end for ever and my life to moan?
    O, thou hast left me all alone!
Thy soul and body, when death's agony
    Besieged around thy noble heart,
    Did not with more reluctance part
Than I, my dearest Friend, do part from thee.

My dearest Friend, would I had died for thee!
Life and this world henceforth will tedious be:
Nor shall I know hereafter what to do
    If once my griefs prove tedious too.
Silent and sad I walk about all day,
    As sullen ghosts stalk speechless by
    Where their hid treasures lie;
Alas! my treasure's gone; why do I stay?

Say, for you saw us, ye immortal lights,
How oft unwearied have we spent the nights,
Till the Ledæan stars, so famed for love,
    Wonder'd at us from above!
We spent them not in toys, in lusts, or wine;
    But search of deep Philosophy,
    Wit, Eloquence, and Poetry—
Arts which I loved, for they, my Friend, were thine.

Ye fields of Cambridge, our dear Cambridge, say
Have ye not seen us walking every day?

ABRAHAM COWLEY

Was there a tree about which did not know
    The love betwixt us
    Henceforth, ye gentle trees, for ever fade;
Or your sad branches thicker join
    And into darksome shades combine,
Dark as the grave wherein my Friend is laid!

Large was his soul: as large a soul as e'er
Submitted to inform a body here;
High as the place 'twas shortly in Heaven to have,
    But low and humble as his grave.
So high that all the virtues there did come,
    As to their chiefest seat
    Conspicuous and great;
So low, that for me too it made a room.

Knowledge he only sought, and so soon caught
As if for him Knowledge had rather sought;
Nor did more learning ever crowded lie
    In such a short mortality.
Whene'er the skilful youth discoursed or writ,
    Still did the notions throng
    About his eloquent tongue;
Nor could his ink flow faster than his wit.

His mirth was the pure spirits of various wit,
Yet never did his God or friends forget;
And when deep talk and wisdom came in view,
    Retired, and gave to them their due.
For the rich help of books he always took,
    Though his own searching mind before
    Was so with notions written o'er,
As if wise Nature had made that her book.

ABRAHAM COWLEY

With as much zeal, devotion, piety,
He always lived, as other saints do die.
Still with his soul severe account he kept,
    Weeping all debts out ere he slept.
Then down in peace and innocence he lay,
    Like the Sun's laborious light,
    Which still in water sets at night,
Unsullied with his journey of the day.

But happy Thou, ta'en from this frantic age,
Where ignorance and hypocrisy does rage!
A fitter time for Heaven no soul e'er chose—
    The place now only free from those.
There 'mong the blest thou dost for ever shine;
    And wheresoe'er thou casts thy view
    Upon that white and radiant crew,
See'st not a soul clothed with more light than thine.

353. *The Wish*

WELL then! I now do plainly see
    This busy world and I shall ne'er agree.
The very honey of all earthly joy
Does of all meats the soonest cloy;
    And they, methinks, deserve my pity
Who for it can endure the stings,
The crowd and buzz and murmurings,
    Of this great hive, the city.

Ah, yet, ere I descend to the grave
May I a small house and large garden have;
And a few friends, and many books, both true,
Both wise, and both delightful too!

ABRAHAM COWLEY

    And since love ne'er will from me flee,
A Mistress moderately fair,
And good as guardian angels are,
    Only beloved and loving me.

O fountains! when in you shall I
Myself eased of unpeaceful thoughts espy?
O fields! O woods! when, when shall I be made
The happy tenant of your shade?
    Here's the spring-head of Pleasure's flood:
Here's wealthy Nature's treasury,
Where all the riches lie that she
    Has coin'd and stamp'd for good.

Pride and ambition here
Only in far-fetch'd metaphors appear;
Here nought but winds can hurtful murmurs scatter,
And nought but Echo flatter.
    The gods, when they descended, hither
From heaven did always choose their way:
And therefore we may boldly say
    That 'tis the way too thither.

How happy here should I
And one dear She live, and embracing die!
She who is all the world, and can exclude
In deserts solitude.
    I should have then this only fear:
Lest men, when they my pleasures see,
Should hither throng to live like me,
    And so make a city here.

ALEXANDER BROME

1620-1666

354. *The Resolve*

TELL me not of a face that's fair,
   Nor lip and cheek that's red,
Nor of the tresses of her hair,
   Nor curls in order laid,
Nor of a rare seraphic voice
   That like an angel sings;
Though if I were to take my choice
   I would have all these things:
But if that thou wilt have me love,
   And it must be a she,
The only argument can move
   Is that she will love me.

The glories of your ladies be
   But metaphors of things,
And but resemble what we see
   Each common object brings.
Roses out-red their lips and cheeks,
   Lilies their whiteness stain;
What fool is he that shadows seeks
   And may the substance gain?
Then if thou'lt have me love a lass,
   Let it be one that's kind:
Else I'm a servant to the glass
   That's with Canary lined.

ANDREW MARVELL

1621-1678

355. *An Horatian Ode*
upon Cromwell's Return from Ireland

THE forward youth that would appear
Must now forsake his Muses dear,
    Nor in the shadows sing
    His numbers languishing.

'Tis time to leave the books in dust,
And oil the unused armour's rust,
    Removing from the wall
    The corslet of the hall.

So restless Cromwell could not cease
In the inglorious arts of peace,
    But through adventurous war
    Urgèd his active star:

And like the three-fork'd lightning, first
Breaking the clouds where it was nurst,
    Did thorough his own side
    His fiery way divide:

For 'tis all one to courage high,
The emulous, or enemy;
    And with such, to enclose
    Is more than to oppose.

Then burning through the air he went
And palaces and temples rent;
    And Cæsar's head at last
    Did through his laurels blast.

ANDREW MARVELL

'Tis madness to resist or blame
The face of angry Heaven's flame ;
    And if we would speak true,
    Much to the man is due,

Who, from his private gardens, where
He lived reservèd and austere
    (As if his highest plot
    To plant the bergamot),

Could by industrious valour climb
To ruin the great work of time,
    And cast the Kingdoms old
    Into another mould ;

Though Justice against Fate complain,
And plead the ancient rights in vain—
    But those do hold or break
    As men are strong or weak—

Nature, that hateth emptiness,
Allows of penetration less,
    And therefore must make room
    Where greater spirits come.

What field of all the civil war
Where his were not the deepest scar ?
    And Hampton shows what part
    He had of wiser art ;

Where, twining subtle fears with hope,
He wove a net of such a scope
    That Charles himself might chase
    To Caresbrooke's narrow case ;

ANDREW MARVELL

That thence the Royal actor borne
The tragic scaffold might adorn:
   While round the armèd bands
   Did clap their bloody hands.

He nothing common did or mean
Upon that memorable scene,
   But with his keener eye
   The axe's edge did try;

Nor call'd the gods, with vulgar spite,
To vindicate his helpless right;
   But bow'd his comely head
   Down, as upon a bed.

This was that memorable hour
Which first assured the forcèd power:
   So when they did design
   The Capitol's first line,

A Bleeding Head, where they begun,
Did fright the architects to run;
   And yet in that the State
   Foresaw its happy fate!

And now the Irish are ashamed
To see themselves in one year tamed:
   So much one man can do
   That does both act and know.

They can affirm his praises best,
And have, though overcome, confest
   How good he is, how just
   And fit for highest trust.

Nor yet grown stiffer with command,
But still in the republic's hand—
    How fit he is to sway
    That can so well obey!

He to the Commons' feet presents
A Kingdom for his first year's rents,
    And, what he may, forbears
    His fame, to make it theirs:

And has his sword and spoils ungirt
To lay them at the public's skirt.
    So when the falcon high
    Falls heavy from the sky,

She, having kill'd, no more doth search
But on the next green bough to perch;
    Where, when he first does lure,
    The falconer has her sure.

What may not then our Isle presume
While victory his crest does plume?
    What may not others fear,
    If thus he crowns each year?

As Cæsar he, ere long, to Gaul,
To Italy an Hannibal,
    And to all States not free
    Shall climacteric be.

The Pict no shelter now shall find
Within his particolour'd mind,
    But, from this valour, sad
    Shrink underneath the plaid;

ANDREW MARVELL

Happy, if in the tufted brake
The English hunter him mistake,
   Nor lay his hounds in near
   The Caledonian deer.

But thou, the war's and fortune's son,
March indefatigably on;
   And for the last effect,
   Still keep the sword erect:

Besides the force it has to fright
The spirits of the shady night,
   The same arts that did gain
   A power, must it maintain.

356.   *A Garden*

Written after the Civil Wars

SEE how the flowers, as at parade,
   Under their colours stand display'd:
Each regiment in order grows,
That of the tulip, pink, and rose.
But when the vigilant patrol
Of stars walks round about the pole,
Their leaves, that to the stalks are curl'd,
Seem to their staves the ensigns furl'd.
Then in some flower's belovèd hut
Each bee, as sentinel, is shut,
And sleeps so too; but if once stirr'd,
She runs you through, nor asks the word.

O thou, that dear and happy Isle,
The garden of the world erewhile,
Thou Paradise of the four seas
Which Heaven planted us to please,
But, to exclude the world, did guard
With wat'ry if not flaming sword;
What luckless apple did we taste
To make us mortal and thee waste!
Unhappy! shall we never more
That sweet militia restore,
When gardens only had their towers,
And all the garrisons were flowers;
When roses only arms might bear,
And men did rosy garlands wear?

357.   *To His Coy Mistress*

HAD we but world enough, and time,
This coyness, Lady, were no crime
We would sit down and think which way
To walk and pass our long love's day.
Thou by the Indian Ganges' side
Shouldst rubies find: I by the tide
Of Humber would complain.   I would
Love you ten years before the Flood,
And you should, if you please, refuse
Till the conversion of the Jews.
My vegetable love should grow
Vaster than empires, and more slow;
An hundred years should go to praise
Thine eyes and on thy forehead gaze;

ANDREW MARVELL

Two hundred to adore each breast,
But thirty thousand to the rest;
An age at least to every part,
And the last age should show your heart.
For, Lady, you deserve this state,
Nor would I love at lower rate.
   But at my back I always hear
Time's wingèd chariot hurrying near;
And yonder all before us lie
Deserts of vast eternity.
Thy beauty shall no more be found,
Nor, in thy marble vault, shall sound
My echoing song: then worms shall try
That long preserved virginity,
And your quaint honour turn to dust,
And into ashes all my lust:
The grave's a fine and private place,
But none, I think, do there embrace.
   Now therefore, while the youthful hue
Sits on thy skin like morning dew,
And while thy willing soul transpires
At every pore with instant fires,
Now let us sport us while we may,
And now, like amorous birds of prey,
Rather at once our time devour
Than languish in his slow-chapt power.
Let us roll all our strength and all
Our sweetness up into one ball,
And tear our pleasures with rough strife
Thorough the iron gates of life:
Thus, though we cannot make our sun
Stand still, yet we will make him run.

slow-chapt] slow-jawed, slowly devouring.

ANDREW MARVELL

358. *The Picture of Little T. C. in a Prospect of Flowers*

SEE with what simplicity
 This nymph begins her golden days!
In the green grass she loves to lie,
And there with her fair aspect tames
The wilder flowers, and gives them names;
 But only with the roses plays,
  And them does tell
What colour best becomes them, and what smell.

Who can foretell for what high cause
 This darling of the gods was born?
Yet this is she whose chaster laws
The wanton Love shall one day fear,
And, under her command severe,
 See his bow broke and ensigns torn.
  Happy who can
Appease this virtuous enemy of man!

O then let me in time compound
 And parley with those conquering eyes,
Ere they have tried their force to wound;
Ere with their glancing wheels they drive
In triumph over hearts that strive,
 And them that yield but more despise:
  Let me be laid,
Where I may see the glories from some shade.

Meantime, whilst every verdant thing
 Itself does at thy beauty charm,

Reform the errors of the Spring;
Make that the tulips may have share
Of sweetness, seeing they are fair,
And roses of their thorns disarm;
    But most procure
That violets may a longer age endure.

But O, young beauty of the woods,
Whom Nature courts with fruits and flowers,
Gather the flowers, but spare the buds;
Lest Flora, angry at thy crime
To kill her infants in their prime,
Do quickly make th' example yours;
    And ere we see,
Nip in the blossom all our hopes and thee.

359. *Thoughts in a Garden*

HOW vainly men themselves amaze
  To win the palm, the oak, or bays,
And their uncessant labours see
Crown'd from some single herb or tree,
Whose short and narrow-vergèd shade
Does prudently their toils upbraid;
While all the flowers and trees do close
To weave the garlands of repose!

Fair Quiet, have I found thee here,
And Innocence thy sister dear?
Mistaken long, I sought you then
In busy companies of men:

ANDREW MARVELL

Your sacred plants, if here below,
Only among the plants will grow:
Society is all but rude
To this delicious solitude.

No white nor red was ever seen
So amorous as this lovely green.
Fond lovers, cruel as their flame,
Cut in these trees their mistress' name:
Little, alas! they know or heed
How far these beauties hers exceed!
Fair trees! wheres'e'er your barks I wound,
No name shall but your own be found.

When we have run our passions' heat,
Love hither makes his best retreat:
The gods, that mortal beauty chase,
Still in a tree did end their race;
Apollo hunted Daphne so
Only that she might laurel grow;
And Pan did after Syrinx speed
Not as a nymph, but for a reed.

What wondrous life in this I lead!
Ripe apples drop about my head;
The luscious clusters of the vine
Upon my mouth do crush their wine;
The nectarine and curious peach
Into my hands themselves do reach;
Stumbling on melons, as I pass,
Ensnared with flowers, I fall on grass.

Meanwhile the mind from pleasure less
Withdraws into its happiness;

ANDREW MARVELL

The mind, that ocean where each kind
Does straight its own resemblance find;
Yet it creates, transcending these,
Far other worlds, and other seas;
Annihilating all that's made
To a green thought in a green shade.

Here at the fountain's sliding foot,
Or at some fruit-tree's mossy root,
Casting the body's vest aside,
My soul into the boughs does glide;
There, like a bird, it sits and sings,
Then whets and combs its silver wings,
And, till prepared for longer flight,
Waves in its plumes the various light.

Such was that happy Garden-state
While man there walk'd without a mate:
After a place so pure and sweet,
What other help could yet be meet!
But 'twas beyond a mortal's share
To wander solitary there:
Two paradises 'twere in one,
To live in Paradise alone.

How well the skilful gard'ner drew
Of flowers and herbs this dial new!
Where, from above, the milder sun
Does through a fragrant zodiac run:
And, as it works, th' industrious bee
Computes its time as well as we.
How could such sweet and wholesome hours
Be reckon'd, but with herbs and flowers!

ANDREW MARVELL

360. *Bermudas*

WHERE the remote Bermudas ride
 In the ocean's bosom unespied,
From a small boat that row'd along
The listening woods received this song:
 'What should we do but sing His praise
That led us through the watery maze
Unto an isle so long unknown,
And yet far kinder than our own?
Where He the huge sea-monsters wracks,
That lift the deep upon their backs,
He lands us on a grassy stage,
Safe from the storms' and prelates' rage:
He gave us this eternal Spring
Which here enamels everything,
And sends the fowls to us in care
On daily visits through the air:
He hangs in shades the orange bright
Like golden lamps in a green night,
And does in the pomegranates close
Jewels more rich than Ormus shows:
He makes the figs our mouths to meet
And throws the melons at our feet;
But apples plants of such a price,
No tree could ever bear them twice.
With cedars chosen by His hand
From Lebanon He stores the land;
And makes the hollow seas that roar
Proclaim the ambergris on shore.
He cast (of which we rather boast)
The Gospel's pearl upon our coast;

And in these rocks for us did frame
A temple where to sound His name.
O, let our voice His praise exalt
Till it arrive at Heaven's vault,
Which thence (perhaps) rebounding may
Echo beyond the Mexique bay!'

Thus sung they in the English boat
A holy and a cheerful note:
And all the way, to guide their chime,
With falling oars they kept the time.

361. *An Epitaph*

ENOUGH; and leave the rest to Fame!
   'Tis to commend her, but to name.
Courtship which, living, she declined,
When dead, to offer were unkind:
Nor can the truest wit, or friend,
Without detracting, her commend.

To say—she lived a virgin chaste
In this age loose and all unlaced;
Nor was, when vice is so allowed,
Of virtue or ashamed or proud;
That her soul was on Heaven so bent,
No minute but it came and went;
That, ready her last debt to pay,
She summ'd her life up every day;
Modest as morn, as mid-day bright,
Gentle as evening, cool as night:
—'Tis true; but all too weakly said.
'Twas more significant, she's dead.

HENRY VAUGHAN
The Retreat

HAPPY those early days, when I
  Shin'd in my Angel-infancy!
Before I understood this place
Appointed for my second race,
Or taught my soul to fancy aught
But a white celestial thought:
When yet I had not walk'd above
A mile or two from my first Love,
And looking back—at that short space—
Could see a glimpse of His bright face:
When on some gilded cloud, or flow'r,
My gazing soul would dwell an hour,
And in those weaker glories spy
Some shadows of eternity:
Before I taught my tongue to wound
My Conscience with a sinful sound,
Or had the black art to dispense
A several sin to ev'ry sense,
But felt through all this fleshly dress
Bright shoots of everlastingness.

O how I long to travel back,
And tread again that ancient track!
That I might once more reach that plain
Where first I left my glorious train;
From whence th' enlightned spirit sees
That shady City of Palm-trees.
But ah! my soul with too much stay
Is drunk, and staggers in the way!

Some men a forward motion love,
But I by backward steps would move;
And when this dust falls to the urn,
In that state I came, return.

363. Peace

MY soul, there is a country
  Far beyond the stars,
Where stands a wingèd sentry
  All skilful in the wars:
There, above noise and danger,
  Sweet Peace sits crown'd with smiles,
And One born in a manger
  Commands the beauteous files.
He is thy gracious Friend,
  And—O my soul, awake!—
Did in pure love descend
  To die here for thy sake.
If thou canst get but thither,
  There grows the flower of Peace,
The Rose that cannot wither,
  Thy fortress, and thy ease.
Leave then thy foolish ranges;
  For none can thee secure
But One who never changes—
  Thy God, thy life, thy cure.

364. The Timber

SURE thou didst flourish once! and many springs,
  Many bright mornings, much dew, many showers,
Pass'd o'er thy head; many light hearts and wings,
  Which now are dead, lodg'd in thy living bowers.

And still a new succession sings and flies;
  Fresh groves grow up, and their green branches shoot
Towards the old and still enduring skies,
  While the low violet thrives at their root.

But thou beneath the sad and heavy line
  Of death, doth waste all senseless, cold, and dark;
Where not so much as dreams of light may shine,
  Nor any thought of greenness, leaf, or bark.

And yet—as if some deep hate and dissent,
  Bred in thy growth betwixt high winds and thee,
Were still alive—thou dost great storms resent
  Before they come, and know'st how near they be.

Else all at rest thou liest, and the fierce breath
  Of tempests can no more disturb thy ease;
But this thy strange resentment after death
  Means only those who broke—in life—thy peace.

365. *Friends Departed*

THEY are all gone into the world of light!
  And I alone sit ling'ring here;
Their very memory is fair and bright,
  And my sad thoughts doth clear.

It glows and glitters in my cloudy breast,
  Like stars upon some gloomy grove,
Or those faint beams in which this hill is drest
  After the sun's remove.

HENRY VAUGHAN

I see them walking in an air of glory,
    Whose light doth trample on my days:
My days, which are at best but dull and hoary,
    Mere glimmering and decays.

O holy Hope! and high Humility,
    High as the heavens above!
These are your walks, and you have show'd them me,
    To kindle my cold love.

Dear, beauteous Death! the jewel of the Just,
    Shining nowhere, but in the dark;
What mysteries do lie beyond thy dust,
    Could man outlook that mark!

He that hath found some fledg'd bird's nest may know,
    At first sight, if the bird be flown;
But what fair well or grove he sings in now,
    That is to him unknown.

And yet as Angels in some brighter dreams
    Call to the soul, when man doth sleep:
So some strange thoughts transcend our wonted themes,
    And into glory peep.

If a star were confin'd into a tomb,
    Her captive flames must needs burn there;
But when the hand that lock'd her up gives room,
    She'll shine through all the sphere.

O Father of eternal life, and all
    Created glories under Thee!
Resume Thy spirit from this world of thrall
    Into true liberty.

HENRY VAUGHAN

Either disperse these mists, which blot and fill
    My perspective still as they pass:
Or else remove me hence unto that hill,
    Where I shall need no glass.

JOHN BUNYAN
1628-1688

366. *The Shepherd Boy sings in the Valley of Humiliation*

HE that is down needs fear no fall,
    He that is low, no pride;
He that is humble ever shall
    Have God to be his guide.

I am content with what I have,
    Little be it or much:
And, Lord, contentment still I crave,
    Because Thou savest such.

Fullness to such a burden is
    That go on pilgrimage:
Here little, and hereafter bliss,
    Is best from age to age.

BALLADS AND SONGS BY UNKNOWN AUTHORS

367. Thomas the Rhymer

TRUE Thomas lay on Huntlie bank;
  A ferlie he spied wi' his e'e;
And there he saw a ladye bright
  Come riding down by the Eildon Tree.

Her skirt was o' the grass-green silk,
  Her mantle o' the velvet fyne;
At ilka tett o' her horse's mane,
  Hung fifty siller bells and nine.

True Thomas he pu'd aff his cap,
  And louted low down on his knee:
'Hail to thee, Mary, Queen of Heaven!
  For thy peer on earth could never be.'

'O no, O no, Thomas,' she said,
  'That name does not belang to me;
I'm but the Queen o' fair Elfland,
  That am hither come to visit thee.

'Harp and carp, Thomas,' she said;
  'Harp and carp along wi' me;
And if ye dare to kiss my lips,
  Sure of your bodie I will be.'

---

ferlie] marvel.   tett] tuft, lock.   harp and carp] play and recite (as a minstrel).

ANONYMOUS

'Betide me weal, betide me woe,
    That weird shall never daunten me.'
Syne he has kiss'd her rosy lips,
    All underneath the Eildon Tree.

'Now ye maun go wi' me,' she said,
    'True Thomas, ye maun go wi' me;
And ye maun serve me seven years,
    Thro' weal or woe as may chance to be.'

She's mounted on her milk-white steed,
    She's ta'en true Thomas up behind;
And aye, whene'er her bridle rang,
    The steed gaed swifter than the wind.

O they rade on, and farther on,
    The steed gaed swifter than the wind;
Until they reach'd a desert wide,
    And living land was left behind.

'Light down, light down now, true Thomas,
    And lean your head upon my knee;
Abide ye there a little space,
    And I will show you ferlies three.

'O see ye not yon narrow road,
    So thick beset wi' thorns and briers?
That is the Path of Righteousness,
    Though after it but few inquires.

'And see ye not yon braid, braid road,
    That lies across the lily leven?
That is the Path of Wickedness,
    Though some call it the Road to Heaven.

leven] ? lawn.

ANONYMOUS

'And see ye not yon bonny road
    That winds about the fernie brae?
That is the Road to fair Elfland,
    Where thou and I this night maun gae.

'But, Thomas, ye sall haud your tongue,
    Whatever ye may hear or see;
For speak ye word in Elfyn-land,
    Ye'll ne'er win back to your ain countrie.'

O they rade on, and farther on,
    And they waded rivers abune the knee;
And they saw neither sun nor moon,
    But they heard the roaring of the sea.

It was mirk, mirk night, there was nae starlight,
    They waded thro' red blude to the knee;
For a' the blude that's shed on the earth
    Rins through the springs o' that countrie.

Syne they came to a garden green,
    And she pu'd an apple frae a tree:
'Take this for thy wages, true Thomas;
    It will give thee the tongue that can never lee.'

'My tongue is my ain,' true Thomas he said;
    'A gudely gift ye wad gie to me!
I neither dought to buy or sell
    At fair or tryst where I might be.

'I dought neither speak to prince or peer,
    Nor ask of grace from fair ladye!'—
'Now haud thy peace, Thomas,' she said,
    'For as I say, so must it be.'

dought] could.

ANONYMOUS

He has gotten a coat of the even cloth,
 And a pair o' shoon of the velvet green;
And till seven years were gane and past,
 True Thomas on earth was never seen.

368. *Sir Patrick Spens*

1. *The Sailing*

THE king sits in Dunfermline town
 Drinking the blude-red wine;
'O whare will I get a skeely skipper
 To sail this new ship o' mine?'

O up and spak an eldern knight,
 Sat at the king's right knee;
'Sir Patrick Spens is the best sailor
 That ever sail'd the sea.'

Our king has written a braid letter,
 And seal'd it with his hand,
And sent it to Sir Patrick Spens,
 Was walking on the strand.

'To Noroway, to Noroway,
 To Noroway o'er the faem;
The king's daughter o' Noroway,
 'Tis thou must bring her hame.'

The first word that Sir Patrick read
 So loud, loud laugh'd he;
The neist word that Sir Patrick read
 The tear blinded his e'e.

368. skeely] skilful.

ANONYMOUS

'O wha is this has done this deed
    And tauld the king o' me,
To send us out, at this time o' year,
    To sail upon the sea?

'Be it wind, be it weet, be it hail, be it sleet,
    Our ship must sail the faem;
The king's daughter o' Noroway,
    'Tis we must fetch her hame.'

They hoysed their sails on Monenday
    Wi' a' the speed they may;
They hae landed in Noroway
    Upon a Wodensday.

II. *The Return*

'Mak ready, mak ready, my merry men
    Our gude ship sails the morn.'
'Now ever alack, my master dear,
    I fear a deadly storm.

'I saw the new moon late yestreen
    Wi' the auld moon in her arm;
And if we gang to sea, master,
    I fear we'll come to harm.'

They hadna sail'd a league, a league,
    A league but barely three,
When the lift grew dark, and the wind blew loud,
    And gurly grew the sea.

The ankers brak, and the topmast lap,
    It was sic a deadly storm:
And the waves cam owre the broken ship
    Till a' her sides were torn.

lift] sky.   lap] sprang.

ANONYMOUS

'Go fetch a web o' the silken claith,
    Another o' the twine,
And wap them into our ship's side,
    And let nae the sea come in.'

They fetch'd a web o' the silken claith,
    Another o' the twine,
And they wapp'd them round that gude ship's side,
    But still the sea came in.

O laith, laith were our gude Scots lords
    To wet their cork-heel'd shoon;
But lang or a' the play was play'd
    They wat their hats aboon.

And mony was the feather bed
    That flatter'd on the faem;
And mony was the gude lord's son
    That never mair cam hame.

O lang, lang may the ladies sit,
    Wi' their fans into their hand,
Before they see Sir Patrick Spens
    Come sailing to the strand!

And lang, lang may the maidens sit
    Wi' their gowd kames in their hair,
A-waiting for their ain dear loves!
    For them they'll see nae mair.

Half-owre, half-owre to Aberdour,
    'Tis fifty fathoms deep;
And there lies gude Sir Patrick Spens,
    Wi' the Scots lords at his feet!

flatter'd] tossed afloat.   kames] combs.

369. *The Lass of Lochroyan*

'O WHA will shoe my bonny foot?
    And wha will glove my hand?
And wha will bind my middle jimp
    Wi' a lang, lang linen band?

'O wha will kame my yellow hair,
    With a haw bayberry kame?
And wha will be my babe's father
    Till Gregory come hame?'

'Thy father, he will shoe thy foot,
    Thy brother will glove thy hand,
Thy mither will bind thy middle jimp
    Wi' a lang, lang linen band.

'Thy sister will kame thy yellow hair,
    Wi' a haw bayberry kame;
The Almighty will be thy babe's father
    Till Gregory come hame.'

'And wha will build a bonny ship,
    And set it on the sea?
For I will go to seek my love,
    My ain love Gregory.'

Up then spak her father dear,
    A wafu' man was he;
'And I will build a bonny ship,
    And set her on the sea.

---

jimp] trim.   kame] comb.   haw bayberry] ? a corruption for 'braw ivory': or bayberry may = laurel-wood.

ANONYMOUS

'And I will build a bonny ship,
    And set her on the sea,
And ye sal gae and seek your love,
    Your ain love Gregory.'

Then he's gart build a bonny ship,
    And set it on the sea,
Wi' four-and-twenty mariners,
    To bear her company.

O he's gart build a bonny ship,
    To sail on the salt sea;
The mast was o' the beaten gold,
    The sails o' cramoisie.

The sides were o' the gude stout a
    The deck o' mountain pine,
The anchor o' the silver shene,
    The ropes o' silken twine.

She hadna sail'd but twenty leagues
    But twenty leagues and three,
When she met wi' a rank reiver,
    And a' his companie.

'Now are ye Queen of Heaven hie
    Come to pardon a' our sin?
Or are ye Mary Magdalane,
    Was born at Bethlam?'

'I'm no the Queen of Heaven hie,
    Come to pardon ye your sin,
Nor am I Mary Magdalane,
    Was born in Bethlam.

cramoisie] crimson.   reiver] robber.

ANONYMOUS

'But I'm the lass of Lochroyan,
   That's sailing on the sea
To see if I can find my love,
   My ain love Gregory.'

'O see na ye yon bonny bower?
   It's a' covered owre wi' tin;
When thou hast sail'd it round about,
   Lord Gregory is within.'

And when she saw the stately tower,
   Shining both clear and bright,
Whilk stood aboon the jawing wave,
   Built on a rock of height,

Says, 'Row the boat, my mariners,
   And bring me to the land,
For yonder I see my love's castle,
   Close by the salt sea strand.'

She sail'd it round, and sail'd it round,
   And loud and loud cried she,
'Now break, now break your fairy charms,
   And set my true-love free.'

She's ta'en her young son in her arms,
   And to the door she's gane,
And long she knock'd, and sair she ca'd.
   But answer got she nane.

'O open, open, Gregory!
   O open! if ye be within;
For here's the lass of Lochroyan,
   Come far fra kith and kin.

ANONYMOUS

'O open the door, Lord Gregory!
  O open and let me in!
The wind blows loud and cauld, Gregory,
  The rain drops fra my chin.

'The shoe is frozen to my foot,
  The glove unto my hand,
The wet drops fra my yellow hair,
  Na langer dow I stand.'

O up then spak his ill mither,
  —An ill death may she die!
'Ye're no the lass of Lochroyan,
  She's far out-owre the sea.

'Awa', awa', ye ill woman,
  Ye're no come here for gude;
Ye're but some witch or wil' warlock,
  Or mermaid o' the flood.'

'I am neither witch nor wil' warlock,
  Nor mermaid o' the sea,
But I am Annie of Lochroyan,
  O open the door to me!'

'Gin ye be Annie of Lochroyan,
  As I trow thou binna she,
Now tell me of some love-tokens
  That pass'd 'tween thee and me.'

'O dinna ye mind, love Gregory,
  As we sat at the wine,
We changed the rings frae our fingers?
  And I can shew thee thine.

dow] can.

ANONYMOUS

'O yours was gude, and gude enough,
    But ay the best was mine,
For yours was o' the gude red gowd,
    But mine o' the diamond fine.

'Yours was o' the gude red gowd,
    Mine o' the diamond fine;
Mine was o' the purest troth,
    But thine was false within.'

'If ye be the lass of Lochroyan,
    As I kenna thou be,
Tell me some mair o' the love-tokens
    Pass'd between thee and me.'

'And dinna ye mind, love Gregory!
    As we sat on the hill,
Thou twin'd me o' my maidenheid,
    Right sair against my will?

'Now open the door, love Gregory!
    Open the door! I pray;
For thy young son is in my arms,
    And will be dead ere day.'

'Ye lie, ye lie, ye ill woman,
    So loud I hear ye lie;
For Annie of the Lochroyan
    Is far out-owre the sea.'

Fair Annie turn'd her round about:
    'Weel, sine that it be sae,
May ne'er woman that has borne a son
    Hae a heart sae fu' o' wae!

ANONYMOUS

'Tak down, tak down that mast o' gowd,
    Set up a mast of tree;
It disna become a forsaken lady
    To sail sae royallie.'

When the cock had crawn, and the day did dawn,
    And the sun began to peep,
Up then raise Lord Gregory,
    And sair, sair did he weep.

'O I hae dream'd a dream, mither,
    I wish it may bring good!
That the bonny lass of Lochroyan
    At my bower window stood.

'O I hae dream'd a dream, mither,
    The thought o't gars me greet!
That fair Annie of Lochroyan
    Lay dead at my bed-feet.'

'Gin it be for Annie of Lochroyan
    That ye mak a' this mane,
She stood last night at your bower-door,
    But I hae sent her hame.'

'O wae betide ye, ill woman,
    An ill death may ye die!
That wadna open the door yoursell
    Nor yet wad waken me.'

O he's gane down to yon shore-side,
    As fast as he could dree,
And there he saw fair Annie's bark
    A rowing owre the sea.

ANONYMOUS

'O Annie, Annie,' loud he cried,
  'O Annie, O Annie, bide!'
But ay the mair he cried 'Annie,'
  The braider grew the tide.

'O Annie, Annie, dear Annie,
  Dear Annie, speak to me!'
But ay the louder he gan call,
  The louder roar'd the sea.

The wind blew loud, the waves rose hie
  And dash'd the boat on shore;
Fair Annie's corpse was in the faem,
  The babe rose never more.

Lord Gregory tore his gowden locks
  And made a wafu' moan;
Fair Annie's corpse lay at his feet,
  His bonny son was gone.

'O cherry, cherry was her cheek,
  And gowden was her hair,
And coral, coral was her lips,
  Nane might with her compare.'

Then first he kiss'd her pale, pale cheek,
  And syne he kiss'd her chin,
And syne he kiss'd her wane, wane lips,
  There was na breath within.

'O wae betide my ill mither,
  An ill death may she die!
She turn'd my true-love frae my door,
  Who cam so far to me.

ANONYMOUS

'O wae betide my ill mither,
    An ill death may she die!
She has no been the deid o' ane,
    But she's been the deid of three.'

Then he's ta'en out a little dart,
    Hung low down by his gore,
He thrust it through and through his heart,
    And words spak never more.

370. *The Dowie Houms of Yarrow*

LATE at een, drinkin' the wine,
    And ere they paid the lawin',
They set a combat them between,
    To fight it in the dawin'.

'O stay at hame, my noble lord!
    O stay at hame, my marrow!
My cruel brother will you betray,
    On the dowie houms o' Yarrow.'

'O fare ye weel, my lady gay!
    O fare ye weel, my Sarah!
For I maun gae, tho' I ne'er return
    Frae the dowie banks o' Yarrow.'

She kiss'd his cheek, she kamed his hair,
    As she had done before, O;
She belted on his noble brand,
    An' he's awa to Yarrow.

---

369. gore] skirt, waist.   *370*. lawin'] reckoning.   marrow] mate, husband or wife.   dowie] doleful.   houms] water-meads.

ANONYMOUS

O he's gane up yon high, high hill—
    I wat he gaed wi' sorrow—
An' in a den spied nine arm'd men,
    I' the dowie houms o' Yarrow.

'O are ye come to drink the wine,
    As ye hae doon before, O?
Or are ye come to wield the brand,
    On the dowie banks o' Yarrow?'

'I am no come to drink the wine,
    As I hae don before, O,
But I am come to wield the brand,
    On the dowie houms o' Yarrow.'

Four he hurt, an' five he slew,
    On the dowie houms o' Yarrow,
Till that stubborn knight came him behind,
    An' ran his body thorrow.

'Gae hame, gae hame, good brother John,
    An' tell your sister Sarah
To come an' lift her noble lord,
    Who's sleepin' sound on Yarrow.'

'Yestreen I dream'd a dolefu' dream;
    I ken'd there wad be sorrow;
I dream'd I pu'd the heather green,
    On the dowie banks o' Yarrow.'

She gaed up yon high, high hill—
    I wat she gaed wi' sorrow—
An' in a den spied nine dead men,
    On the dowie houms o' Yarrow.

ANONYMOUS

She kiss'd his cheek, she kamed his hair,
    As oft she did before, O ;
She drank the red blood frae him ran,
    On the dowie houms o' Yarrow.

'O haud your tongue, my douchter dear,
    For what needs a' this sorrow?
I'll wed you on a better lord
    Than him you lost on Yarrow.'

'O haud your tongue, my father dear,
    An' dinna grieve your Sarah ;
A better lord was never born
    Than him I lost on Yarrow.

'Tak hame your ousen, tak hame your kye,
    For they hae bred our sorrow ;
I wiss that they had a' gane mad
    Whan they cam first to Yarrow.'

371. *Clerk Saunders*

CLERK SAUNDERS and may Margaret
    Walk'd owre yon garden green ;
And deep and heavy was the love
    That fell thir twa between.

'A bed, a bed,' Clerk Saunders said,
    'A bed for you and me ! '
'Fye na, fye na,' said may Margaret,
    'Till anes we married be ! '

'Then I'll take the sword frae my scabbard
    And slowly lift the pin ;
And you may swear, and save your aith,
    Ye ne'er let Clerk Saunders in.

ANONYMOUS

'Take you a napkin in your hand,
    And tie up baith your bonnie e'en,
And you may swear, and save your aith,
    Ye saw me na since late yestreen.'

It was about the midnight hour,
    When they asleep were laid,
When in and came her seven brothers,
    Wi' torches burning red:

When in and came her seven brothers,
    Wi' torches burning bright:
They said, 'We hae but one sister,
    And behold her lying with a knight

Then out and spake the first o' them,
    'I bear the sword shall gar him die.
And out and spake the second o' them
    'His father has nae mair but he.'

And out and spake the third o' them,
    'I wot that they are lovers dear.'
And out and spake the fourth o' them,
    'They hae been in love this mony a .'

Then out and spake the fifth o' them,
    'It were great sin true love to twain.'
And out and spake the sixth o' them,
    'It were shame to slay a sleeping man.'

Then up and gat the seventh o' them,
    And never a word spake he;
But he has striped his bright brown brand
    Out through Clerk Saunders' fair bodye.

striped] thrust.

ANONYMOUS

Clerk Saunders he started, and Margaret she turn'd
    Into his arms as asleep she lay;
And sad and silent was the night
    That was atween thir twae.

And they lay still and sleepit sound
    Until the day began to daw';
And kindly she to him did say,
    'It is time, true love, you were awa'.'

But he lay still, and sleepit sound,
    Albeit the sun began to sheen;
She look'd atween her and the wa',
    And dull and drowsie were his e'en.

Then in and came her father dear;
    Said, 'Let a' your mourning be;
I'll carry the dead corse to the clay,
    And I'll come back and comfort thee.'

'Comfort weel your seven sons,
    For comforted I will never be:
I ween 'twas neither knave nor loon
    Was in the bower last night wi' me.'

The clinking bell gaed through the town,
    To carry the dead corse to the clay;
And Clerk Saunders stood at may Margaret's window,
    I wot, an hour before the day.

'Are ye sleeping, Marg'ret?' he says,
    'Or are ye waking presentlie?
Give me my faith and troth again,
    I wot, true love, I gied to thee.'

ANONYMOUS

'Your faith and troth ye sall never get,
    Nor our true love sall never twin,
Until ye come within my bower,
    And kiss me cheik and chin.'

'My mouth it is full cold, Marg'ret;
    It has the smell, now, of the ground;
And if I kiss thy comely mouth,
    Thy days of life will not be lang.

'O cocks are crowing a merry midnight;
    I wot the wild fowls are boding day;
Give me my faith and troth again,
    And let me fare me on my way.'

'Thy faith and troth thou sallna get,
    And our true love sall never twin,
Until ye tell what comes o' women,
    I wot, who die in strong traivelling?'

'Their beds are made in the heavens high,
    Down at the foot of our good Lord's knee,
Weel set about wi' gillyflowers;
    I wot, sweet company for to see.

'O cocks are crowing a merry midnight;
    I wot the wild fowls are boding day;
The psalms of heaven will soon be sung,
    And I, ere now, will be miss'd away.'

Then she has taken a crystal wand,
    And she has stroken her troth thereon;
She has given it him out at the shot-window,
    Wi' mony a sad sigh and heavy groan.

twin] part in two.

ANONYMOUS

'I thank ye, Marg'ret; I thank ye, Marg'ret;
   And ay I thank ye heartilie;
Gin ever the dead come for the quick,
   Be sure, Marg'ret, I'll come for thee.'

It's hosen and shoon, and gown alone,
   She climb'd the wall, and follow'd him,
Until she came to the green forest,
   And there she lost the sight o' him.

'Is there ony room at your head, Saunders?
   Is there ony room at your feet?
Or ony room at your side, Saunders,
   Where fain, fain, I wad sleep?'

'There's nae room at my head, Marg'ret,
   There's nae room at my feet;
My bed it is fu' lowly now,
   Amang the hungry worms I sleep.

'Cauld mould is my covering now,
   But and my winding-sheet;
The dew it falls nae sooner down
   Than my resting-place is weet.

'But plait a wand o' bonny birk,
   And lay it on my breast;
And shed a tear upon my grave,
   And wish my saul gude rest.'

Then up and crew the red, red cock,
   And up and crew the gray:
''Tis time, 'tis time, my dear Marg'ret,
   That you were going away.

'And fair Marg'ret, and rare Marg'ret,
 And Marg'ret o' veritie,
Gin e'er ye love another man,
 Ne'er love him as ye did me.'

372. *Fair Annie*

THE reivers they stole Fair Annie,
 As she walk'd by the sea;
But a noble knight was her ransom soon,
 Wi' gowd and white monie.

She bided in strangers' land wi' him,
 And none knew whence she cam;
She lived in the castle wi' her love,
 But never told her name.

'It's narrow, narrow, mak your bed,
 And learn to lie your lane;
For I'm gaun owre the sea, Fair Annie,
 A braw Bride to bring hame.
Wi' her I will get gowd and gear,
 Wi' you I ne'er gat nane.

'But wha will bake my bridal bread,
 Or brew my bridal ale?
And wha will welcome my bright Bride,
 That I bring owre the dale?'

'It's I will bake your bridal bread,
 And brew your bridal ale;
And I will welcome your bright Bride,
 That you bring owre the dale.'

ANONYMOUS

'But she that welcomes my bright Bride
    Maun gang like maiden fair;
She maun lace on her robe sae jimp,
    And comely braid her hair.

'Bind up, bind up your yellow hair,
    And tie it on your neck;
And see you look as maiden-like
    As the day that first we met.'

'O how can I gang maiden-like,
    When maiden I am nane?
Have I not borne six sons to thee,
    And am wi' child again?'

'I'll put cooks into my kitchen,
    And stewards in my hall,
And I'll have bakers for my bread,
    And brewers for my ale;
But you're to welcome my bright Bride,
    That I bring owre the dale.'

Three months and a day were gane and past,
    Fair Annie she gat word
That her love's ship was come at last,
    Wi' his bright young Bride aboard.

She's ta'en her young son in her arms,
    Anither in her hand;
And she's gane up to the highest tower,
    Looks over sea and land.

jimp] trim.

ANONYMOUS

'Come doun, come doun, my mother dear,
    Come aff the castle wa'!
I fear if langer ye stand there,
    Ye'll let yoursell doun fa'.'

She's ta'en a cake o' the best bread,
    A stoup o' the best wine,
And a' the keys upon her arm,
    And to the yett is gane.

'O ye're welcome hame, my ain gude lord,
    To your castles and your towers
Ye're welcome hame, my ain gude l,
    To your ha's, but and your bow
And welcome to your hame, fair]
    For a' that's here is yours.'

'O whatna lady's that, my lord,
    That welcomes you and me?
Gin I be lang about this place,
    Her friend I mean to be.'

Fair Annie served the lang tables
    Wi' the white bread and the wi
But ay she drank the wan water
    To keep her colour fine.

And she gaed by the first table,
    And smiled upon them a';
But ere she reach'd the second table,
    The tears began to fa'.

yett] gate.

ANONYMOUS

She took a napkin lang and white,
    And hung it on a pin;
It was to wipe away the tears,
    As she gaed out and in.

When bells were rung and mass was sung,
    And a' men bound for bed,
The bridegroom and the bonny Bride
    In ae chamber were laid.

Fair Annie's ta'en a harp in her hand,
    To harp thir twa asleep;
But ay, as she harpit and she sang,
    Fu' sairly did she weep.

'O gin my sons were seven rats,
    Rinnin' on the castle wa',
And I mysell a great grey cat,
    I soon wad worry them a'!

'O gin my sons were seven hares,
    Rinnin' owre yon lily lea,
And I mysell a good greyhound,
    Soon worried they a' should be!'

Then out and spak the bonny young Bride,
    In bride-bed where she lay:
'That's like my sister Annie,' she says;
    'Wha is it doth sing and play?

'I'll put on my gown,' said the new-come Bride,
    'And my shoes upon my feet;
I will see wha doth sae sadly sing,
    And what is it gars her greet.

ANONYMOUS

'What ails you, what ails you, my housekeeper,
   That ye mak sic a mane?
Has ony wine-barrel cast its girds,
   Or is a' your white bread gane?'

'It isna because my wine is spilt,
   Or that my white bread's gane;
But because I've lost my true love's love,
   And he's wed to anither ane.'

'Noo tell me wha was your father?' she says,
   'Noo tell me wha was your mother?
And had ye ony sister?' she says,
   'And had ye ever a brother?'

'The Earl of Wemyss was my father,
   The Countess of Wemyss my mother,
Young Elinor she was my sister dear,
   And Lord John he was my brother.'

'If the Earl of Wemyss was your father,
   I wot sae was he mine;
And it's O my sister Annie!
   Your love ye sallna tyne.

'Tak your husband, my sister dear;
   You ne'er were wrang'd for me,
Beyond a kiss o' his merry mouth
   As we cam owre the sea.

'Seven ships, loaded weel,
   Cam owre the sea wi' me;
Ane o' them will tak me hame,
   And six I'll gie to thee.'

tyne] lose.

ANONYMOUS

373. *Edward, Edward*

'WHY does your brand sae drop wi' blude,
  Edward, Edward?
Why does your brand sae drop wi' blude,
  And why sae sad gang ye, O?'
'O I hae kill'd my hawk sae gude,
  Mither, mither;
O I hae kill'd my hawk sae gude,
  And I had nae mair but he, O.'

'Your hawk's blude was never sae red,
  Edward, Edward;
Your hawk's blude was never sae red,
  My dear son, I tell thee, O.'
'O I hae kill'd my red-roan steed,
  Mither, mither;
O I hae kill'd my red-roan steed,
  That erst was sae fair and free, O.'

'Your steed was auld, and ye hae got mair,
  Edward, Edward;
Your steed was auld, and ye hae got mair;
  Some other dule ye dree, O.'
'O I hae kill'd my father dear,
  Mither, mither;
O I hae kill'd my father dear,
  Alas, and wae is me, O!'

dule ye dree] grief you suffer.

ANONYMOUS

'And whatten penance will ye dree for that,
    Edward, Edward?
Whatten penance will ye dree for that?
    My dear son, now tell me, O.'
'I'll set my feet in yonder boat,
    Mither, mither;
I'll set my feet in yonder boat,
    And I'll fare over the sea, O.'

'And what will ye do wi' your tow'rs and your ha',
    Edward, Edward?
And what will ye do wi' your tow'rs and your ha',
    That were sae fair to see, O?'
'I'll let them stand till they doun fa',
    Mither, mither;
I'll let them stand till they doun fa',
    For here never mair maun I be, O.'

'And what will ye leave to your bairns and your wife,
    Edward, Edward?
And what will ye leave to your bairns and your wife,
    When ye gang owre the sea, O?'
'The warld's room: let them beg through life,
    Mither, mither;
The warld's room: let them beg through life;
    For them never mair will I see, O.'

'And what will ye leave to your ain mither dear,
    Edward, Edward?
And what will ye leave to your ain mither dear,
    My dear son, now tell me, O?'

ANONYMOUS

'The curse of hell frae me sall ye bear,
    Mither, mither;
The curse of hell frae me sall ye bear:
    Sic counsels ye gave to me, O!'

374. Edom o' Gordon

IT fell about the Martinmas,
    When the wind blew shrill and cauld,
Said Edom o' Gordon to his men,
    'We maun draw to a hauld.

'And what a hauld sall we draw to,
    My merry men and me?
We will gae to the house o' the Rodes,
    To see that fair ladye.'

The lady stood on her castle wa',
    Beheld baith dale and down;
There she was ware of a host of men
    Cam riding towards the town.

'O see ye not, my merry men a',
    O see ye not what I see?
Methinks I see a host of men;
    I marvel wha they be.'

She ween'd it had been her lovely lord,
    As he cam riding hame;
It was the traitor, Edom o' Gordon,
    Wha reck'd nae sin nor shame.

town] stead.

ANONYMOUS

She had nae sooner buskit hersell,
    And putten on her gown,
But Edom o' Gordon an' his men
    Were round about the town.

They had nae sooner supper set,
    Nae sooner said the grace,
But Edom o' Gordon an' his men
    Were lighted about the place.

The lady ran up to her tower-head,
    Sae fast as she could hie,
To see if by her fair speeches
    She could wi' him agree.

'Come doun to me, ye lady gay,
    Come doun, come doun to me;
This night sall ye lig within mine arms,
    To-morrow my bride sall be.'

'I winna come down, ye fals Gordon,
    I winna come down to thee;
I winna forsake my ain dear lord,
    That is sae far frae me.'

'Gie owre your house, ye lady fair,
    Gie owre your house to me;
Or I sall brenn yoursel therein,
    But and your babies three.'

'I winna gie owre, ye fals Gordon,
    To nae sic traitor as yee;
And if ye brenn my ain dear babes,
    My lord sall mak ye dree.

buskit] attired.

ANONYMOUS

'Now reach my pistol, Glaud, my man,
    And charge ye weel my gun;
For, but an I pierce that bluidy butcher,
    My babes, we been undone!'

She stood upon her castle wa',
    And let twa bullets flee:
She miss'd that bluidy butcher's heart,
    And only razed his knee.

'Set fire to the house!' quo' fals Gordon,
    All wud wi' dule and ire:
'Fals lady, ye sall rue this deid
    As ye brenn in the fire!'

'Wae worth, wae worth ye, Jock, my man!
    I paid ye weel your fee;
Why pu' ye out the grund-wa' stane,
    Lets in the reek to me?

'And e'en wae worth ye, Jock, my man!
    I paid ye weel your hire;
Why pu' ye out the grund-wa' stane,
    To me lets in the fire?'

'Ye paid me weel my hire, ladye,
    Ye paid me weel my fee:
But now I'm Edom o' Gordon's man—
    Maun either do or die.'

O then bespake her little son,
    Sat on the nurse's knee:
Says, 'Mither dear, gie owre this house,
    For the reek it smithers me.'

wud] mad.   **grund-wa']** ground-wall.

ANONYMOUS

'I wad gie a' my gowd, my bairn,
    Sae wad I a' my fee,
For ae blast o' the western wind,
    To blaw the reek frae thee.'

O then bespake her dochter dear—
    She was baith jimp and sma':
'O row me in a pair o' sheets,
    And tow me owre the wa'!'

They row'd her in a pair o' sheets,
    And tow'd her owre the wa';
But on the point o' Gordon's spear
    She gat a deadly fa'.

O bonnie, bonnie was her mouth,
    And cherry were her cheiks,
And clear, clear was her yellow hair,
    Whereon the red blood dreips.

Then wi' his spear he turn'd her owre;
    O gin her face was wane!
He said, 'Ye are the first that e'er
    I wish'd alive again.'

He turn'd her owre and owre again;
    O gin her skin was white!
'I might hae spared that bonnie face
    To hae been some man's delight.

'Busk and boun, my merry men a',
    For ill dooms I do guess;
I canna look in that bonnie face
    As it lies on the grass.'

jimp] slender, trim.   row] roll, wrap.   Busk and boun] trim up and prepare to go.

ANONYMOUS

'Wha looks to freits, my master dear,
    It's freits will follow them;
Let it ne'er be said that Edom o' Gordon
    Was daunted by a dame.'

But when the lady saw the fire
    Come flaming owre her head,
She wept, and kiss'd her children twain,
    Says, 'Bairns, we been but dead.'

The Gordon then his bugle blew,
    And said, 'Awa', awa'!
This house o' the Rodes is a' in a flame;
    I hauld it time to ga'.'

And this way lookit her ain dear lord,
    As he cam owre the lea;
He saw his castle a' in a lowe,
    As far as he could see.

Then sair, O sair, his mind misgave,
    And all his heart was wae:
'Put on, put on, my wighty men,
    Sae fast as ye can gae.

'Put on, put on, my wighty men,
    Sae fast as ye can drie!
For he that's hindmost o' the thrang
    Sall ne'er get good o' me.'

Then some they rade, and some they ran,
    Out-owre the grass and bent;
But ere the foremost could win up,
    Baith lady and babes were brent.

freits] ill omens.   lowe] flame.   wighty] stout, doughty.

ANONYMOUS

And after the Gordon he is gane,
  Sae fast as he might drie;
And soon i' the Gordon's foul heart's blude
  He's wroken his dear ladye.

375. *The Queen's Marie*

MARIE HAMILTON's to the kirk gane,
  Wi' ribbons in her hair;
The King thought mair o' Marie Hamilton
  Than ony that were there.

Marie Hamilton's to the kirk gane
  Wi' ribbons on her breast;
The King thought mair o' Marie Hamilton
  Than he listen'd to the priest.

Marie Hamilton's to the kirk gane,
  Wi' gloves upon her hands;
The King thought mair o' Marie Hamilton
  Than the Queen and a' her lands.

She hadna been about the King's court
  A month, but barely one,
Till she was beloved by a' the King's court
  And the King the only man.

She hadna been about the King's court
  A month, but barely three,
Till frae the King's court Marie Hamilton,
  Marie Hamilton durstna be.

wroken] avenged.

ANONYMOUS

The King is to the Abbey gane,
    To pu' the Abbey tree,
To scale the babe frae Marie's heart;
    But the thing it wadna be.

O she has row'd it in her apron,
    And set it on the sea—
'Gae sink ye or swim ye, bonny babe,
    Ye'se get nae mair o' me.'

Word is to the kitchen gane,
    And word is to the ha',
And word is to the noble room
    Amang the ladies a',
That Marie Hamilton's brought to bed,
    And the bonny babe's miss'd and awa'.

Scarcely had she lain down again,
    And scarcely fa'en asleep,
When up and started our gude Queen
    Just at her bed-feet;
Saying—'Marie Hamilton, where's your babe?
    For I am sure I heard it greet.'

'O no, O no, my noble Queen!
    Think no sic thing to be;
'Twas but a stitch into my side,
    And sair it troubles me!'

'Get up, get up, Marie Hamilton:
    Get up and follow me;
For I am going to Edinburgh town,
    A rich wedding for to see.'

row'd] rolled, wrapped.   greet] cry.

ANONYMOUS

O slowly, slowly rase she up,
   And slowly put she on;
And slowly rade she out the way
   Wi' mony a weary groan.

The Queen was clad in scarlet,
   Her merry maids all in green;
And every town that they cam to,
   They took Marie for the Queen.

'Ride hooly, hooly, gentlemen,
   Ride hooly now wi' me!
For never, I am sure, a wearier burd
   Rade in your companie.'—

But little wist Marie Hamilton,
   When she rade on the brown,
That she was gaen to Edinburgh town,
   And a' to be put down.

'Why weep ye so, ye burgess wives,
   Why look ye so on me?
O I am going to Edinburgh town,
   A rich wedding to see.'

When she gaed up the tolbooth stairs,
   The corks frae her heels did flee;
And lang or e'er she cam down again,
   She was condemn'd to die.

When she cam to the Netherbow port,
   She laugh'd loud laughters three;
But when she came to the gallows foot
   The tears blinded her e'e.

hooly] gently.

ANONYMOUS

'Yestreen the Queen had four Maries,
   The night she'll hae but three;
There was Marie Seaton, and Marie Beaton,
   And Marie Carmichael, and me.

'O often have I dress'd my Queen
   And put gowd upon her hair;
But now I've gotten for my reward
   The gallows to be my share.

'Often have I dress'd my Queen
   And often made her bed;
But now I've gotten for my reward
   The gallows tree to tread.

'I charge ye all, ye mariners,
   When ye sail owre the faem,
Let neither my father nor mother get wit
   But that I'm coming hame.

'I charge ye all, ye mariners,
   That sail upon the sea,
That neither my father nor mother get wit
   The dog's death I'm to die.

'For if my father and mother got wit,
   And my bold brethren three,
O mickle wad be the gude red blude
   This day wad be spilt for me!

'O little did my mother ken,
   The day she cradled me,
The lands I was to travel in
   Or the death I was to die!

376. Binnorie

THERE were twa sisters sat in a bour;
    Binnorie, O Binnorie!
There cam a knight to be their wooer,
    By the bonnie milldams o' Binnorie.

He courted the eldest with glove and ring,
But he lo'ed the youngest abune a thing.

The eldest she was vexèd sair,
And sair envied her sister fair.

Upon a morning fair and clear,
She cried upon her sister dear:

'O sister, sister, tak my hand,
And let's go down to the river-strand.'

She's ta'en her by the lily hand,
And led her down to the river-strand.

The youngest stood upon a stane,
The eldest cam and push'd her in.

'O sister, sister, reach your hand!
And ye sall be heir o' half my land:

'O sister, reach me but your glove!
And sweet William sall be your love.'

Sometimes she sank, sometimes she swam,
Until she cam to the miller's dam.

Out then cam the miller's son,
And saw the fair maid soummin' in.

'O father, father, draw your dam!
There's either a mermaid or a milk-white swan.'

soummin'] swimming.

ANONYMOUS

The miller hasted and drew his dam,
And there he found a drown'd woman.

You couldna see her middle sma',
Her gowden girdle was sae braw.

You couldna see her lily feet,
Her gowden fringes were sae deep.

All amang her yellow hair
A string o' pearls was twisted rare.

You couldna see her fingers sma',
Wi' diamond rings they were cover'd a'.

And by there cam a harper fine,
That harpit to the king at dine.

And when he look'd that lady on,
He sigh'd and made a heavy moan.

He's made a harp of her breast-bane,
Whose sound wad melt a heart of stane.

He's ta'en three locks o' her yellow hair,
And wi' them strung his harp sae rare.

He went into her father's hall,
And there was the court assembled all.

He laid his harp upon a stane,
And straight it began to play by lane.

'O yonder sits my father, the King,
And yonder sits my mother, the Queen;

'And yonder stands my brother Hugh,
And by him my William, sweet and true.'

But the last tune that the harp play'd then—
  Binnorie, O Binnorie!
Was, 'Woe to my sister, false Helèn!'
  By the bonnie milldams o' Binnorie.

377. *The Bonnie House o' Airlie*

IT fell on a day, and a bonnie simmer day,
  When green grew aits and barley,
That there fell out a great dispute
  Between Argyll and Airlie.

Argyll has raised an hunder men,
  An hunder harness'd rarely,
And he's awa' by the back of Dunkell,
  To plunder the castle of Airlie.

Lady Ogilvie looks o'er her bower-window,
  And O but she looks warely!
And there she spied the great Argyll,
  Come to plunder the bonnie house of Airlie.

'Come down, come down, my Lady Ogilvie,
  Come down and kiss me fairly:'
'O I winna kiss the fause Argyll,
  If he shouldna leave a standing stane in Airlie.'

He hath taken her by the left shoulder,
  Says, 'Dame, where lies thy dowry?'
'O it's east and west yon wan water side,
  And it's down by the banks of the Airlie.'

They hae sought it up, they hae sought it down,
    They hae sought it maist severely,
Till they fand it in the fair plum-tree
    That shines on the bowling-green of Airlie.

He hath taken her by the middle sae small,
    And O but she grat sairly!
And laid her down by the bonnie burn-side,
    Till they plunder'd the castle of Airlie.

'Gif my gude lord war here this night,
    As he is with King Charlie,
Neither you, nor ony ither Scottish lord,
    Durst avow to the plundering of Airlie.

'Gif my gude lord war now at hame,
    As he is with his king,
There durst nae a Campbell in a' Argyll
    Set fit on Airlie green.

'Ten bonnie sons I have borne unto him,
    The eleventh ne'er saw his daddy;
But though I had an hunder mair,
    I'd gie them a' to King Charlie!'

378. *The Wife of Usher's Well*

THERE lived a wife at Usher's well,
    And a wealthy wife was she;
She had three stout and stalwart sons,
    And sent them o'er the sea.

ANONYMOUS

They hadna been a week from her,
   A week but barely ane,
When word came to the carline wife
   That her three sons were gane.

They hadna been a week from her,
   A week but barely three,
When word came to the carline wife
   That her sons she'd never see.

'I wish the wind may never cease.
   Nor fashes in the flood,
Till my three sons come hame to me,
   In earthly flesh and blood!'

It fell about the Martinmas,
   When nights are lang and mirk,
The carline wife's three sons came hame,
   And their hats were o' the birk.

It neither grew in syke nor ditch,
   Nor yet in ony sheugh;
But at the gates o' Paradise
   That birk grew fair eneugh.

'Blow up the fire, my maidens!
   Bring water from the well!
For a' my house shall feast this night,
   Since my three sons are well.'

And she has made to them a bed,
   She's made it large and wide;
And she's ta'en her mantle her about,
   Sat down at the bedside.

fashes] troubles.   syke] marsh.   sheugh] trench.

ANONYMOUS

Up then crew the red, red cock,
  And up and crew the gray;
The eldest to the youngest said.
  ''Tis time we were away.'

The cock he hadna craw'd but once,
  And clapp'd his wings at a',
When the youngest to the eldest said,
  'Brother, we must awa'.

'The cock doth craw, the day doth daw,
  The channerin' worm doth chide;
Gin we be miss'd out o' our place,
  A sair pain we maun bide.'

'Lie still, lie still but a little wee while,
  Lie still but if we may;
Gin my mother should miss us when she wakes,
  She'll go mad ere it be day.'

'Fare ye weel, my mother dear!
  Fareweel to barn and byre!
And fare ye weel, the bonny lass
  That kindles my mother's fire!'

379.   *The Three Ravens*

THERE were three ravens sat on a tree,
  They were as black as they might be.

The one of them said to his make,
  'Where shall we our breakfast take?'

378. channerin'] fretting.   *379.* make] mate.

ANONYMOUS

'Down in yonder greene field
There lies a knight slain under his shield;

'His hounds they lie down at his feet,
So well they can their master keep;

'His hawks they flie so eagerly,
There's no fowl dare come him nigh.'

Down there comes a fallow doe
As great with young as she might goe.

She lift up his bloudy head
And kist his wounds that were so red.

She gat him up upon her back
And carried him to earthen lake.

She buried him before the prime,
She was dead herself ere evensong time.

God send every gentleman
Such hounds, such hawks, and such a leman.

380.   *The Twa Corbies*

(SCOTTISH VERSION)

AS I was walking all alane
I heard twa corbies making a mane:
The tane unto the tither did say,
'Whar sall we gang and dine the day?'

380. corbies] ravens.

ANONYMOUS

'—In behint yon auld fail dyke
I wot there lies a new-slain knight;
And naebody kens that he lies there
But his hawk, his hound, and his lady fair.

'His hound is to the hunting gane,
His hawk to fetch the wild-fowl hame,
His lady's ta'en anither mate,
So we may mak our dinner sweet.

'Ye'll sit on his white hause-bane,
And I'll pike out his bonny blue e'en:
Wi' ae lock o' his gowden hair
We'll theek our nest when it grows bare.

'Mony a one for him maks mane,
But nane sall ken whar he is gane:
O'er his white banes, when they are bare,
The wind sall blaw for evermair.'

381. *A Lyke-Wake Dirge*

THIS ae nighte, this ae nighte,
—*Every nighte and alle,*
Fire and fleet and candle-lighte,
And Christe receive thy saule.

When thou from hence away art past,
—*Every nighte and alle,*
To Whinny-muir thou com'st at last;
And Christe receive thy saule.

380. fail] turf. hause] neck. theek] thatch. *381.* fleet] house-room.

ANONYMOUS

If ever thou gavest hosen and shoon,
—*Every nighte and alle,*
Sit thee down and put them on;
And Christe receive thy saule.

If hosen and shoon thou ne'er gav'st nane
—*Every nighte and alle,*
The whinnes sall prick thee to the bare bane;
And Christe receive thy saule.

From Whinny-muir when thou may'st pass,
—*Every nighte and alle,*
To Brig o' Dread thou com'st at last;
And Christe receive thy saule.

From Brig o' Dread when thou may'st pass,
—*Every nighte and alle,*
To Purgatory fire thou com'st at last;
And Christe receive thy saule.

If ever thou gavest meat or drink,
—*Every nighte and alle,*
The fire sall never make thee shrink;
And Christe receive thy saule.

If meat or drink thou ne'er gav'st nane,
—*Every nighte and alle,*
The fire will burn thee to the bare bane;
And Christe receive thy saule.

This ae nighte, this ae nighte,
—*Every nighte and alle,*
Fire and fleet and candle-lighte,
And Christe receive thy saule.

ANONYMOUS

382.   *The Seven Virgins.*

A CAROL

ALL under the leaves and the leaves of life
    I met with virgins seven,
And one of them was Mary mild,
    Our Lord's mother of Heaven.

'O what are you seeking, you seven fair maids,
    All under the leaves of life?
Come tell, come tell, what seek you
    All under the leaves of life?'

'We're seeking for no leaves, Thomas,
    But for a friend of thine;
We're seeking for sweet Jesus Christ,
    To be our guide and thine.'

'Go down, go down, to yonder town,
    And sit in the gallery,
And there you'll see sweet Jesus Christ
    Nail'd to a big yew-tree.'

So down they went to yonder town
    As fast as foot could fall,
And many a grievous bitter tear
    From the virgins' eyes did fall.

'O peace, Mother, O peace, Mother,
    Your weeping doth me grieve:
I must suffer this,' He said,
    'For Adam and for Eve.

'O Mother, take you John Evangelist
  All for to be your son,
And he will comfort you sometimes,
  Mother, as I have done.'

'O come, thou John Evangelist,
  Thou'rt welcome unto me;
But more welcome my own dear Son,
  Whom I nursed on my knee.'

Then He laid His head on His right shoulder,
  Seeing death it struck Him nigh—
'The Holy Ghost be with your soul,
  I die, Mother dear, I die.'

O the rose, the gentle rose,
  And the fennel that grows so green!
God give us grace in every place
  To pray for our king and queen.

Furthermore for our enemies all
  Our prayers they should be strong:
Amen, good Lord; your charity
  Is the ending of my song.

383. *Two Rivers*

SAYS Tweed to Till—
  'What gars ye rin sae still?'
Says Till to Tweed—
'Though ye rin with speed
  And I rin slaw,
For ae man that ye droon
  I droon twa.'

ANONYMOUS

384.   *Cradle Song*

O MY deir hert, young Jesus sweit,
 Prepare thy creddil in my spreit,
And I sall rock thee in my hert
And never mair from thee depart.

But I sall praise thee evermoir
With sangis sweit unto thy gloir;
The knees of my hert sall I bow,
And sing that richt *Balulalow!*

385.   *The Call*

MY blood so red
 For thee was shed,
Come home again, come home again;
My own sweet heart, come home again!
 You've gone astray
 Out of your way,
Come home again, come home again!

386.   *The Bonny Earl of Murray*

YE Highlands and ye Lawlands,
 O where hae ye been?
They hae slain the Earl of Murray,
 And hae laid him on the green.

Now wae be to thee, Huntley!
 And whairfore did ye sae!
I bade you bring him wi' you,
 But forbade you him to slay.

ANONYMOUS

He was a braw gallant,
    And he rid at the ring;
And the bonny Earl of Murray,
    O he might hae been a king!

He was a braw gallant,
    And he play'd at the ba';
And the bonny Earl of Murray
    Was the flower amang them a'!

He was a braw gallant,
    And he play'd at the gluve;
And the bonny Earl of Murray,
    O he was the Queen's luve!

O lang will his Lady
    Look owre the Castle Downe,
Ere she see the Earl of Murray
    Come sounding through the town!

387. *Helen of Kirconnell*

I WISH I were where Helen lies,
    Night and day on me she cries;
O that I were where Helen lies,
    On fair Kirconnell lea!

Curst be the heart that thought the thought,
And curst the hand that fired the shot,
When in my arms burd Helen dropt,
    And died to succour me!

O think na ye my heart was sair,
When my Love dropp'd and spak nae mair!
There did she swoon wi' meikle care,
    On fair Kirconnell lea.

ANONYMOUS

As I went down the water side,
None but my foe to be my guide,
None but my foe to be my guide,
   On fair Kirconnell lea;

I lighted down my sword to draw,
I hackèd him in pieces sma',
I hackèd him in pieces sma',
   For her sake that died for me.

O Helen fair, beyond compare!
I'll mak a garland o' thy hair,
Shall bind my heart for evermair,
   Until the day I die!

O that I were where Helen lies!
Night and day on me she cries;
Out of my bed she bids me rise,
   Says, 'Haste, and come to me!'

O Helen fair! O Helen chaste!
If I were with thee, I'd be blest,
Where thou lies low and taks thy rest,
   On fair Kirconnell lea.

I wish my grave were growing green,
A winding-sheet drawn owre my e'en,
And I in Helen's arms lying,
   On fair Kirconnell lea.

I wish I were where Helen lies!
Night and day on me she cries;
And I am weary of the skies,
   For her sake that died for me.

ANONYMOUS

388. *Waly, Waly*

O WALY, waly, up the bank,
   And waly, waly, doun the brae,
And waly, waly, yon burn-side,
   Where I and my Love wont to gae!
I lean'd my back unto an aik,
   I thocht it was a trustie tree;
But first it bow'd and syne it brak—
   Sae my true love did lichtlie me.

O waly, waly, gin love be bonnie
   A little time while it is new!
But when 'tis auld it waxeth cauld,
   And fades awa' like morning dew.
O wherefore should I busk my heid,
   Or wherefore should I kame my hair?
For my true Love has me forsook,
   And says he'll never lo'e me mair.

Now Arthur's Seat sall be my bed,
   The sheets sall ne'er be 'filed by me;
Saint Anton's well sall be my drink;
   Since my true Love has forsaken me.
Marti'mas wind, when wilt thou blaw,
   And shake the green leaves aff the tree?
O gentle Death, when wilt thou come?
   For of my life I am wearìe.

'Tis not the frost, that freezes fell,
   Nor blawing snaw's inclemencie,
'Tis not sic cauld that makes me cry;
   But my Love's heart grown cauld to me.

When we cam in by Glasgow toun,
    We were a comely sicht to see;
My Love was clad in the black velvèt,
    And I mysel in cramasie.

But had I wist, before I kist,
    That love had been sae ill to win,
I had lock'd my heart in a case o' gowd,
    And pinn'd it wi' a siller pin.

And O! if my young babe were born,
    And set upon the nurse's knee;
And I mysel were dead and gane,
    And the green grass growing over me!

389. *Barbara Allen's Cruelty*

IN Scarlet town, where I was born,
    There was a fair maid dwellin',
Made every youth cry *Well-a-way!*
    Her name was Barbara Allen.

All in the merry month of May,
    When green buds they were swellin',
Young Jemmy Grove on his death-bed lay,
    For love of Barbara Allen.

He sent his man in to her then,
    To the town where she was dwellin',
'O haste and come to my master dear,
    If your name be Barbara Allen.'

So slowly, slowly rase she up,
    And slowly she came nigh him,
And when she drew the curtain by—
    'Young man, I think you're dyin'.'

388. cramasie] crimson.

'O it's I am sick and very very sick,
  And it's all for Barbara Allen.'
'O the better for me ye'se never be,
  Tho' your heart's blood were a-spillin'!
'O dinna ye mind, young man,' says she,
  'When the red wine ye were fillin',
That ye made the healths go round and round,
  And slighted Barbara Allen?'

He turn'd his face unto the wall,
  And death was with him dealin':
'Adieu, adieu, my dear friends all,
  And be kind to Barbara Allen!'

As she was walking o'er the fields,
  She heard the dead-bell knellin';
And every jow the dead-bell gave
  Cried 'Woe to Barbara Allen.'

'O mother, mother, make my bed,
  O make it saft and narrow:
My love has died for me to-day,
  I'll die for him to-morrow.

'Farewell,' she said, 'ye virgins all,
  And shun the fault I fell in:
Henceforth take warning by the fall
  Of cruel Barbara Allen.'

390. *Pipe and Can*

I

THE Indian weed witherèd quite;
  Green at morn, cut down at night;
Shows thy decay: all flesh is hay:
  Thus think, then drink Tobacco.

389. jow] beat, toll.

ANONYMOUS

And when the smoke ascends on high,
Think thou behold'st the vanity
Of worldly stuff, gone with a puff:
 Thus think, then drink Tobacco.

But when the pipe grows foul within,
Think of thy soul defiled with sin,
And that the fire doth it require:
 Thus think, then drink Tobacco.

The ashes, that are left behind,
May serve to put thee still in mind
That unto dust return thou must:
 Thus think, then drink Tobacco.

II

WHEN as the chill Charokko blows,
 And Winter tells a heavy tale;
When pyes and daws and rooks and crows
Sit cursing of the frosts and snows;
 Then give me ale.

Ale in a Saxon rumkin then,
 Such as will make grimalkin prate;
Bids valour burgeon in tall men,
Quickens the poet's wit and pen,
 Despises fate.

Ale, that the absent battle fights,
 And frames the march of Swedish drum,
Disputes with princes, laws, and rights,
What's done and past tells mortal wights,
 And what's to come.

Charokko] Scirocco.

ANONYMOUS

Ale, that the plowman's heart up-keeps
　And equals it with tyrants' thrones,
That wipes the eye that over-weeps,
And lulls in sure and dainty sleeps
　　　Th' o'er-wearied bones.

Grandchild of Ceres, Bacchus' daughter,
　Wine's emulous neighbour, though but stale,
Ennobling all the nymphs of water,
And filling each man's heart with laughter—
　　　Ha! give me ale!

391. *Love will find out the Way*

OVER the mountains
　And over the waves,
Under the fountains
　And under the graves;
Under floods that are deepest,
　Which Neptune obey,
Over rocks that are steepest,
　Love will find out the way.

When there is no place
　For the glow-worm to lie,
When there is no space
　For receipt of a fly;
When the midge dares not venture
　Lest herself fast she lay,
If Love come, he will enter
　And will find out the way.

ANONYMOUS

You may esteem him
  A child for his might;
Or you may deem him
  A coward for his flight;
But if she whom Love doth honour
  Be conceal'd from the day—
Set a thousand guards upon her,
  Love will find out the way.

Some think to lose him
  By having him confined;
And some do suppose him,
  Poor heart! to be blind;
But if ne'er so close ye wall him,
  Do the best that ye may,
Blind Love, if so ye call him,
  He will find out his way.

You may train the eagle
  To stoop to your fist;
Or you may inveigle
  The Phœnix of the east;
The lioness, you may move her
  To give over her prey;
But you'll ne'er stop a lover—
  He will find out the way.

If the earth it should part him,
  He would gallop it o'er;
If the seas should o'erthwart him,
  He would swim to the shore;
Should his Love become a swallow,
  Through the air to stray,
Love will lend wings to follow,
  And will find out the way.

ANONYMOUS

    There is no striving
        To cross his intent;
    There is no contriving
        His plots to prevent;
    But if once the message greet him
        That his True Love doth stay,
    If Death should come and meet him,
        Love will find out the way!

392. *Phillada flouts Me*

O WHAT a plague is love!
    How shall I bear it?
She will inconstant prove,
    I greatly fear it.
She so torments my mind
    That my strength faileth,
And wavers with the wind
    As a ship saileth.
Please her the best I may,
She loves still to gainsay;
Alack and well-a-day!
    Phillada flouts me.

At the fair yesterday
    She did pass by me;
She look'd another way
    And would not spy me:
I woo'd her for to dine,
    But could not get her;
Will had her to the wine—
    He might entreat her.

ANONYMOUS

With Daniel she did dance,
On me she look'd askance:
O thrice unhappy chance!
Phillada flouts me.

Fair maid, be not so coy,
Do not disdain me!
I am my mother's joy:
Sweet, entertain me!
She'll give me, when she dies,
All that is fitting:
Her poultry and her bees,
And her goose sitting,
A pair of mattrass beds,
And a bag full of shreds;
And yet, for all this guedes,
Phillada flouts me!

She hath a clout of mine
Wrought with blue coventry,
Which she keeps for a sign
Of my fidelity:
But i' faith, if she flinch
She shall not wear it;
To Tib, my t'other wench,
I mean to bear it.
And yet it grieves my heart
So soon from her to part:
Death strike me with his dart!
Phillada flouts me.

Thou shalt eat crudded cream
All the year lasting,

guedes] goods, property of any kind.

ANONYMOUS

And drink the crystal stream
   Pleasant in tasting;
Whig and whey whilst thou lust,
   And bramble-berries,
Pie-lid and pastry-crust,
   Pears, plums, and cherries.
Thy raiment shall be thin,
Made of a weevil's skin—
Yet all's not worth a pin!
   Phillada flouts me.

In the last month of May
   I made her posies;
I heard her often say
   That she loved roses.
Cowslips and gillyflowers
   And the white lily
I brought to deck the bowers
   For my sweet Philly.
But she did all disdain,
And threw them back again;
Therefore 'tis flat and plain
   Phillada flouts me.

Fair maiden, have a care,
   And in time take me;
I can have those as fair
   If you forsake me:
For Doll the dairy-maid
   Laugh'd at me lately,
And wanton Winifred
   Favours me greatly.

ANONYMOUS

One throws milk on my clothes,
T'other plays with my nose;
What wanting signs are those?
　　Phillada flouts me.

I cannot work nor sleep
　　At all in season:
Love wounds my heart so deep
　　Without all reason.
I 'gin to pine away
　　In my love's shadow,
Like as a fat beast may,
　　Penn'd in a meadow.
I shall be dead, I fear,
Within this thousand year:
And all for that my dear
　　Phillada flouts me.

WILLIAM STRODE
1602-1645

393. Chloris in the Snow

I SAW fair Chloris walk alone,
　When feather'd rain came softly down,
As Jove descending from his Tower
To court her in a silver shower:
The wanton snow flew to her breast,
Like pretty birds into their nest,
But, overcome with whiteness there,
For grief it thaw'd into a tear:
　　Thence falling on her garments' hem,
　　To deck her, froze into a gem.

THOMAS STANLEY
1625-1678

394. The Relapse

O TURN away those cruel eyes,
    The stars of my undoing!
Or death, in such a bright disguise,
    May tempt a second wooing.

Punish their blind and impious pride,
    Who dare contemn thy glory;
It was my fall that deified
    Thy name, and seal'd thy story.

Yet no new sufferings can prepare
    A higher praise to crown thee;
Though my first death proclaim thee fair,
    My second will unthrone thee.

Lovers will doubt thou canst entice
    No other for thy fuel,
And if thou burn one victim twice,
    Both think thee poor and cruel.

THOMAS D'URFEY
1653-1723

395. Chloe Divine

CHLOE's a Nymph in flowery groves,
    A Nereid in the streams;
Saint-like she in the temple moves,
    A woman in my dreams.

Love steals artillery from her eyes,
    The Graces point her charms;
Orpheus is rivall'd in her voice,
    And Venus in her arms.

THOMAS D'URFEY

Never so happily in one
    Did heaven and earth combine:
And yet 'tis flesh and blood alone
    That makes her so divine.

CHARLES COTTON
1630-1687

396. To Cœlia

WHEN, Cœlia, must my old day set,
    And my young morning rise
In beams of joy so bright as yet
    Ne'er bless'd a lover's eyes?
My state is more advanced than when
    I first attempted thee:
I sued to be a servant then,
    But now to be made free.

I've served my time faithful and true,
    Expecting to be placed
In happy freedom, as my due,
    To all the joys thou hast:
Ill husbandry in love is such
    A scandal to love's power,
We ought not to misspend so much
    As one poor short-lived hour.

Yet think not, sweet, I'm weary grown,
    That I pretend such haste;
Since none to surfeit e'er was known
    Before he had a taste:
My infant love could humbly wait
    When, young, it scarce knew how
To plead; but grown to man's estate,
    He is impatient now.

KATHERINE PHILIPS ('ORINDA')
1631-1664

397. *To One persuading a Lady to Marriage*

FORBEAR, bold youth; all's heaven here,
   And what you do aver
To others courtship may appear,
   'Tis sacrilege to her.
She is a public deity;
   And were't not very odd
She should dispose herself to be
   A petty household god?

First make the sun in private shine
   And bid the world adieu,
That so he may his beams confine
   In compliment to you:
But if of that you do despair,
   Think how you did amiss
To strive to fix her beams which are
   More bright and large than his.

JOHN DRYDEN
1631-1700

398. *Ode*

To the Pious Memory of the accomplished young lady, Mrs. Anne Killigrew, excellent in the two sister arts of Poesy and Painting

THOU youngest virgin-daughter of the skies,
   Made in the last promotion of the blest;
Whose palms, new pluck'd from Paradise,
In spreading branches more sublimely rise,

JOHN DRYDEN

Rich with immortal green above the rest:
Whether, adopted to some neighbouring star,
Thou roll'st above us, in thy wandering race,
   Or, in procession fixt and regular,
   Mov'd with the heaven's majestic pace;
   Or, call'd to more superior bliss,
Thou tread'st with seraphims the vast abyss:
Whatever happy region is thy place,
Cease thy celestial song a little space;
Thou wilt have time enough for hymns divine,
   Since Heaven's eternal year is thine.
Hear, then, a mortal Muse thy praise rehearse,
       In no ignoble verse;
But such as thy own voice did practise here,
When thy first-fruits of Poesy were given,
To make thyself a welcome inmate there;
   While yet a young probationer,
       And candidate of heaven.

   If by traduction came thy mind,
   Our wonder is the less, to find
A soul so charming from a stock so good;
Thy father was transfus'd into thy blood:
So wert thou born into the tuneful strain,
An early, rich, and inexhausted vein.
   But if thy pre-existing soul
   Was form'd at first with myriads more,
It did through all the mighty poets roll
   Who Greek or Latin laurels wore,
And was that Sappho last, which once it was before.
   If so, then cease thy flight, O heaven-born mind!
Thou hast no dross to purge from thy rich ore:
Nor can thy soul a fairer mansion find,

JOHN DRYDEN

Than was the beauteous frame she left behind :
Return, to fill or mend the quire of thy celestial kind.

  May we presume to say, that, at thy birth,
New joy was sprung in heaven as well as here on earth?
For sure the milder planets did combine
On thy auspicious horoscope to shine,
And even the most malicious were in trine.
  Thy brother-angels at thy birth
  Strung each his lyre, and tun'd it high,
  That all the people of the sky
Might know a poetess was born on earth ;
  And then, if ever, mortal ears
  Had heard the music of the spheres.
And if no clust'ring swarm of bees
On thy sweet mouth distill'd their golden dew,
  'Twas that such vulgar miracles
  Heaven had not leisure to renew :
For all the blest fraternity of love
Solemniz'd there thy birth, and kept thy holiday above.

  O gracious God! how far have we
Profan'd thy heavenly gift of Poesy!
Made prostitute and profligate the Muse,
Debas'd to each obscene and impious use,
Whose harmony was first ordain'd above,
For tongues of angels and for hymns of love!
O wretched we! why were we hurried down
  This lubrique and adulterate age
  (Nay, added fat pollutions of our own),
  To increase the streaming ordures of the stage?
What can we say to excuse our second fall?
Let this thy Vestal, Heaven, atone for all!
Her Arethusian stream remains unsoil'd,

JOHN DRYDEN

Unmixt with foreign filth, and undefil'd;
Her wit was more than man, her innocence a child.

 Art she had none, yet wanted none,
  For Nature did that want supply:
 So rich in treasures of her own,
  She might our boasted stores defy:
Such noble vigour did her verse adorn,
That it seem'd borrow'd, where 'twas only born.
Her morals, too, were in her bosom bred,
 By great examples daily fed,
What in the best of books, her father's life, she read.
And to be read herself she need not fear;
Each test, and every light, her Muse will bear,
Though Epictetus with his lamp were there.
Even love (for love sometimes her Muse exprest)
Was but a lambent flame which play'd about her breast,
 Light as the vapours of a morning dream;
So cold herself, whilst she such warmth exprest,
 'Twas Cupid bathing in Diana's stream. . . .

 Now all those charms, that blooming grace,
The well-proportion'd shape, and beauteous face,
Shall never more be seen by mortal eyes;
In earth the much-lamented virgin lies.
Not wit, nor piety could fate prevent;
Nor was the cruel destiny content
To finish all the murder at a blow,
To sweep at once her life and beauty too;
But, like a harden'd felon, took a pride
 To work more mischievously slow,
 And plunder'd first, and then destroy'd.
O double sacrilege on things divine,

JOHN DRYDEN

To rob the relic, and deface the shrine!
    But thus Orinda died:
Heaven, by the same disease, did both translate;
As equal were their souls, so equal was their fate.

Meantime, her warlike brother on the seas
His waving streamers to the winds displays,
And vows for his return, with vain devotion, pays.
    Ah, generous youth! that wish forbear,
    The winds too soon will waft thee here!
    Slack all thy sails, and fear to come,
Alas, thou know'st not, thou art wreck'd at home!
No more shalt thou behold thy sister's face,
Thou hast already had her last embrace.
But look aloft, and if thou kenn'st from far,
Among the Pleiads a new kindl'd star,
If any sparkles than the rest more bright,
'Tis she that shines in that propitious light.

When in mid-air the golden trump shall sound,
    To raise the nations under ground;
When, in the Valley of Jehoshaphat,
The judging God shall close the book of Fate,
    And there the last assizes keep
    For those who wake and those who sleep;
    When rattling bones together fly
    From the four corners of the sky;
When sinews o'er the skeletons are spread,
Those cloth'd with flesh, and life inspires the dead;
The sacred poets first shall hear the sound,
    And foremost from the tomb shall bound,
For they are cover'd with the lightest ground;
And straight, with inborn vigour, on the wing,

Like mounting larks, to the new morning sing.
There thou, sweet Saint, before the quire shalt go,
As harbinger of Heaven, the way to show,
The way which thou so well hast learn'd below.

399. *A Song for St. Cecilia's Day, 1687*

FROM harmony, from heavenly harmony,
    This universal frame began:
  When nature underneath a heap
    Of jarring atoms lay,
    And could not heave her head,
The tuneful voice was heard from high,
    'Arise, ye more than dead!'
Then cold, and hot, and moist, and dry,
  In order to their stations leap,
    And Music's power obey.
From harmony, from heavenly harmony,
    This universal frame began:
    From harmony to harmony
Through all the compass of the notes it ran,
The diapason closing full in Man.

What passion cannot Music raise and quell?
    When Jubal struck the chorded shell,
  His listening brethren stood around,
    And, wondering, on their faces fell
  To worship that celestial sound:
Less than a God they thought there could not dwell
    Within the hollow of that shell,
    That spoke so sweetly, and so well.
What passion cannot Music raise and quell?

JOHN DRYDEN

    The trumpet's loud clangour
        Excites us to arms,
      With shrill notes of anger,
        And mortal alarms.
The double double double beat
      Of the thundering drum
    Cries Hark! the foes come;
Charge, charge, 'tis too late to retreat!

    The soft complaining flute,
    In dying notes, discovers
    The woes of hopeless lovers,
Whose dirge is whisper'd by the warbling lute.

    Sharp violins proclaim
Their jealous pangs and desperation,
Fury, frantic indignation,
Depth of pains, and height of passion,
  For the fair, disdainful dame.

    But O, what art can teach,
    What human voice can reach,
      The sacred organ's praise?
    Notes inspiring holy love,
Notes that wing their heavenly ways
    To mend the choirs above.

  Orpheus could lead the savage race;
  And trees unrooted left their place,
    Sequacious of the lyre;
But bright Cecilia rais'd the wonder higher:
When to her organ vocal breath was given,
  An angel heard, and straight appear'd
    Mistaking Earth for Heaven.

JOHN DRYDEN

Grand Chorus.

As from the power of sacred lays
    The spheres began to move,
And sung the great Creator's praise
    To all the Blest above;
So when the last and dreadful hour
This crumbling pageant shall devour,
The trumpet shall be heard on high,
The dead shall live, the living die,
And Music shall untune the sky!

400. *Ah, how sweet it is to love!*

AH, how sweet it is to love!
    Ah, how gay is young Desire!
And what pleasing pains we prove
    When we first approach Love's fire!
Pains of love be sweeter far
Than all other pleasures are.

Sighs which are from lovers blown
    Do but gently heave the heart:
Ev'n the tears they shed alone
    Cure, like trickling balm, their smart:
Lovers, when they lose their breath,
Bleed away in easy death.

Love and Time with reverence use,
    Treat them like a parting friend;
Nor the golden gifts refuse
    Which in youth sincere they send:
For each year their price is more,
And they less simple than before.

JOHN DRYDEN

Love, like spring-tides full and high,
    Swells in every youthful vein;
But each tide does less supply,
    Till they quite shrink in again:
If a flow in age appear,
'Tis but rain, and runs not clear.

401. Hidden Flame

I FEED a flame within, which so torments me
    That it both pains my heart, and yet contents me:
'Tis such a pleasing smart, and I so love it,
That I had rather die than once remove it.

Yet he, for whom I grieve, shall never know it;
My tongue does not betray, nor my eyes show it.
Not a sigh, nor a tear, my pain discloses,
But they fall silently, like dew on roses.

Thus, to prevent my Love from being cruel,
My heart's the sacrifice, as 'tis the fuel;
And while I suffer this to give him quiet,
My faith rewards my love, though he deny it.

On his eyes will I gaze, and there delight me;
While I conceal my love no frown can fright me.
To be more happy I dare not aspire,
Nor can I fall more low, mounting no higher.

JOHN DRYDEN

402. *Song to a Fair Young Lady, going out of the Town in the Spring*

ASK not the cause why sullen Spring
  So long delays her flowers to bear;
Why warbling birds forget to sing,
  And winter storms invert the year:
Chloris is gone; and fate provides
To make it Spring where she resides.

Chloris is gone, the cruel fair;
  She cast not back a pitying eye:
But left her lover in despair
  To sigh, to languish, and to die:
Ah! how can those fair eyes endure
To give the wounds they will not cure?

Great God of Love, why hast thou made
  A face that can all hearts command,
That all religions can invade,
  And change the laws of every land?
Where thou hadst plac'd such power before,
Thou shouldst have made her mercy more.

When Chloris to the temple comes,
  Adoring crowds before her fall;
She can restore the dead from tombs
  And every life but mine recall.
I only am by Love design'd
To be the victim for mankind.

CHARLES WEBBE
c. 1673

403. *Against Indifference*

MORE love or more disdain I crave;
   Sweet, be not still indifferent:
O send me quickly to my grave,
   Or else afford me more content!
Or love or hate me more or less,
For love abhors all lukewarmness.

Give me a tempest if 'twill drive
   Me to the place where I would be;
Or if you'll have me still alive,
   Confess you will be kind to me.
Give hopes of bliss or dig my grave:
More love or more disdain I crave.

SIR GEORGE ETHEREGE
1635-1691

404. *Song*

LADIES, though to your conquering eyes
   Love, owes his chiefest victories,
And borrows those bright arms from you
With which he does the world subdue,
Yet you yourselves are not above
The empire nor the griefs of love.

Then rack not lovers with disdain,
Lest Love on you revenge their pain:
You are not free because you're fair:
The Boy did not his Mother spare.
Beauty's but an offensive dart:
It is no armour for the heart.

SIR GEORGE ETHEREGE

405. *To a Lady asking him how long he would love her*

IT is not, Celia, in our power
  To say how long our love will last;
It may be we within this hour
  May lose those joys we now do taste;
The Blessèd, that immortal be,
From change in love are only free.

Then since we mortal lovers are,
  Ask not how long our love will last;
But while it does, let us take care
  Each minute be with pleasure past:
Were it not madness to deny
To live because we're sure to die?

THOMAS TRAHERNE
1637?-1674

406. *News*

NEWS from a foreign country came
  As if my treasure and my wealth lay there;
So much it did my heart inflame,
'Twas wont to call my Soul into mine ear;
    Which thither went to meet
      The approaching sweet,
    And on the threshold stood
To entertain the unknown Good.
    It hover'd there
  As if 'twould leave mine ear,

THOMAS TRAHERNE

And was so eager to embrace
  The joyful tidings as they came,
'Twould almost leave its dwelling-place
  To entertain that same.

As if the tidings were the things,
My very joys themselves, my foreign treasure—
Or else did bear them on their wings—
With so much joy they came, with so much pleasure.
  My Soul stood at that gate
    To recreate
  Itself with bliss, and to
Be pleased with speed. A fuller view
    It fain would take,
  Yet journeys back would make
Unto my heart; as if 'twould fain
  Go out to meet, yet stay within
  To fit a place to entertain
    And bring the tidings in.

What sacred instinct did inspire
My soul in childhood with a hope so strong?
What secret force moved my desire
To expect my joys beyond the seas, so young?
    Felicity I knew
    Was out of view,
    And being here alone,
I saw that happiness was gone
    From me! For this
  I thirsted absent bliss,
And thought that sure beyond the seas,
  Or else in something near at hand—
I knew not yet—since naught did please
  I knew—my Bliss did stand.

THOMAS TRAHERNE

  But little did the infant dream
That all the treasures of the world were by:
  And that himself was so the cream
And crown of all which round about did lie.
    Yet thus it was: the Gem,
      The Diadem,
    The ring enclosing all
  That stood upon this earthly ball,
    The Heavenly eye,
   Much wider than the sky,
  Wherein they all included were,
  The glorious Soul, that was the King
Made to possess them, did appear
   A small and little thing!

THOMAS FLATMAN
1637-1688

407. *The Sad Day*

O THE sad day!
  When friends shall shake their heads, and say
Of miserable me—
'Hark, how he groans!
Look, how he pants for breath!
See how he struggles with the pangs of death!'
When they shall say of these dear eyes—
'How hollow, O how dim they be!
Mark how his breast doth rise and swell
Against his potent enemy!'
When some old friend shall step to my bedside,
Touch my chill face, and thence shall gently slide.

THOMAS FLATMAN

But—when his next companions say
'How does he do? What hopes?'—shall turn away,
Answering only, with a lift-up hand—
'Who can his fate withstand?'

Then shall a gasp or two do more
Than e'er my rhetoric could before:
Persuade the world to trouble me no more!

CHARLES SACKVILLE, EARL OF DORSET
1638-1706

408.   *Song*

*Written at Sea, in the First Dutch War (1665), the
night before an Engagement.*

TO all you ladies now at land
   We men at sea indite;
But first would have you understand
   How hard it is to write:
The Muses now, and Neptune too,
We must implore to write to you—
   With a fa, la, la, la, la.

For though the Muses should prove kind,
   And fill our empty brain,
Yet if rough Neptune rouse the wind
   To wave the azure main,
Our paper, pen, and ink, and we,
Roll up and down our ships at sea—
   With a fa, la, la, la, la.

EARL OF DORSET

Then if we write not by each post,
  Think not we are unkind;
Nor yet conclude our ships are lost
  By Dutchmen or by wind:
Our tears we'll send a speedier way.
The tide shall bring them twice a day—
  With a fa, la, la, la, la.

The King with wonder and surprise
  Will swear the seas grow bold,
Because the tides will higher rise
  Than e'er they did of old:
But let him know it is our tears
Bring floods of grief to Whitehall stairs—
  With a fa, la, la, la, la.

Should foggy Opdam chance to know
  Our sad and dismal story,
The Dutch would scorn so weak a foe,
  And quit their fort at Goree:
For what resistance can they find
From men who've left their hearts behind?—
  With a fa, la, la, la, la.

Let wind and weather do its worst,
  Be you to us but kind;
Let Dutchmen vapour, Spaniards curse,
  No sorrow we shall find:
'Tis then no matter how things go,
Or who's our friend, or who's our foe—
  With a fa, la, la, la, la.

To pass our tedious hours away
  We throw a merry main,
Or else at serious ombre play;
  But why should we in vain

EARL OF DORSET

Each other's ruin thus pursue?
We were undone when we left you—
    With a fa, la, la, la, la.

But now our fears tempestuous grow
    And cast our hopes away;
Whilst you, regardless of our woe,
    Sit careless at a play:
Perhaps permit some happier man
To kiss your hand, or flirt your fan—
    With a fa, la, la, la, la.

When any mournful tune you hear,
    That dies in every note
As if it sigh'd with each man's care
    For being so remote,
Think then how often love we've made
To you, when all those tunes were play'd—
    With a fa, la, la, la, la.

In justice you cannot refuse
    To think of our distress,
When we for hopes of honour lose
    Our certain happiness:
All those designs are but to prove
Ourselves more worthy of your love—
    With a fa, la, la, la, la.

And now we've told you all our loves,
    And likewise all our fears,
In hopes this declaration moves
    Some pity for our tears:
Let's hear of no inconstancy—
We have too much of that at sea—
    With a fa, la, la, la, la.

SIR CHARLES SEDLEY
1639-1701

409. *To Chloris*

AH, Chloris! that I now could sit
  As unconcern'd as when
Your infant beauty could beget
  No pleasure, nor no pain!
When I the dawn used to admire,
  And praised the coming day,
I little thought the growing fire
  Must take my rest away.

Your charms in harmless childhood lay
  Like metals in the mine;
Age from no face took more away
  Than youth conceal'd in thine.
But as your charms insensibly
  To their perfection prest,
Fond love as unperceived did fly,
  And in my bosom rest.

My passion with your beauty grew,
  And Cupid at my heart,
Still as his mother favour'd you,
  Threw a new flaming dart:
Each gloried in their wanton part;
  To make a lover, he
Employ'd the utmost of his art—
  To make a beauty, she.

410. *To Celia*

NOT, Celia, that I juster am
  Or better than the rest!
For I would change each hour, like the
  Were not my heart at rest.

SIR CHARLES SEDLEY

But I am tied to very thee
  By every thought I have;
Thy face I only care to see,
  Thy heart I only crave.

All that in woman is adored
  In thy dear self I find—
For the whole sex can but afford
  The handsome and the kind.

Why then should I seek further store,
  And still make love anew?
When change itself can give no more,
  'Tis easy to be true!

APHRA BEHN
1640-1689

411. *Song*

LOVE in fantastic triumph sate
  Whilst bleeding hearts around him flow'd,
For whom fresh pains he did create
  And strange tyrannic power he show'd:
From thy bright eyes he took his fires,
  Which round about in sport he hurl'd;
But 'twas from mine he took desires
  Enough t' undo the amorous world.

From me he took his sighs and tears,
  From thee his pride and cruelty;
From me his languishments and fears,
  And every killing dart from thee.
Thus thou and I the god have arm'd
  And set him up a deity;
But my poor heart alone is harm'd,
  Whilst thine the victor is, and free!

APHRA BEHN

412. *The Libertine*

A THOUSAND martyrs I have made,
   All sacrificed to my desire,
A thousand beauties have betray'd
   That languish in resistless fire:
The untamed heart to hand I brought,
And fix'd the wild and wand'ring thought.

I never vow'd nor sigh'd in vain,
   But both, tho' false, were well received;
The fair are pleased to give us pain,
   And what they wish is soon believed:
And tho' I talk'd of wounds and smart,
Love's pleasures only touch'd my heart.

Alone the glory and the spoil
   I always laughing bore away;
The triumphs without pain or toil,
   Without the hell the heaven of joy;
And while I thus at random rove
Despise the fools that whine for love.

JOHN WILMOT, EARL OF ROCHESTER
1647-1680

413. *Return*

ABSENT from thee, I languish still;
   Then ask me not, When I return?
The straying fool 'twill plainly kill
   To wish all day, all night to mourn.

Dear, from thine arms then let me fly,
  That my fantastic mind may prove
The torments it deserves to try,
  That tears my fix'd heart from my love.

When, wearied with a world of woe,
  To thy safe bosom I retire,
Where love, and peace, and truth does flow,
  May I contented there expire!

Lest, once more wandering from that heaven,
  I fall on some base heart unblest;
Faithless to thee, false, unforgiven—
  And lose my everlasting rest.

414. *Love and Life*

ALL my past life is mine no more;
  The flying hours are gone,
Like transitory dreams given o'er,
Whose images are kept in store
  By memory alone.

The time that is to come is not;
  How can it then be mine?
The present moment's all my lot;
And that, as fast as it is got,
  Phillis, is only thine.

Then talk not of inconstancy,
  False hearts, and broken vows;
If I by miracle can be
This live-long minute true to thee,
  'Tis all that Heaven allows.

EARL OF ROCHESTER

415.   *Constancy*

I CANNOT change as others do,
   Though you unjustly scorn;
Since that poor swain that sighs for you
   For you alone was born.
No, Phillis, no; your heart to move
   A surer way I'll try;
And, to revenge my slighted love,
   Will still love on and die.

When kill'd with grief Amyntas lies,
   And you to mind shall call
The sighs that now unpitied rise,
   The tears that vainly fall—
That welcome hour, that ends this smart,
   Will then begin your pain;
For such a faithful tender heart
   Can never break in vain.

416.   *To His Mistress*

(After Quarles)

WHY dost thou shade thy lovely face? O why
   Does that eclipsing hand of thine deny
The sunshine of the Sun's enlivening eye?

Without thy light what light remains in me?
Thou art my life; my way, my light's in thee;
I live, I move, and by thy beams I see.

Thou art my life—if thou but turn away
My life's a thousand deaths. Thou art my way—
Without thee, Love, I travel not but stray.

EARL OF ROCHESTER

My light thou art—without thy glorious sight
My eyes are darken'd with eternal night.
My Love, thou art my way, my life, my light.

Thou art my way; I wander if thou fly.
Thou art my light; if hid, how blind am I!
Thou art my life; if thou withdraw'st, I die.

My eyes are dark and blind, I cannot see:
To whom or whither should my darkness flee,
But to that light?—and who's that light but thee?

If I have lost my path, dear lover, say,
Shall I still wander in a doubtful way?
Love, shall a lamb of Israel's sheepfold stray?

My path is lost, my wandering steps do stray;
I cannot go, nor can I safely stay;
Whom should I seek but thee, my path, my way?

And yet thou turn'st thy face away and fly'st me!
And yet I sue for grace and thou deny'st me!
Speak, art thou angry, Love, or only try'st me?

Thou art the pilgrim's path, the blind man's eye,
The dead man's life. On thee my hopes rely:
If I but them remove, I surely die.

Dissolve thy sunbeams, close thy wings and stay!
See, see how I am blind, and dead, and stray!
—O thou that art my life, my light, my way!

Then work thy will! If passion bid me flee,
My reason shall obey, my wings shall be
Stretch'd out no farther than from me to thee!

JOHN SHEFFIELD, DUKE OF BUCKINGHAMSHIRE
1649-1720

417. *The Reconcilement*

COME, let us now resolve at last
    To live and love in quiet;
We'll tie the knot so very fast
    That Time shall ne'er untie it.

The truest joys they seldom prove
    Who free from quarrels live:
'Tis the most tender part of love
    Each other to forgive.

When least I seem'd concern'd, I took
    No pleasure nor no rest;
And when I feign'd an angry look,
    Alas! I loved you best.

Own but the same to me—you'll find
    How blest will be our fate.
O to be happy—to be kind—
    Sure never is too late!

418. *On One who died discovering her Kindness*

SOME vex their souls with jealous pain,
    While others sigh for cold disdain:
Love's various slaves we daily see—
Yet happy all compared with me!

DUKE OF BUCKINGHAMSHIRE

Of all mankind I loved the best
A nymph so far above the rest
That we outshined the Blest above;
In beauty she, as I in love.

And therefore They, who could not bear
To be outdone by mortals here,
Among themselves have placed her now,
And left me wretched here below.

All other fate I could have borne,
And even endured her very scorn;
But oh! thus all at once to find
That dread account—both dead and kind!
What heart can hold? If yet I live,
'Tis but to show how much I grieve.

THOMAS OTWAY
1652-1685

419.   *The Enchantment*

I DID but look and love awhile,
   'Twas but for one half-hour;
Then to resist I had no will,
   And now I have no power.

To sigh and wish is all my ease;
   Sighs which do heat impart
Enough to melt the coldest ice,
   Yet cannot warm your heart.

O would your pity give my heart
   One corner of your breast,
'Twould learn of yours the winning art,
   And quickly steal the rest.

JOHN OLDHAM

1653-1683

420. *A Quiet Soul*

THY soul within such silent pomp did keep,
  As if humanity were lull'd asleep;
So gentle was thy pilgrimage beneath,
  Time's unheard feet scarce make less noise,
  Or the soft journey which a planet goes:
Life seem'd all calm as its last breath.
  A still tranquillity so hush'd thy breast,
    As if some Halcyon were its guest,
    And there had built her nest;
  It hardly now enjoys a greater rest.

JOHN CUTTS, LORD CUTTS

1661-1707

421. *Song*

ONLY tell her that I love:
  Leave the rest to her and Fate:
Some kind planet from above
May perhaps her pity move:
  Lovers on their stars must wait.—
Only tell her that I love!

Why, O why should I despair!
  Mercy's pictured in her eye:
If she once vouchsafe to hear,
Welcome Hope and farewell Fear!
  She's too good to let me die.—
Why, O why should I despair?

MATTHEW PRIOR
1664-1721

422. *The Question to Lisetta*

WHAT nymph should I admire or trust,
But Chloe beauteous, Chloe just?
What nymph should I desire to see,
But her who leaves the plain for me?
To whom should I compose the lay,
But her who listens when I play?
To whom in song repeat my cares,
But her who in my sorrow shares?
For whom should I the garland make,
But her who joys the gift to take,
And boasts she wears it for my sake?
In love am I not fully blest?
Lisetta, prithee tell the rest.

LISETTA'S REPLY

Sure Chloe just, and Chloe fair,
Deserves to be your only care;
But, when you and she to-day
Far into the wood did stray,
And I happen'd to pass by,
Which way did you cast your eye?
But, when your cares to her you sing,
You dare not tell her whence they spring;
Does it not more afflict your heart,
That in those cares she bears a part?
When you the flowers for Chloe twine,
Why do you to her garland join
The meanest bud that falls from mine?
Simplest of swains! the world may see
Whom Chloe loves, and who loves me.

MATTHEW PRIOR

423. *To a Child of Quality,*
Five Years Old, 1704. The Author then Forty

LORDS, knights, and squires, the numerous band
    That wear the fair Miss Mary's fetters,
Were summoned by her high command
    To show their passions by their letters.

My pen amongst the rest I took,
    Lest those bright eyes, that cannot read,
Should dart their kindling fire, and look
    The power they have to be obey'd.

Nor quality, nor reputation,
    Forbid me yet my flame to tell;
Dear Five-years-old befriends my passion,
    And I may write till she can spell.

For, while she makes her silkworms beds
    With all the tender things I swear;
Whilst all the house my passion reads,
    In papers round her baby's hair;

She may receive and own my flame;
    For, though the strictest prudes should know it,
She'll pass for a most virtuous dame,
    And I for an unhappy poet.

Then too, alas! when she shall tear
    The rhymes some younger rival sends,
She'll give me leave to write, I fear,
    And we shall still continue friends.

For, as our different ages move,
    'Tis so ordain'd (would Fate but mend it!),
That I shall be past making love
    When she begins to comprehend it.

424.   *Song*

THE merchant, to secure his treasure,
  Conveys it in a borrow'd name:
Euphelia serves to grace my measure;
  But Chloe is my real flame.

My softest verse, my darling lyre,
  Upon Euphelia's toilet lay;
When Chloe noted her desire
  That I should sing, that I should play.

My lyre I tune, my voice I raise;
  But with my numbers mix my sighs:
And while I sing Euphelia's praise,
  I fix my soul on Chloe's eyes.

Fair Chloe blush'd: Euphelia frown'd:
  I sung, and gazed: I play'd, and trembled:
And Venus to the Loves around
  Remark'd, how ill we all dissembled.

425.   *On My Birthday, July 21*

I, MY dear, was born to-day—
  So all my jolly comrades say:
They bring me music, wreaths, and mirth,
And ask to celebrate my birth:
Little, alas! my comrades know
That I was born to pain and woe;
To thy denial, to thy scorn,
Better I had ne'er been born:
I wish to die, even whilst I say—
'I, my dear, was born to-day.'

I, my dear, was born to-day:
Shall I salute the rising ray,
Well-spring of all my joy and woe?
Clotilda, thou alone dost know.
Shall the wreath surround my hair?
Or shall the music please my ear?
Shall I my comrades' mirth receive,
And bless my birth, and wish to live?
Then let me see great Venus chase
Imperious anger from thy face;
Then let me hear thee smiling say—
'Thou, my dear, wert born to-day.'

426. *The Lady who offers her Looking-Glass to Venus*

VENUS, take my votive glass:
　Since I am not what I was,
What from this day I shall be,
Venus, let me never see.

427.　　*A Letter*
to Lady Margaret Cavendish Holles-Harley, when a Child

MY noble, lovely, little Peggy,
　Let this my First Epistle beg ye,
At dawn of morn, and close of even,
To lift your heart and hands to Heaven.
In double duty say your prayer:
Our Father first, then *Notre Père*.

And, dearest child, along the day,
In every thing you do and say,
Obey and please my lord and lady,
So God shall love and angels aid ye.

If to these precepts you attend,
No second letter need I send,
And so I rest your constant friend.

428. *For my own Monument*

AS doctors give physic by way of prevention,
    Mat, alive and in health, of his tombstone took care;
For delays are unsafe, and his pious intention
    May haply be never fulfill'd by his heir.

Then take Mat's word for it, the sculptor is paid;
    That the figure is fine, pray believe your own eye;
Yet credit but lightly what more may be said,
    For we flatter ourselves, and teach marble to lie.

Yet counting as far as to fifty his years,
    His virtues and vices were as other men's are;
High hopes he conceived, and he smother'd great fears,
    In a life parti-colour'd, half pleasure, half care.

Nor to business a drudge, nor to faction a slave,
    He strove to make int'rest and freedom agree;
In public employments industrious and grave,
    And alone with his friends, Lord! how merry was he!

Now in equipage stately, now humbly on foot,
    Both fortunes he tried, but to neither would trust;
And whirl'd in the round as the wheel turn'd about,
    He found riches had wings, and knew man was but dust.

MATTHEW PRIOR

This verse, little polish'd, tho' mighty sincere,
  Sets neither his titles nor merit to view;
It says that his relics collected lie here,
  And no mortal yet knows too if this may be true.
Fierce robbers there are that infest the highway,
  So Mat may be kill'd, and his bones never found;
False witness at court, and fierce tempests at sea,
  So Mat may yet chance to be hang'd or be drown'd.
If his bones lie in earth, roll in sea, fly in air,
  To Fate we must yield, and the thing is the same;
And if passing thou giv'st him a smile or a tear,
  He cares not—yet, prithee, be kind to his fame.

WILLIAM WALSH
1663-1708

429.   *Rivals*

OF all the torments, all the cares,
  With which our lives are curst;
Of all the plagues a lover bears,
  Sure rivals are the worst!
By partners in each other kind
  Afflictions easier grow;
In love alone we hate to find
  Companions of our woe.

Sylvia, for all the pangs you see
  Are labouring in my breast,
I beg not you would favour me,
  Would you but slight the rest!
How great soe'er your rigours are,
  With them alone I'll cope;
I can endure my own despair,
  But not another's hope.

LADY GRISEL BAILLIE
1665-1746

430. *Werena my Heart's licht I wad dee*

THERE ance was a may, and she lo'ed na men;
She biggit her bonnie bow'r doun in yon glen;
But now she cries, Dool and a well-a-day!
Come doun the green gait and come here away!

When bonnie young Johnnie cam owre the sea,
He said he saw naething sae lovely as me;
He hecht me baith rings and mony braw things—
And werena my heart's licht, I wad dee.

He had a wee titty that lo'ed na me,
Because I was twice as bonnie as she;
She raised sic a pother 'twixt him and his mother
That werena my heart's licht, I wad dee.

The day it was set, and the bridal to be:
The wife took a dwam and lay doun to dee;
She maned and she graned out o' dolour and pain,
Till he vow'd he never wad see me again.

His kin was for ane of a higher degree,
Said—What had he do wi' the likes of me?
Appose I was bonnie, I wasna for Johnnie—
And werena my heart's licht, I wad dee.

They said I had neither cow nor calf,
Nor dribbles o' drink rins thro' the draff,
Nor pickles o' meal rins thro' the mill-e'e—
And werena my heart's licht, I wad dee.

may] maid. biggit] built. gait] way, path. hecht] promised. titty] sister. dwam] sudden illness. appose] suppose. pickles] small quantities.

LADY GRISEL BAILLIE

His titty she was baith wylie and slee:
She spied me as I cam owre the lea;
And then she ran in and made a loud din—
Believe your ain e'en, an ye trow not me.

His bonnet stood ay fu' round on his brow,
His auld ane look'd ay as well as some's new:
But now he lets 't wear ony gait it will hing,
And casts himsel dowie upon the corn bing.

And now he gaes daund'ring about the dykes,
And a' he dow do is to hund the tykes:
The live-lang nicht he ne'er steeks his e'e—
And werena my heart's licht, I wad dee.

Were I but young for thee, as I hae been,
We should hae been gallopin' doun in yon green,
And linkin' it owre the lily-white lea—
And wow, gin I were but young for thee!

WILLIAM CONGREVE
1670-1729

431. *False though She be*

FALSE though she be to me and love,
  I'll ne'er pursue revenge;
For still the charmer I approve,
  Though I deplore her change.

In hours of bliss we oft have met:
  They could not always last;
And though the present I regret,
  I'm grateful for the past.

430. hing] hang.   dowie] dejectedly.   hund the tykes] direct the dogs.   steeks] closes.   linkin'] tripping.

WILLIAM CONGREVE

432. *A Hue and Cry after Fair Amoret*

FAIR Amoret is gone astray—
  Pursue and seek her, ev'ry lover;
I'll tell the signs by which you may
  The wand'ring Shepherdess discover.

Coquette and coy at once her air,
  Both studied, tho' both seem neglected;
Careless she is, with artful care,
  Affecting to seem unaffected.

With skill her eyes dart ev'ry glance,
  Yet change so soon you'd ne'er suspect them,
For she'd persuade they wound by chance,
  Tho' certain aim and art direct them.

She likes herself, yet others hates
  For that which in herself she prizes;
And, while she laughs at them, forgets
  She is the thing that she despises.

JOSEPH ADDISON

1672-1719

433. *Hymn*

THE spacious firmament on high,
  With all the blue ethereal sky,
And spangled heavens, a shining frame,
Their great Original proclaim.
Th' unwearied Sun from day to day
Does his Creator's power display;
And publishes to every land
The work of an Almighty hand.

JOSEPH ADDISON

Soon as the evening shades prevail,
The Moon takes up the wondrous tale;
And nightly to the listening Earth
Repeats the story of her birth:
Whilst all the stars that round her burn,
And all the planets in their turn,
Confirm the tidings as they roll,
And spread the truth from pole to pole.

What though in solemn silence all
Move round the dark terrestrial ball;
What though nor real voice nor sound
Amidst their radiant orbs be found?
In Reason's ear they all rejoice,
And utter forth a glorious voice;
For ever singing as they shine,
'The Hand that made us is divine.'

ISAAC WATTS
1674-1748
434. *The Day of Judgement*

WHEN the fierce North-wind with his airy forces
    Rears up the Baltic to a foaming fury;
And the red lightning with a storm of hail comes
                  Rushing amain down;

How the poor sailors stand amazed and tremble,
While the hoarse thunder, like a bloody trumpet,
Roars a loud onset to the gaping waters
                  Quick to devour them.

ISAAC WATTS

Such shall the noise be, and the wild disorder
(If things eternal may be like these earthly),
Such the dire terror when the great Archangel
                Shakes the creation;

Tears the strong pillars of the vault of Heaven,
Breaks up old marble, the repose of princes,
Sees the graves open, and the bones arising,
                Flames all around them.

Hark, the shrill outcries of the guilty wretches!
Lively bright horror and amazing anguish
Stare thro' their eyelids, while the living worm lies
                Gnawing within them.

Thoughts, like old vultures, prey upon their heart-strings,
And the smart twinges, when the eye beholds the
Lofty Judge frowning, and a flood of vengeance
                Rolling 'afore him.

Hopeless immortals! how they scream and shiver,
While devils push them to the pit wide-yawning
Hideous and gloomy, to receive them headlong
                Down to the centre!

Stop here, my fancy: (all away, ye horrid
Doleful ideas!) come, arise to Jesus,
How He sits God-like! and the saints around Him
                Throned, yet adoring!

O may I sit there when He comes triumphant,
Dooming the nations! then ascend to glory,
While our Hosannas all along the passage
                Shout the Redeemer.

ISAAC WATTS

435.   *A Cradle Hymn*

HUSH! my dear, lie still and slumber,
  Holy angels guard thy bed!
Heavenly blessings without number
  Gently falling on thy head.

Sleep, my babe; thy food and raiment,
  House and home, thy friends provide;
All without thy care or payment:
  All thy wants are well supplied.

How much better thou'rt attended
  Than the Son of God could be,
When from heaven He descended
  And became a child like thee!

Soft and easy is thy cradle:
  Coarse and hard thy Saviour lay,
When His birthplace was a stable
  And His softest bed was hay.

Blessèd babe! what glorious features—
  Spotless fair, divinely bright!
Must He dwell with brutal creatures?
  How could angels bear the sight?

Was there nothing but a manger
  Cursèd sinners could afford
To receive the heavenly stranger?
  Did they thus affront their Lord?

ISAAC WATTS

Soft, my child: I did not chide thee,
    Though my song might sound too hard;
'Tis thy mother sits beside thee,
    And her arms shall be thy guard.

Yet to read the shameful story
    How the Jews abused their King,
How they served the Lord of Glory,
    Makes me angry while I sing.

See the kinder shepherds round Him,
    Telling wonders from the sky!
Where they sought Him, there they found Him,
    With His Virgin mother by.

See the lovely babe a-dressing;
    Lovely infant, how He smiled!
When He wept, the mother's blessing
    Soothed and hush'd the holy child.

Lo, He slumbers in His manger,
    Where the hornèd oxen fed:
Peace, my darling; here's no danger,
    Here's no ox anear thy bed.

'Twas to save thee, child, from dying,
    Save my dear from burning flame,
Bitter groans and endless crying,
    That thy blest Redeemer came.

May'st thou live to know and fear Him,
    Trust and love Him all thy days;
Then go dwell for ever near Him,
    See His face, and sing His praise!

Milton Keynes UK
Ingram Content Group UK Ltd.
UKHW031647170724
445742UK00001B/32